Dear Heather~
I wish you a Bounty of
happy meals with good
friends and loving family~
Valerie Hart
♡

The Bounty of Central Florida

Valerie Hart

ISBN #0-9748676-0-8

LCCN #2004090226

First Printing — April 2004

WIMMER
COOKBOOKS

ConsolidatedGraphics
800.548.2537
www.wimmerco.com

Grateful Appreciation

Alexandra Hart Bosshardt, MPS, RD, LD/N, whose talents and perseverance have enabled her to combine her role of homemaker and devoted parent, while earning notoriety in her career, both of which have brought honor to her and pride to our family.

Gregory Hart, who continually interrupted his schedule as a Database Engineer to spend endless hours on the telephone and traveled between Tampa and Mount Dora for five years "unglitching" my computer mishaps and creating simple programs to organize the format of this book.

Katherine Hart Kelsey, whose delicious perceptions, coupled with love and compassion, make me proud to be her friend.

My Buddy for forty-five years, who craves hot dogs, steak and fried potatoes, but patiently endures alligator tail, wild birds and fierce crabs crawling in the sink, and who has been my source of inspiration and the kindest critic I have ever known.

Photographer Mel Victor and his daughter, Donna.

Photographer Jack Hardman

Grateful appreciation to Ineke Zonnenberg

Prologue

Until we moved to Mount Dora, my comprehension of Central Florida was that of an elongated peninsula en route to Miami and Key West. From the window of a plane on a clear day, one could ascertain the uninhabitable topography of the Everglades swamp. The city of Orlando was detected only by smatterings of small clusters of lights that twinkled from below. Then, a little mouse migrated from California during the sixties to create a booming metropolis of diversification and sophistication.

Even after Disney invaded the area, citrus was the only commodity known outside of Florida. The uncultivated land appeared doomed to cypress trees, scrub pines and lakes teeming with alligators. All that sand and heat were no match for the rich dark soil of the north. Only local folk waited anxiously for the first weeks in May when the succulent sweet corn ripened in Zellwood. Only a few agriculturalists were privy to Florida's experimentation in the early sixties with some of the first organically grown vegetables in the country. And, all but the Texans and Florida ranchers were unaware that the area was known as a cattle center, and particularly for birthing cattle, thousands of which are still shipped to Texas. The cattle ranchers cracked whips to move the herds of cows. The ability to whip a horsefly from an animal without touching its flesh was carried from father to son until all who lived in the area became known as "Florida Crackers".

The metamorphosis of south Florida's countryside from farmlands to housing projects, golf courses and shopping malls is disquieting to those of us who treasure our rural atmosphere. We fearfully liken these developers to the barbaric Goths who crossed the Rhine River to sack Rome in 410 AD. We see their armies moving up the coast, leveling the citrus groves, polluting our natural spring waters and displacing our wild life into extinction. During the last twenty years, people looking to escape from the confusion of Miami relocated in Orlando. Unfortunately, they brought their city values with them. Raccoons, possums, alligators, bobcats and snakes were not welcomed neighbors, so they were removed or obliterated. People are now retreating from the big city of Orlando to settle in Clermont, Eustis, Tavares, Leesburg, and Mount Dora. We tell them, "If you cannot live with country creatures, stay in the city", but they will not heed our warning. They will settle among us with their "gated communities", plowing through our groves and woods and replacing them with super discount stores, strip malls, fast food eateries and gas stations as they have done in Winter Park and Altamonte Springs.

This book is dedicated to all those who love and protect our natural resources with my plea and prayers for responsible growth with ample allocation of private and county funds for the future propagation of Central Florida's bounty of farmlands and wildlife.

Table of Contents

Bananas

The Florida banana is a small, fat, sweet and more succulent baby version of the imported variety found in the supermarkets.

RECIPES:

Banana Bourbon Bread Pudding

Banana Pudding

Banana Raisin Pudding

Banana Fritters

Banana Rum Custard Pudding

Hazelnut Meringue Cookies

Banana Cake

Flaming Bananas

Banana Bourbon Bread Pudding

Yield: Approximately 8 Servings

9 slices French or country white bread, cut into quarters

3-4 Florida finger bananas

½ cup dark seedless raisins

4 whole eggs, graded jumbo

¼ cup light brown sugar

2 ounces bourbon whiskey

½ ounce Triple Sec liqueur

6 tablespoons melted butter

2 cups 4-percent whole buttermilk

Cinnamon/nutmeg/sugar

1 quart baking dish

1. Preheat oven to 350°F.

2. Slice and cut bread into quarters, leaving the crusts intact. Peel and slice bananas. Combine bread and bananas in a 1-quart baking dish.

3. Beat next 6 ingredients together and toss with the bread. Sprinkle cinnamon, nutmeg and sugar over the top. Place dish in a pan of water for the pan to sit in while baking.

4. Bake 1 hour. Serve hot or warm with sweetened whipped cream on the side.

Alternate method: Slice bread, leaving it whole and layer it with the bananas and custard mixture.

Banana Pudding

Yield: 6 Servings

1 cup coffee cream

5 extra large egg yolks

1½ cups whole milk

3½ tablespoons cornstarch

½ teaspoon salt

½ cup granulated sugar

1 teaspoon vanilla extract

As many vanilla wafers as it takes

8 yellow but firm Dwarf Cavendish or finger bananas

1 quart baking dish

Meringue:

5 extra large egg whites

¼ teaspoon cream of tartar

3 tablespoons granulated sugar

1. Preheat oven to 425°F.

2. With a wire whisk, stir the coffee cream into the egg yolks until blended. Stir in the milk.

3. Combine cornstarch, salt and ½ cup of the sugar in the top of a double boiler over medium-high heat. Stir in the milk mixture a little at a time with the whisk. Cook, stirring, until mixture thickens.

4. Remove from heat and add vanilla.

5. Place a layer of vanilla wafers, flat side up, in the bottom of the baking dish. Slice the bananas and cover the wafers. Spoon a thin layer of mixture over. Repeat 2 or 3 times, depending on depth of dish, ending with pudding on top.

6. Beat egg whites until foamy. Add cream of tartar. Continue beating until thick. Add 3 tablespoons sugar and beat until stiff peaks form. Spread over the top of the pudding, pulling up peaks with a spoon. Or, pipe circles and rosettes with a bag fitted with a fluted piping tube.

7. Bake 5 minutes. Remove from oven to cool. Serve warm or refrigerate 1 hour to serve cold.

Banana Raisin Pudding

Yield: 6-8 Servings

4 extra large eggs, beaten with a pinch of salt

1 quart whole milk

1 tablespoon vanilla extract

1 cup granulated sugar

4 very firm yellow finger bananas (or 2 of the more common, larger variety)

2½ ounces golden seedless raisins (½ cup)

2 quart deep glass casserole dish

Sprinkling of grated nutmeg and cinnamon

1.   Preheat oven to 350°F.

2.   Beat eggs with a pinch of salt. Slowly beat in milk, vanilla and sugar until well blended. Slice bananas rather thick and add. Add raisins.

3.   Pour into the casserole dish. Grate nutmeg and cinnamon over the top. Place dish in a pan of water to reach ⅓ up the dish. Bake 55-60 minutes, or until set and a knife inserted in the center comes out clean.

This recipe can be divided into 8 1 cup baking dishes. Cook time will change to approximately 30 minutes.

Banana Fritters

Yield: Approximately 6 Fritters

1 pound bananas (approximately 4 finger bananas or 2 of the larger variety)

1 tablespoon granulated sugar

¼ cup whole milk

¼ cup all-purpose flour

1 heaping teaspoon baking powder

¼ teaspoon grated nutmeg

¼ teaspoon salt

1 tablespoon vegetable oil

1.   Purée bananas in a blender to measure 1 cup. Add sugar and milk and blend again. Add flour with baking powder, nutmeg and salt and blend again. Push excess flour from sides and blend again. Refrigerate 1 hour.

2.   Heat vegetable oil in a large, shallow skillet. Spoon in banana mixture. Cook on both sides until brown, turning with a spatula.

Note: These can be difficult to turn over. Even if they don't look perfect, you'll like the flavor.

Banana Rum Custard Pudding

Yield: 4 Servings

5 extra large egg yolks

1 cup coffee cream

½ cup granulated sugar

2 tablespoons dark brown sugar

Pinch of salt

1 cup whole milk

1 tablespoon cornstarch

1 teaspoon vanilla extract

3 Florida finger bananas, ripe but still firm

3 tablespoons dark rum

Cinnamon

Sweetened whipped cream

1. Separate eggs, saving the whites tightly covered in the refrigerator for Hazelnut Meringue Cookies (recipe follows).

2. Beat yolks with the coffee cream until incorporated. Add sugars and salt and slowly mix in the whole milk. Stir in the cornstarch.

3. Cook in a saucepan over medium heat, stirring alternately with a wooden spoon and wire whisk until mixture thickens a bit. Do not allow it to boil or it will curdle. Stir in vanilla. Pour through a strainer into individual martini glasses or saucer champagne glasses. Refrigerate until very cold.

4. Cut bananas into approximately ⅑-inch slices. Pour rum over to marinate 30 minutes.

5. Spoon bananas and rum over custard. Sprinkle with cinnamon and top with a dollop of sweetened whipped cream.

Hazelnut Meringue Cookies

Yield: Approximately 24 Cookies

1 cup sugar

4 tablespoons cornstarch

6 extra large egg whites, room temperature

¼ teaspoon cream of tartar

8 ounces finely-chopped hazelnuts

Pastry bag fitted with a large fluted tube

1. Preheat oven to 200°F. Set the rack ⅓ from the bottom.

2. Line baking sheets with parchment paper.

3. Combine the sugar with the cornstarch.

4. Beat egg whites with an electric mixer on highest speed 30 seconds until foamy. Add cream of tartar and beat until soft peaks form. Add the sugar mixture, 1 tablespoon at a time. Beat until whites are very stiff and shiny, 4-6 minutes.

5. Stir in finely-chopped hazelnuts.

6. Fill the pastry bag with the mixture and, in one movement, pipe three circles on top of each other, bringing each to a point in the center. Create even rows of meringue circles ½-inch apart on the parchment.

7. Bake meringues 3 hours without opening the oven door. Turn off oven. Leave meringues inside closed oven overnight. Store in an airtight container.

Banana Cake

Yield: 3 (8x3½-inch) loaves or 2 (8x8-inch) square pans or 5 (3½x6x2-inch) mini loaves

The shape of this technically makes it Banana Bread. It can, however, be baked in 2 (8-inch) cake pans and frosted with Lemon Frosting (recipe page 53).

1 teaspoon baking soda

2 teaspoons double acting baking powder

2 cups sifted all-purpose flour

½ pound butter, softened to room temperature

2 cups granulated sugar

4 extra large eggs, room temperature

1 tablespoon vanilla extract

¼ teaspoon almond extract

½ cup sour cream

2 cups ripe bananas (4 commercial bananas or 6-7 Finger bananas)

1. Preheat oven to 350°F.

2. Sift together the soda, baking powder and flour.

3. Beat butter, adding sugar slowly on low speed. Turn speed to high and beat until white. Turn beaters off occasionally to scrape the sides and bottom with a rubber spatula.

4. Add eggs, one at a time, on medium speed until well-blended, scraping the sides of the bowl after each addition. Add vanilla and almond extracts.

5. Add sour cream on low speed. Mixture may appear to "curdle". (This will disappear in the baking.)

6. Purée bananas in a blender and beat in immediately.

7. Add flour mixture on low speed. Turn off beaters. Scrape bowl. Beat again on medium speed for a few seconds, or until flour is incorporated. Do not over-beat. Over-beating of flour makes a cake "tough".

8. Pour into 2 square pans or 3 small loaf pans. Set a rack ⅓ from the bottom of the oven and bake as follows:

   a. 8-inch loaves 40-45 minutes

   b. mini loaves and square pans 30-35 minutes

Vanilla found in supermarkets generally is one-fold, or "normal". Vanilla found in gourmet shops is generally two-fold, reflected by the price. If you have two-fold vanilla extract, you may cut back the measurement from 1 tablespoon to 2 teaspoons.

Note: Ripe mango or peach purée may be substituted for the bananas, or combined. Exchange orange extract for the almond listed above.

This is a favorite Jamaican dessert. The Florida banana is a small, fat, sweet and more succulent baby version of the imported variety found in the supermarket.

Flaming Bananas

Yield: 6 Servings

6 tablespoons unsalted butter

3 tablespoons light brown sugar

2 teaspoons grated Red Valencia or Blood Orange rind

⅛ teaspoon grated nutmeg

¼ teaspoon cinnamon

1 tablespoon Meyer lemon juice

½ cup orange juice

6 Dwarf Cavendish bananas, yellow but firm

½ cup light rum

1. Melt butter with the sugar, orange rind and nutmeg in a shallow pan over a fire. Add the orange and lemon juices and cook, stirring, until hot.

2. Slice the bananas lengthwise and place them into the pan, spooning the mixture over as you add each one. Turn the bananas over one time and cook approximately 5 minutes, or until they begin to soften. Heat the rum to the boiling point. Immediately ignite the rum with a match or long lighter used for gas barbecues. Pour the rum over the bananas into the sauce. Spoon over the bananas. Divide among 6 plates and serve immediately.

Note: Ripe pineapple spears may be added to this recipe.

Berries

Mama raccoon followed by three or more cubs, or "kits" as some refer to them, has no problem walking directly past me to grab my early May blueberries while I watch.

RECIPES:

Berry-a-Trifle

Pastry Cream (Crème Patisserie)

Blueberry Custard Pie

Cold Berry Soup

Low Fat Blueberry Coffee Cake

Turn of the Century Blueberry Streusel

Zabaglione with Berries

Strawberry Salad

Intoxicated Strawberry Ice Cream

Strawberry Pie

Strawberry Mousse

Strawberry Bread Pudding

Strawberry Peach Yogurt Soup

Strawberry Soup with Crème Fraîche

Crème Fraîche

Strawberry Fluff: A Diet Dessert

Strawberry Tiramisu

Strawberry Cassis Jam

Strawberry Shortcake
with Strawberry Butter

Strawberry Butter

Bodacious Berries and Gratuitous Grapes

These bounties of nature must be carefully guarded as they burst into maturity lest they be stolen in the night by the multitude of birds, raccoons, and our resident gray fox, that has enough red in its coat to fool us into believing it's a rare specimen from the Panhandle. The gopher turtle who claimed the property many years before us burrows new holes around the field to let us know he still has title. On occasion our dog meets him face to face, but never lays a paw on him out of respect. I haven't seen our two brown rabbits since a neighboring bobcat began prowling around late at night, and I suspect foul play. But, that's what the real world is all about. I guess it can be accurately called the balance of nature. Animals and plants live together in a variety of communities called ecosystems. Within the ecosystems animals live in what we call habitat, interacting to take care of their needs. Plant eating animals keep the plants in balance. Their meat-eating predators keep the plant-eaters in balance. Unfortunately, the greedy and prolific raccoons think they own my plants. They have more nerve than spoiled children. Some of these unwanted creatures are the size of baby bears. They are brazen to the extent of absurdity. Mama raccoon followed by three or more cubs (or "kits" as some refer to them) has no problem walking directly past me to grab my early May blueberries and late July grapes while I watch. I shout to the trees for a predator hawk to soar down and grab one of her toddling furry fiends, but none are in sight. And, so I share because that's what it's all about.

There are serious vineyards in Central Florida. Lakeridge Winery, just outside Clermont on U.S. Highway 27 North, and San Sebastian Winery, on King Street in St. Augustine, are becoming contenders for America's national wine industry with two wines, in particular. A fruity white revealing an aftertaste of spice and oak is named Blanc Du Bois Reserve. This varietals label, named from a hybrid developed in Florida, was selected by wine experts as one of the 40 best of 2,147 wines from nineteen countries. Stover Reserve is similar to a Sauvignon Blanc, and has also received acclaim. Because these vineyards have been producing less than twenty years, their production is still that of a 'cottage industry'.

I have no intention of competing with Florida's wine industry, or even of trying my hand at fermenting these luscious specimens. My proficiency is that of boiling and straining to produce jelly by following instructions included within the pectin box, although there are few grapes left to cook after family, friends and critters have their fill.

Berry-a-Trifle

Yield: 8-10 Servings

Genoise Cake (recipe, page 248) or
   Citrus Sunshine Cake (recipe, page 71)

Double recipe Pastry Cream (recipe follows)

2 cups Lake County blueberries

2 cups Lake County strawberries

1 cup kumquat preserves (recipe, page 44)

½ cup chopped, toasted pecans

½ pint heavy cream

1 tablespoon granulated sugar

2 quart glass trifle bowl on a stand, or deep
   glass bowl

1. Make Genoise or Sunshine Cake, or purchase a white cake at the market.

2. Prepare Crème Patisserie.

3. Measure the bowl and cut the cake into enough slices for 2 layers and to cover the inside perimeter of the bowl. 4. Spread a thin layer of kumquat preserves over each slice. Cover the bottom and sides of the bowl with the cake slices.

5. Cover with ½ of the Crème Patisserie. Cover the Crème Patisserie with ½ of the blueberries and strawberries. Cover with remaining cake slices. Cover with the rest of the Crème Patisserie. Cover with the remaining blueberries and strawberries.

6. Chop the pecans and toast them on a baking sheet in a preheated 250°F oven 15 minutes. Cool and sprinkle over the top of the trifle.

7. Whip the cream with 1 tablespoon granulated sugar. Spoon the cream into a piping bag fitted with a #4B fluted tip and create a border with rosettes around the top by squeezing out little circles with peaks. Refrigerate several hours, but not overnight.

Note: The beauty of this dessert is seeing the layers through the glass. These bowls are available in discount pottery stores as well as gourmet shops.

Pastry Cream: (Crème Patisserie)

Yield: 2 Cups

5 extra large egg yolks

⅓ cup granulated sugar

⅛ teaspoon salt

3½ tablespoons cornstarch

2 cups whole milk

2 teaspoons vanilla extract

Optional: 1 ounce semi-sweet chocolate for chocolate pastry cream

1. Separate eggs, making sure no white membrane remains around the yolks. Reserve the whites for Pecan Meringue Cookies (recipe, page 120) or Strawberry Fluff: A Diet Dessert (recipe, page 31).

2. Combine sugar, salt and cornstarch and sift into a saucepan. Add ¼ cup of the milk and stir to combine. Stir in remaining milk.

3. Cook, stirring, over medium heat until mixture is hot. Stir 2 tablespoons of the hot mixture into the yolks before adding the yolks to the saucepan. Cook the mixture, stirring constantly with a wooden spoon and smoothing with a wire whisk until thick. If custard begins to stick to the bottom of the pan, lower heat. (Chocolate may be added at this time.) Stir in vanilla and remove from stove. Cover tightly with plastic film to cool.

4. Fill cake layers, or use the custard for trifle with fruit, or fill cream puffs (Pâte à Choux, recipe, page 158), or as a custard topped with fresh fruit for pies, or with the addition of 1 ounce chocolate, spoon it into cups for the best chocolate pudding ever.

Note: If custard forms lumps that will not smooth with a wire whisk, remove from heat and strain. If you concentrate on what you are doing and go about it slowly, there should be no problem. The secret is patience.

Blueberry Custard Pie

Yield: 9-inch Pie

Custard:

Baked crust of Sablé Pastry (recipe, page 265)

⅓ cup granulated sugar

3½ tablespoons cornstarch

6 extra large egg yolks, beaten

2 cups whole 4 percent milk

1 tablespoon vanilla extract

1. Bake pie crust and cool to room temperature.

2. Mix sugar with cornstarch in a small pot.

3. Separate eggs, saving the whites for Hazelnut Meringue Cookies (recipe, page 12). Beat egg yolks. Beat in ½ cup of the milk.

4. Stir remaining milk into the sugar mixture and cook over medium heat, stirring constantly, until mixture is smooth and thick.

5. Add a bit of the hot mixture to the egg yolk mixture before adding it to the pot. After adding the egg yolk mixture, stir until thick and smooth alternating a wire whisk with a wooden spoon to smooth and stir from the bottom. Stir in the vanilla and remove from the heat. When custard has cooled to room temperature, fill pie shell.

Blueberry Topping:

1 pint Florida blueberries

4 tablespoons sugar

½ cup water

1 tablespoon cornstarch

¼ cup cool water

1 pint extra large blueberries to top

1. Boil 1 pint blueberries with the sugar and water until they pop open. Stir often during the cooking. Strain them through a sieve and return them to the pot.

2. Dissolve the cornstarch in ¼ cup cool water and stir into the blueberry sauce. Bring to a boil, stirring, until mixture thickens. Remove from the heat to cool completely.

3. Fold ½ the extra large blueberries into the sauce and cover the custard. Sprinkle remaining blueberries over. Refrigerate until very cold.

Note: This pie is best served the day it is made.

Cold Berry Soup

Yield: 8-10 Servings

1 pound ripe, sweet Plant City strawberries

1 quart Lake County blueberries

2 tablespoons Meyer lemon juice

½ cup water

1 bottle white Blanc du Bois wine* (see note at bottom)

Handful fresh mint leaves, minced

1. Clean berries and set aside. On highest speed of an electric blender, purée strawberries in batches with lemon juice and water. Strain through a large mesh strainer into a container.

2. Stir in wine and mint leaves with a whisk to smooth. Taste. If necessary, add a few tablespoons honey, sugar or sugar substitute.

3. Refrigerate several hours.

4. Ladle into individual bowls, topping each with a handful of blueberries. Place a strawberry in the center of each bowl. A dollop of Crème Fraîche may be swirled into the soup before adding the berries.

*Note: Florida's reputation as a wine producer may be in its infancy, but the hybrid grape developed by a University of Florida grape breeder thirty years ago has begun to receive attention in international wine competitions. Lakeridge Winery in Lake County has produced a Blanc du Bois white wine with a slightly spicy flavor resembling a German Riesling. Actually, wine production in our little peninsula known for sand and citrus began in the 1500s with the Spanish settlers, who brought the plants from Europe.

Low Fat Blueberry Coffee Cake

Yield: 12-16 Squares

1½ cups all-purpose flour
¾ cup granulated sugar
2 teaspoons baking powder
½ teaspoon salt
8 ounces blueberry yogurt

½ cup vegetable oil
2 extra large graded eggs
½ cup sugar mixed with 1 teaspoon cinnamon
2 pints fresh Florida blueberries

1. Sift the first 4 ingredients together

2. Add yogurt, oil and eggs. Beat 1 minute with a hand electric mixer on medium speed.

3. Pour into a 9x9-inch greased or non-stick baking pan or aluminum foil pan.

4. Sprinkle sugar-cinnamon mixture over the top.

5. Bake in a preheated 350°F oven 35-40 minutes, or until a toothpick comes out dry. Sprinkle blueberries over the top. Sprinkle with additional cinnamon-sugar. Turn oven to broil. Broil until hot and bubbly.

6. Cut into squares and serve with the reserved blueberries on the side.

Turn of the Century Blueberry Streusel

(The Nineteenth Century, when great-grandma didn't measure ingredients.)

Yield: Approximately 8 Servings

The Batter:

2 cups all-purpose flour

½ cup plus 1 tablespoon granulated sugar

1 tablespoon baking powder

¼ teaspoon salt

1 jumbo graded egg, beaten

½ cup softened butter

½ cup 4-percent whole milk

1 cup Florida ripe blueberries

1 cup chopped Florida pecans

9-inch square baking pan

The Streusel Topping:

½ cup granulated sugar

⅓ cup all-purpose flour

¼ cup cold butter

1. Preheat oven to 375°F.

2. Sift flour with the sugar, baking powder and salt and set aside.

3. With an electric beater, beat in egg and softened butter. Beat in milk in a slow, steady, stream, until mixture is smooth, cleaning the sides of the bowl with a spatula several times.

4. Fold in blueberries and pecans by hand.

5. Spread into a 9-inch baking pan.

6. Make Streusel by combining the sugar with the flour. Cut the butter into tiny pieces and chop into the sugar-flour until mixture is crumbly. Sprinkle over the batter.

7. Bake 30-35 minutes and check doneness by inserting a wooden pick into the center. If it comes out clean, the cake is done. If it is still wet and sticky, leave the cake to cook another 5 minutes.

Warm Zabaglione with Berries

Yield: 4 Servings

2 cups Central Florida blueberries, blackberries, sliced strawberries, or a combination

4 jumbo graded egg yolks

½ cup sweet Marsala wine (or cream sherry or Dubonnet)

3 tablespoons granulated sugar

¼ cup coffee cream

Optional: 1 ounce semi-sweet chocolate

1. Divide the berries into saucer champagne cups or dessert bowls.

2. Beat the egg yolks, wine and sugar in a bowl set in a pot half-filled with simmering water. You may use a hand electric beater, old fashioned egg beater, or a wire whisk. If you have a copper bowl, you will achieve greater volume. Beat until mixture triples in volume, becoming thick and creamy. Stir coffee cream in slowly, adding only enough to create a thinner consistency.

3. Spoon Zabaglione over the berries.

4. Shave the chocolate on top and serve immediately.

Note: This recipe may be doubled, but it is easier and faster to work it as an individual recipe. Keep the first covered over warm water until the second is ready to serve.

Cold Zabaglione with Berries

Yield: 4 Servings

16 ladyfingers

2 cups strawberries or blueberries, or a combination

1 cup heavy cream

1 teaspoon granulated sugar

6 extra large graded egg yolks

3 tablespoons granulated sugar

½ cup sweet Marsala wine (or cream sherry or Dubonnet)

1. Stand 4 ladyfingers around the outside edge of 4 long-stemmed wine glasses. Divide the berries to fill the bottom of the glasses, reserving a few for top decoration.

2. Whip the cream. When it is almost thick, add 1 teaspoon sugar and continue beating until very thick. Refrigerate.

3. Combine the egg yolks with 3 tablespoons sugar and the wine in a glass or copper bowl set over simmering water. Beat on high speed of an electric mixer or with a wire whisk until mixture has tripled in volume, becoming thick and creamy. Remove from heat to cool to room temperature.

4. When custard has cooled, fold in the whipped cream. Spoon over the berries and serve.

Note: Do not fill glasses with mixture in advance. If necessary, prepare the glasses with the berries and ladyfingers and refrigerate the finished Zabaglione until ready to serve.

Strawberry Salad

Yield: 4 Servings

½ cup chopped Festival strawberries

1 tablespoon Meyer lemon juice

1 tablespoon orange blossom honey

1 teaspoon white balsamic vinegar

Pinch salt

Mixed baby salad greens of choice

2 or more tablespoons toasted chopped pecans

Whole strawberries to garnish

8 thin slices Camembert or Brie or chunks of
    goat cheese

1. Remove stems and chop strawberries coarse.

2. Combine lemon juice, honey, balsamic vinegar and salt. Stir in strawberries to create strawberry dressing. Do this several hours in advance of serving. Refrigerate.

3. Divide cold salad greens onto 4 plates. Spoon strawberry dressing over.

4. Sprinkle with pecans. Place 1 whole berry on the top of each.

5. Set 2 slices cheese on opposite edges of each plate.

Intoxicated Strawberry Ice Cream

Yield: 6-8 Servings

3 cups Camarosa strawberries, separated

½ pint heavy cream for whipping

2 tablespoons granulated sugar

2 ounces brandy

2 ounces Grand Marnier liqueur

1 cup vanilla ice cream

1 cup strawberry sherbet

1. Mash half the strawberries and set aside. Cut the other half into large slices, leaving 1 whole berry to top each serving.

2. Beat the cream and sugar together until very thick.

3. Combine the brandy and liqueur with the ice cream and sherbet in a bowl and beat on low speed until mixed. Fold in the whipped cream. Fold in the mashed strawberries. Refrigerate 1 hour or longer.

4. Spoon into saucer champagne or Margarita glasses surrounded with the sliced berries. Set a whole berry on the top of each to serve.

Strawberry Pie

Crust:

2 cups self-rising flour

½ teaspoon salt

1½ sticks plus 2 tablespoons cold, unsalted butter, cut into tiny bits

⅓ cup ice water

1. Preheat oven to 350°F.

2. Combine flour, salt and butter in a food processor. Blend into coarse meal. Remove to a bowl. Add water, working quickly to form the mixture into a ball. Dust with flour. Roll out to ¼-inch thickness. Fill the bottom and sides of a 9-inch pie plate. Chill or freeze. Remove from refrigerator and immediately place into the oven. Bake 10-12 minutes. Cool before filling.

Filling:

⅓ cup granulated sugar

3½ tablespoons cornstarch

2 cups whole milk

5 jumbo egg yolks

1 tablespoon vanilla extract

3. Combine sugar with cornstarch. Pour a little milk into the yolks and stir to blend. Add remaining milk and pour through a strainer into a saucepan. Stir in sugar-cornstarch mixture.

4. Heat mixture, stirring constantly. Continue cooking over medium heat, until very thick. Stir in vanilla. Cool to room temperature. Fill cold pastry crust.

Topping:

12 ounces red currant jelly

3 tablespoons Port wine

2 tablespoons Crème de Cassis liqueur

1 or more pints large Camarosa (bed of red) strawberries

5. Combine jelly, wines and liqueur in a small saucepan. Heat, stirring, until smooth. Reduce heat to simmer. Simmer until mixture thickens a bit. Do not overcook. Cool to room temperature.

6. Dip strawberries individually into the sauce and set them on top of the custard. Refrigerate until very cold.

Note: Strawberries may also be sliced and tossed in the sauce to top.

Strawberry Mousse

Yield: 2 quarts - Approximately 8 Servings

3 pints freshly picked Camarosa (Bed of Red) strawberries

Juice of ½ lemon

2½ pints heavy cream for whipping, very cold

1⅓ cups 10X powdered confectioners sugar

2 tablespoons clear strawberry jelly, melted and cooled

½ cup Kirsch liqueur

2 tablespoons unflavored gelatin

½ cup lukewarm water

2-quart soufflé dish

½ pint heavy cream for whipping

1 tablespoon granulated sugar

1. Cut a sheet of wax paper or aluminum foil to wrap around the outside of the soufflé dish. Cut it deep enough to create a triple fold 4-inches deep. Secure it to the dish with tape. This is called a "collar".

2. Slice 2 pints of the strawberries and toss with the lemon juice.

3. Whip the cream with the confectioners sugar until very thick.

4. Stir the liquid jelly into the cream. Stir in the Kirsch.

5. Soften gelatin in ½ cup lukewarm water and stir it into the jelly mixture.

6. Stir in the strawberries.

7. Rub liquid vegetable oil into the mold before filling it with the mixture.

8. Refrigerate overnight.

9. Beat ½ pint heavy cream with 1 tablespoon granulated sugar until very thick. Fill a piping bag outfitted with a fluted tube and decorate the top of the soufflé with rosettes.

10. Slice the remaining pint of strawberries. Sprinkle with a tablespoon of granulated sugar and fill a bowl to serve on the side.

Strawberry Bread Pudding

Yield: 6-8 Servings

1 pint ripe Festival or Camarosa strawberries from Lake County

⅓ cup Crème de Cassis liqueur

1 loaf French bread, approximately 1 pound or less

1 quart whole milk

3 tablespoons melted butter

4 jumbo graded eggs

3 cups granulated sugar

2 tablespoons vanilla extract

9½x14x2½-inch baking dish

Cinnamon-sugar to sprinkle over the top (7 parts sugar to 2 parts cinnamon)

1. Preheat oven to 350°F.

2. Slice strawberries and toss with the Cassis.

3. Slice bread thick and cut into cubes. Heat milk to the boiling point. Pour over the bread and let soak until soft.

4. Pour melted butter into the bottom of the baking pan.

5. Beats eggs with the sugar and vanilla. Stir into bread mixture. Pour into buttered dish. Cover the top with the strawberry liqueur mixture. Sprinkle the top with cinnamon-sugar.

6. Bake 1 hour, or until a knife comes out clean.

The Camarosa (Bed of Red) strawberry is not quite as sweet as the Festival, but equally delicious. Larger and heartier, it will hold several days, whereas Festival must be eaten within twenty-four hours for peak flavor and quality. The Camarosa works best in shakes and pies and shortcake, and makes marvelous jam.

Strawberry Peach Yogurt Soup

Yield: Approximately 6 Cups

4 cups cleaned Camarosa (Bed of Red)
   strawberries, sliced
¼ cup granulated sugar
2 tablespoons lemon juice

½ cup unflavored yogurt
½ cup heavy cream
2 large peaches, peeled and finely diced

1. Place strawberries in a blender and purée. Remove to a bowl. Add sugar, lemon juice, yogurt and cream. Refrigerate until very cold. Stir in the peaches directly before serving.

Strawberry Soup with Crème Fraîche

Yield: 6 Servings

2 cups puréed strawberries
1 teaspoon lemon juice
2 tablespoons apricot, peach or orange liqueur
¼ teaspoon cinnamon
2 tablespoons coffee cream

2 tablespoons whole milk
Pinch of salt
6 tablespoons Crème Fraîche
Chopped mint leaves (Lemon mint leaves are
   best)

1. Combine puréed strawberries, lemon juice, liqueur and cinnamon in a bowl. Stir in cream and milk and a pinch of salt. Refrigerate until very cold.

2. Spoon into individual bowls. Spoon a tablespoon of Crème Fraîche on top of each and sprinkle with chopped mint leaves.

Crème Fraîche

Yield: 2 cups

2 cups heavy cream

⅓ cup whole buttermilk

Optional: ¼ cup sour cream

1. Do not whip the heavy cream. Combine the buttermilk and heavy cream and heat slowly to exactly 85°F, or lukewarm. This may be done on top of the stove, or in a microwave. If the cream is cold, microwave on high 40 seconds. Stir. Microwave another 30 seconds. Insert a thermometer to test the temperature. If too cool or too hot, mixture will not thicken.

2. Pour into a glass jar or plastic container. Cover and allow to rest in a warm place 24 hours. Refrigerate overnight. If mixture has not thickened sufficiently, stir in sour cream.

Note: Crème Fraîche will keep until the expiration of the ingredients within.

Strawberry Fluff: A Diet Dessert

Yield: 4-6 Servings

1 pint sweet, ripe strawberries

¼ cup Kirschwasser cherry brandy

3 jumbo graded egg whites

½ teaspoon cream of tartar

½ cup sifted 10X confectioners powdered sugar

1. Push the strawberries through a fine strainer into a bowl to extract the juices. Stir in the Kirschwasser.

2. Beat the egg whites with the cream of tartar on highest speed of an electric mixer until very thick. Add the sifted sugar slowly and continue beating for 10 more seconds.

3. Fold the strawberry juice into the whites slowly with a spatula until blended. Spoon into individual ice cream cups and freeze.

Note: This dessert should be made the same day as it is served for peak quality.

The simple test of a good berry is its aroma. If it smells like a strawberry, it will taste like a strawberry. Our newest local specie they call Festival is juicy and luscious beyond comparison and it has no need of embellishment. Pick it. Take a bite. Let the ambrosial juices permeate your taste buds and drip down your throat. Or, if you are able to restrain yourself, take them home to serve with whipped cream or ice cream.

This recipe comes from Christina Tozzi Manari, Florence, Italy.

Strawberry Tiramisu

Yield: 4-6 Servings

2 jumbo graded egg yolks

¼ cup granulated sugar

2 tablespoons espresso or very strong coffee

2 tablespoons cream sherry or Marsala wine

8 ounces mascarpone cheese

1 cup heavy cream

1 tablespoon granulated sugar

1 cup thinly sliced Central Florida strawberries

4-6 Italian ladyfingers, or 8-12 halves

4-6 individual saucer champagne glasses, ramekins or glass serving dish

1. Beat the egg yolks and sugar in a bowl over simmering water until cream-colored and thick, approximately 10 minutes. Cool to room temperature.
2. Beat the coffee and sherry into the mascarpone cheese and fold into the yolk mixture.
3. Whip the cream with 1 tablespoon sugar until thick. Fold ⅓ of the whipped cream into the mascarpone mixture.
4. Set the ladyfingers flat side up on the bottom of individual glasses or line the bottom and sides of a glass serving dish.
5. Slice the strawberries thin and place a layer or two over the ladyfingers.
6. Cover the strawberries with the mascarpone mixture.
7. Cover with the remaining sliced strawberries. Cover the top with remaining whipped cream. (If you are adept with a pastry bag, insert a fluted tube and pipe swirls around the top with rosettes.) To finish: Insert a ladyfinger on a slant into the top of each. Refrigerate 1 hour or longer.

Note: Mascarpone is called "cream cheese" in Italy. It is, however, quite different. It is not as sweet or white and has a more pronounced flavor. It is also expensive to purchase in America. A light or whipped cream cheese could be substituted for part of the mascarpone or a greater amount of heavy cream could be incorporated into the mixture. American ladyfingers have the consistency of a thin batter cake. Italian ladyfingers are harder and have the crunch of a vanilla cookie. Vanilla wafers may be substituted in the absence of Italian ladyfingers.

"Tiramisu" translates as "pick me up" in Italian, most likely because of the addition of strong coffee.

Strawberry season begins in late December in Central Florida and continues until the end of March. Most of the berries found in our supermarkets come from Plant City in Hillsborough County. The berries grown in Lake County are sold at roadside stands and U-Pick farms. Far Reach Ranch in Tavares and Oak Haven Farms on Wolf Branch Road a few miles outside Mount Dora cater to the U-Pick crowd with acres of Festival and Camarosa strawberries. Far Reach Ranch grows blueberries for commercial sales and Oak Haven is growing Christmas trees to cut down for people in our area. Oak Haven also bottles jams and offers the thirsty amateur strawberry picker strawberry milkshakes and shortcake.

Strawberry Cassis Jam

Yield: 12 (½-pint) jars

4 pounds ripe (10 cups puréed) Camarosa strawberries

¼ cup Meyer lemon juice

4 cups granulated sugar (5 for sweeter jam)

5 packages Sure Jell®

1 cup Crème de Cassis liqueur

1. Wipe or wash strawberries. Purée in a food processor or blender. Pour into a pot.

2. Add lemon juice and sugar and bring to a boil. Boil 30 seconds only.

3. Combine Sure Jell® with Crème de Cassis in a separate saucepan. Heat, stirring, until smooth. Pour into strawberry mixture. Boil 1 minute only, stirring.

4. Immediately fill and seal jars according to directions on package.

Note: An easy method of sterilizing the jars is to run them through the rinse cycle of the dishwasher without soap.

Strawberry Shortcake with Strawberry Butter

2 cups all-purpose flour

2 tablespoons baking powder

½ teaspoon salt

2 tablespoons granulated sugar

¼ pound butter or solid vegetable shortening

¾ cup whole milk

1 pint Plant City strawberries

1. Preheat oven to 450°F.

2. Sift flour with baking powder, salt and sugar.

3. Mix in shortening with a fork or pastry blender.

4. Work milk into mixture.

5. Place on a lightly floured surface. Roll out into approximately 1-inch thickness. Cut into rounds with a cookie cutter or inverted glass.

6. Bake 12-15 minutes, or until golden. Split biscuits to fill with chopped strawberries.

7. Spoon Strawberry Butter over to serve.

Strawberry Butter

Yield: Approximately ½ cup

½ cup mashed strawberries

¼ cup 10X powdered confectioners sugar, sifted

½ teaspoon lemon juice

¼ pound unsalted butter, softened

1. Combine strawberries, sugar and lemon juice in a food processor or blender, or mash together with a fork for a cruder mixture.

2. Incorporate the berry mixture into the butter.

Note: Strawberry Butter may be spooned into a crock and served with breakfast biscuits.

Grapes

The Muscadine grape is native to Florida and southeastern United States. It was the first grape to be cultivated in North America. Anyone in our area can grow these cluster type grapes. Just pound some stakes into the ground twenty feet apart in an open area with direct sunlight.

Grapes

The Muscadine grape we planted in the open field adjacent to our grove is native to Florida and southeastern United States. It was the first grape to be cultivated in North America. Anyone in our area can grow these cluster type grapes in our sandy soil. Just pound some stakes into the ground twenty feet apart in an open area with direct sunlight. Next, purchase some heavy wire and run it from the top of each stake to the next. Nature produces the large marble-shaped ambrosia with very little help from me. Because these grapes grow on their own root system, I simply cut a vine from someone else's yard or my own stock, stick the open end into a hole, and saturate it with water. It helps to fertilize several times a year with a commercial 10-10-10, but it's not necessary to use pesticides on this insect and disease tolerant sustainable fruit, which allows the children a picnic right at the vine. We grow two varieties of Muscadine, the female Fry that produces a huge global shaped fruit that turns from green to light bronze when fully ripe, and a smaller grape, that has a reddish-purple hue and a similar taste sensation to the northern Concorde variety. Both are perfect for jams and jellies. Some folk even try their hand at making wine, which is a fun hobby for personal consumption, but a poor business investment that usually ends as a disastrous endeavor.

Muscadine Jam with Marsala

Yield: Fills 8 (½-Pint) Jelly Jars

3½ cups strained juice from the Fry Muscadine grape (Approximately 3 pounds whole grapes)

6 quart non-reactive pot

½ sweet Marsala wine

Fine mesh strainer or jelly bag or 3 layers cheesecloth

7-7½ cups granulated sugar, depending on sweetness of grapes

1 pouch liquid fruit pectin (3 ounces)

1. Prepare lids and jars as directed in the pectin box instructions.

2. Pick a combination of ripe and almost ripe firm grapes. Wash and remove stems from grapes. Set into the pot with the Marsala wine. Cover and cook over low heat approximately 20 minutes, or until grapes are very soft. Cool 30 minutes.

3. Mash grapes with a potato masher to extract the juice.

4. Wet and ring out 3 layers of cheesecloth Hold it over a large bowl and pour the grapes and juice in, pulling the cloth up into a bundle. When all the juice has dripped through, stir the grapes with a wooden spoon to get all the juice. Discard the grape skins and seeds. Cover the bowl of juice and let it sit several hours so any sediment will fall to the bottom. Strain through the cheesecloth again into the pot.

5. If you cannot find cheesecloth, let the grape juice flow through a large fine mesh strainer. Push as much juice through as possible. Discard the grape skins and seeds and strain a second time. Cover the bowl of juice and let it sit several hours so any sediment will fall to the bottom. Strain again into the pot.

6. Bring the juice to the boiling point. Add the sugar and stir until it reaches the boiling point again. Add the liquid pectin, stirring, as it comes to a full boil. Boil, stirring, for 1 minute. Remove from the heat and immediately skim off any foam from the top.

7. Ladle quickly into prepared jars, filling ⅛th from the tops. Wipe any excess from the tops with wet paper towels. Seal tightly and turn upside down for 5 minutes. Turn upright. As jars begin to cool, press the center of their lids with your fingers. They should pop and then settle flat. If any remain puffy, they must be refrigerated. Otherwise, store in a cool, dry, dark place. Refrigerate jelly after opening.

Note: If you eliminate the Marsala wine, use 3⅔ cups juice and ⅓ cup Meyer lemon juice.

The combination of Italy's favorite Arborio rice with Florida's favorite Muscadine grape makes an outstanding first course or side dish to any dinner. Risotto, which was once found only in specialty stores, is now creeping onto the shelves of supermarkets. This rice is prepared differently than the long-grain variety Americans are accustomed to cooking. Whereas long-grain rice and water are combined at the beginning to boil together, the starchiness of risotto makes it necessary to add the liquid slowly, stirring constantly so the rice will not stick together and burn. The texture is also different. Long-grain rice is soft when cooked. The creamy kernels of Arborio have a firm texture. If it is cooked too long, the texture will become starchy rather than soft. Fresh herbs are a necessity for this recipe.

Risotto with Muscadine Grapes

Yield: Approximately 4 Servings

1 cup peeled and seeded Muscadine grapes

2 tablespoons unsalted butter

1 Florida sweet onion, minced

1½ cups Italian Arborio rice

1 teaspoon salt

⅛ teaspoon white pepper

2 cups dry white wine

1 cup chicken broth

2 cups boiling water

1 tablespoon finely-chopped basil leaves

1 teaspoon finely-chopped thyme leaves

1 teaspoon finely-chopped tarragon leaves

1. Peel the skin from the grapes with a sharp paring knife. Make a slit in each and remove the seeds. Set aside.

2. Melt the butter in a heavy pot or one with a non-stick bottom. Add the onion and cook over very low heat until soft, but not colored. Add the rice and toss with the onion.

3. Stir in the salt and pepper. Add the wine. Cook over medium heat, stirring often, until the liquid is absorbed. Add the chicken broth, ½ cup at a time, stirring often until the liquid is absorbed. Do the same with the water. Continue cooking and stirring until the liquid is absorbed.

4. Stir in the grapes, basil, thyme and tarragon and remove from the heat. Do not allow the rice to stand. It must be served immediately.

Kumquats

In China, kumquats are called "Gam Gat Sue". Gam rhymes with the Chinese word for gold. Gat rhymes with the Chinese word for luck. The tiny green leaves symbolize wealth as the word "Lu" (green) rhymes with the Chinese word for wealth. The shape of the kumquat is their symbol of unity and perfection. The Chinese New Year is ushered in with kumquats on the table to insure good fortune, prosperity and happiness.

RECIPES:

Irish Kumquat Jam

Kumquat Happy Jam

Kumquat Preserves and Sauce For Duck

Kumquat Chutney

Spicy Kumquat Relish

Kumquat Muffins

Roundquats in Rum

Mixed Fruit Jam

Getting Rid of Kumquats

Kumquats here, kumquats there, kumquats are falling everywhere. Delicious little creatures piled under the trees, splattering up our driveways and rotting in our yards. The cold snap has ripened them to perfection. It's time to reap the harvest. We eat the sweet skins and suck the small bit of tart juice, cook jams and chutneys and sauces for lamb and poultry and pork and fish until we've had our fill. But they just keep blooming! Waste not. Want not. Like Halloween pranksters or commodities come due, we sneak up to our neighbors' porches and dump bags with little notes telling them to "enjoy" the bounty we share. And they call to thank us and ask what the dickens they are supposed to do with them all. We don't care. It's not our problem any longer. We inform them that five kumquats have only 60 calories and contain vitamins A and C and leave them to their own devices.

In China, kumquats are called "Gam Gat Sue". Gam rhymes with the Chinese word for gold. Gat rhymes with the Chinese word for luck. The tiny green leaves symbolize wealth as the word "Lu" (green) rhymes with the Chinese word for wealth. The shape of the kumquat is their symbol of unity and perfection. The Chinese New Year is ushered in with kumquats on the table to insure good fortune, prosperity, and happiness.

The best quality kumquats have firm, bright orange skins and are fairly large. Don't bother with any that are too small, or that have become soft or wrinkled. Kumquats with stems still attached may be stored in the refrigerator up to one month. Point of information: There are several varieties of kumquats. We are most familiar with the Nagami kumquat. It bears bright orange fruit and does best in warmer areas. The Meiwa is the sweetest of the kumquats. Its fruit is round, with sweet, tender skin and a sweet tangy center. It also does best in hotter locations. Orangequats, sliced into thin rounds, are a wonderful mix of tender, sweet skin with sharp tangy centers. Limequats are cold-hardy versions of Key limes, with unique red skin and flesh. Then there's the Marumi, a tiny round, tart fruit. And, the one most familiar to South Florida, the Calamondin, which is lovely to use in centerpieces, but requires an unprecedented amount of sugar to create jams and jellies.

We grow two varieties of this succulent fruit in our grove: the oval Nagami kumquat and the Meiwa, which we refer to as 'round-quat'. Although different in size, shape, flavor, and foliage, we consider them half-brothers under the skin. Our Roundquat trees produce large fruit with a thicker skin than the kumquat, and definitely sweeter than the kumquat, although a good cold snap will ripen both to lushness.

Kumquats and other acidic foods (citrus, tomatoes) must be cooked in "non-reactive" pots. Stainless steel and enamel (that is not chipped) are non-reactive, as is glass. Glass, however, is a poor conductor of heat, even though it retains heat well after food is cooked. A reactive pot or pan is one made from a material that reacts chemically with other foods. Aluminum and copper are the two most common reactive materials used to manufacture pots and pans. Cast-iron is also reactive. Lightweight aluminum reacts with acidic foods, imparting a metallic taste, and can discolor light-colored soups and sauces, especially if stirred with a metal spoon or wire whisk. Do not cook or store light-colored foods in aluminum cookware. Anodized aluminum has a hard, corrosion-resistant surface that helps prevent discoloration.

However you decide to cook kumquats, working with them is a hassle. Most have very little juice and large seeds within a heavy membrane, leaving only the sweet rind for jellies and jams. Each little piece of fruit must be washed. They should then be covered with hot water, brought to a boil for thirty seconds and drained under cold, running water to remove the acid taste. Then they must be split to remove the seeds, pith, and membrane, after which they must be pulverized in a food processor. If kumquats are left whole, each must be cross-slit on the top or slit from top to bottom so they will not "collapse" and wither after cooking. It's a tricky and time-consuming business to preserve these little gems. Incorporating them within a sauce for poultry, fish or pork is much easier. Drop them into boiling water for thirty seconds, rinse and split to remove the seeds, or just leave them whole. A super, easy glaze for poultry or pork is the mixture of kumquats, chopped or whole, with orange marmalade, a little lemon juice and orange liqueur. Combine in a pot and cook over low heat, stirring, until well mixed. Brush or spoon the mixture over chicken or pork the last fifteen minutes of cooking. Serve remaining sauce on the side.

If you're searching for a refreshing dessert, divide my recipe for Kumquats in Rum in half. Do not bother to preserve in jars. Refrigerate until very cold and serve them with fresh pineapple cubes over sherbet or on toothpicks. There is absolutely nothing better to top off a beautiful dinner.

Irish Kumquat Jam

Yield: 10 Pints

7 pounds kumquats

1½ pounds crystallized ginger

7 pounds granulated sugar

1 cup Irish whiskey

6 ounces liquid fruit pectin (2 pouches Certo®)

1. Pick fully ripe, firm, bright orange kumquats. Discard those which are light in color, withered or soft. Taste several to insure peak flavor.

2. Scrub kumquats well. Cover with water in a large soup pot. Bring to a boil, stirring several times. Drain and rinse with cold water.

3. With a small, sharp knife, slit each kumquat and remove the seeds and membrane, leaving just the skins.

4. Place the ginger into a food processor in batches and grind into tiny pieces. Remove to the pot.

5. Place the kumquats into the food processor in batches and pulverize. Return to the pot.

6. Stir in 3 pounds of the sugar. Stir in the whiskey. If you do not have Irish whiskey, substitute Scotch whiskey. Allow mixture to stand several hours, stirring occasionally.

7. Bring to a slow boil over medium heat, stirring constantly. Do not leave your post for even a short time, or sugar mixture will stick to the bottom of the pot and burn. Continue to stir until mixture begins to boil. It will be very thick.

8. Add remaining sugar and bring to a boil, stirring constantly. Add fruit pectin all at once. Continue stirring, while mixture bubbles, 1 minute. Remove from the heat immediately. Fill sterilized jars while mixture is very hot. Wipe around the tops with wet paper toweling to remove sticky fruit residue. Cap the jars tightly.

9. Set jars into a pot of boiling water for thirty seconds. Remove, dry and turn jars upside down for 30 minutes. Turn right side up.

10. Store at a cool room temperature. Refrigerate after opening.

If I could standardize a recipe I liked best, I would market my kumquat preserves and become a rich lady. However, my taste preference changes each time. More ginger. Less ginger. Sweet. Slightly tart. Add liquor. Who needs liquor? Thick consistency. Thin consistency. And, so, each batch has slightly different proportions. And, each time, it's better than the time before. All of which only proves that you can't go wrong with a kumquat.

Kumquat Happy Jam

Yield: 12 (½-Pint) Jars

7 pounds kumquats

1 pound sugar-glazed ginger, chopped

1 cup pasteurized Florida orange juice

¼ cup Triple Sec liqueur

¼ cup bourbon whiskey

4 pounds granulated sugar

Optional: 5 boxes (packets) Sure Jell® pectin

1. Boil whole kumquats in water to cover 1 minute. Drain and rinse under cold water. Cut into halves and remove pulp and seeds. Pulverize in a food processor or through a meat grinder in batches.

2. Soak ginger in cool water 15 minutes, or until softened. Pulverize in a food processor or through a meat grinder.

3. Return to pot and stir in orange juice, Triple Sec, bourbon, chopped ginger, and half the sugar. Allow to sit at least 15 minutes.

4. Bring to a boil, stirring. Reduce heat to medium. Cook, uncovered, 45 minutes, stirring often. Lower heat if jam begins to stick to the bottom.

5. Add Sure Jell® and remaining sugar. Bring to a boil, stirring. Boil 1 minute only and fill ½-pint jars according to directions.

Note: If you leave out the orange juice and cook the kumquat mixture longer, the consistency will thicken by itself, eliminating the need for any pectin at the end.

Kumquats gain momentum when mixed with a solution of sugar, ginger and rum

Kumquat Preserves and Sauce for Duck

Yield: 6 (8-Ounce) Jars

4½ pounds ripe kumquats

8 ounces fresh ginger

5 pounds granulated sugar (4½ cups)

¾ cup water

3 sticks cinnamon, broken into large pieces

1. Wash kumquats. If they have been sprayed, add a bit of liquid detergent to the water. Rinse well. Put in large pot in water to cover. Bring to a boil. Boil 1 minute. Drain in a colander under cold, running water. Return to the pot and cover again with water. Boil 10 minutes. Drain and rinse again. Pop out the insides and discard, keeping the skins only.

2. Chop the skins fine by hand or in a food processor. Remove to a large pot.

3. Peel the ginger and chop fine by hand or in the food processor. Add to the kumquats.

4. Stir in the sugar, water, rum and cinnamon. Bring to a slow boil over medium heat, stirring often. When mixture begins to boil, reduce heat to low and cover the pot. Boil gently 40 minutes, stirring often. Lower heat to simmer if mixture begins to stick to the bottom.

5. Fill jars according to instructions. Make sure the caps are screwed on very tightly. Refrigerate after preserves have cooled completely.

Sauce for Duck:

Combine 2 cups preserves with ¼ cup Grand Marnier® liqueur in a saucepan. Stir to a boil. Reduce heat to simmer and keep warm until ready to serve.

Kumquat Chutney

Yield: 8 (½-Pint) Jars

3 pounds whole kumquats (approximately 8 cups)

1 pound sweet Florida white onions

1½ pounds combined green, yellow, red, and/or orange bell peppers

12 ounce bottle hot banana peppers

4 ounces peeled fresh gingerroot, grated or minced fine

½ pound chopped crystallized ginger

1 large head garlic

Juice and finely chopped rind of 3 Key limes

1 tablespoon plus 1 teaspoon ground cinnamon

1 teaspoon ground cloves

1 teaspoon ground allspice

1 pound golden raisins

½ cup apple cider vinegar

2 pounds light brown sugar

Salt to taste

1. Prepare jars according to directions.

2. Wash kumquats well and cover with water in a large pot. Bring to a rolling boil. Pour off water and rinse kumquats under cold, running water. Allow to cool. Slice and remove the insides. If they contain juice, remove seeds and membrane only. Transfer in batches to a food processor and chop. Return to the pot.

3. Chop the onions, peppers, and ginger to the small chunky stage. Remove and peel the cloves from the garlic head. Pulverize in a food processor. Add all to the pot with the kumquats.

4. Add remaining ingredients. Allow to stand 15 minutes. Bring to a slow boil, stirring so ingredients will not stick to the bottom. Reduce heat to simmer. Cook slowly, covered with the lid on a slant to release the steam. Stir often and continue cooking 1 hour.

5. Fill jars immediately according to directions.

Note: Renninger's indoor - outdoor Antique emporium and Twin Markets are Mount Dora's weekend tourist attractions. Ginger, dried fruits and nuts can be purchased at "Oh Nuts" for a fraction of the cost of most stores.

Spicy Kumquat Relish

Yield: Approximately 2 Cups

1 pound ripe kumquats

¼ cup thinly sliced crystallized ginger ("Oh Nuts", Renninger's Twin Markets on Hwy 441 in Mount Dora)

1 cup light brown sugar

2 tablespoons apple cider vinegar

¼ cup golden raisins

¼ teaspoon dried crushed red pepper, or 6 ounce can green chili peppers

¼ cup chopped dried apricots

1. Boil kumquats 30 seconds. Rinse under cold running water. Slice in half lengthwise and remove seeds. Combine with remaining ingredients.

2. Cook in a non-reactive pot or slow-cook crockpot on low heat at least 2 hours. Cool. Serve with pork, chicken or fish.

Kumquat Muffins

Yield: 12 Regular Sized Muffins

1 cup whole kumquats

1½ cups all-purpose flour

¾ cup white cornmeal

2 tablespoons baking powder

¾ cup granulated sugar

3 jumbo eggs, beaten

¾ cup vegetable oil (not solid)

¾ cup whole milk

1. Preheat oven to 350°F.

2. Bring kumquats to a full boil in water to cover. Boil 30 seconds. Rinse under cold, running water. Repeat procedure. Cut kumquats in half and remove seeds and membranes. Dice by hand or in the food processor. Set aside.

3. Spray or grease muffin tins. Or, line them with paper cups.

4. Sift flour, cornmeal, baking powder and sugar together. Beat eggs and stir in. Stir in oil and milk until just combined.

5. Stir in diced kumquats. Be careful not to over-mix or the result will be tough muffins with holes in the centers.

6. Bake 15-20 minutes, or until a toothpick comes out clean.

Roundquats in Rum

Yield: 4 12-Ounce (1 pint) Jars

48 roundquats (or large kumquats)	1 whole cinnamon stick
Water to cover	1 cup dark rum
4 ounces crystallized ginger	¼ cup Triple Sec Liqueur
1½ cups water	4 12-ounce jam jars
3 cups granulated sugar	

1. Wash roundquats well to remove any dirt. Slit each lengthwise from top to bottom to expose seeds. Cut only to the center so it appears as though roundquat is whole. This will keep the fruit from collapsing.

2. Cover with water in a large pot. Bring to a boil. Set aside.

3. Cut the ginger into thin strips and set aside.

4. Combine the water, sugar and cinnamon and bring to a boil, uncovered, over high heat. Reduce heat to medium-high and boil gently, stirring occasionally, until mixture begins to thicken. Stir in the rum and triple sec and continue to boil 2 minutes longer. Add ginger strips and bring to a quick boil, stirring. Remove from the heat and stir the roundquats into the hot syrup with a slotted spoon.

5. Fill jars according to instructions, making sure tops are screwed on very tightly. Refrigerate for peak quality.

6. Serve very cold with fresh pineapple cubes for a superb finish to any dinner.

Mixed Fruit Jam

7 half pint jars

2 pounds kumquats

3 pounds Hamlin oranges (or another sweet orange)

3 Key limes

2 cups granulated sugar

1 box Sure Jell® fruit pectin

3½ cups granulated sugar

1. Wash fruit well. Remove the skin from the kumquats and discard the seeds. Place in a food processor and pulverize. Pour into a non-reactive pot.

2. Slice oranges in half. Remove seeds and cut the pulp into pieces to fit into the food processor. Cut the limes into small pieces with their skin and combine with the orange pulp. Turn the machine on-off several times. Add to the pot.

3. Stir in 2 cups sugar and bring to a boil, stirring. Lower heat to medium and boil gently 10 minutes, stirring often. Skim off foam that rises to the top.

4. Stir in Sure Jell® and bring to a boil. Stir in 3½ cups sugar all at once. Bring to a boil, stirring. Boil 1 minute, stirring often. Remove from heat and fill sterilized jars according to directions.

Citrus

The fragrance of blossoms fills the air, producing an aphrodisiac from the thousands of trees proclaiming their superiority over Lake County.

RECIPES:

Bread Pudding with Lemon or
Whiskey Sauce

Lemon Sauce

Whiskey Sauce

Bearss Lemon Torte

Lemon Frosting

Bearss Buttermilk Ices

Avgholemono Soup

Butternut Squash Soup

Victor's Gift

Lemon Curd

Citrus Cheesecake Brownies

Lemon Liqueur

Plum Pudding

Citrus - Lemons, Meyer and Bearss

March has arrived in Central Florida like a gentle lamb bearing clear skies and the promise of balmy air as her apology for the icy cold of January and February that almost sucked away the last breath of life from the citrus. The fragrance of blossoms fills the air, producing an aphrodisiac from the thousands of trees proclaiming their superiority over Lake County.

Within the myriad of white flowers are four Meyer lemon trees clothed in a grand couturier lilac that triumphs over all the others. The intensity of their aroma can only be described as euphoric. There is absolutely no descriptive adjective worthy of the privilege of this experience.

If there is one fruit that truly pleases, the Meyer lemon succeeds. Less acidic than the Eureka and Lisbon variety of lemon, it enhances ice water, creates a pleasant tasting lemonade that requires less sugar than the Bearss lemon, acts as a natural sweetener for the local strawberries now in bloom, and tempers the strong flavor of game and fish. It is an absolutely marvelous gift of nature.

The Meyer lemon is also much larger than other varieties, growing to the size of an orange as it turns from green to bright yellow when ripe, and then to orange at the almost overripe state. The branches that grow bushy and low to the ground become so overburdened from the weight of their prolific tenants, that it becomes necessary to lie prone under them to pluck the fruit. Our lemons are almost seedless. One lemon can yield over a half cup of juice.

Bread Pudding with Lemon or Whiskey Sauce

Yield: Approximately 12 Servings. Recipe may be cut in half.

1 loaf French bread (approximately 1 pound or less)

1 cup black or golden raisins

1½ quarts whole milk

3 tablespoons melted butter

4 jumbo graded eggs

3 cups granulated sugar

2 tablespoons vanilla extract

Optional: 1 teaspoon bourbon whiskey

9½ x 14 x 2½ (approximately) baking dish

1 teaspoon butter to rub around dish

Cinnamon-sugar to sprinkle (7 parts sugar mixed with 2 parts cinnamon)

1. Preheat oven to 350°F.

2. Slice bread ¾-inch thick and cut into cubes. Combine with raisins.

3. Heat milk to the boiling point and pour over the bread and raisins. Leave them to soak until very soft.

4. Pour melted butter into the bottom of the baking pan.

5. Beat eggs with the sugar and vanilla (bourbon). Stir into bread mixture. Butter the dish and pour in the pudding. Sprinkle heavily with the cinnamon-sugar mixture.

6. Bake 1 hour, or until a knife comes out clean.

7. Serve with warm Whiskey Sauce or Lemon Sauce.

Lemon Sauce

Yield: ¾ Cup to serve as an accompaniment to berries or puddings

2 tablespoons Meyer lemon juice

1 tablespoon grated lemon peel

½ cup water

⅓ cup granulated sugar

1 teaspoon cornstarch dissolved in ¼ cup cool water

1 tablespoon vanilla extract

1. Combine ingredients in a saucepan and cook over medium heat, stirring, until thickened.

Whiskey Sauce

Yield: Approximately 1 Cup

¾ cup granulated sugar
1 jumbo graded egg
¼ cup water

¼ pound melted butter
¾ cup bourbon or rum

1. Combine the sugar, egg and water in the top of a double boiler or in a bowl set over simmering water. Slowly pour in the melted butter, beating vigorously. Add the bourbon or rum and continue beating until mixture thickens slightly. Cover tightly and keep warm until ready to serve.

Bearss Lemon Torte

Yield: 12-14 Servings

Genoise Cake, baked in 2 10-inch pans
   (recipe, page 248)
¾ cup cornstarch
2½ cups granulated sugar

¼ teaspoon salt
3 cups boiling water
¾ cup unstrained juice from Bearss lemons
8 extra large or 7 jumbo graded eggs yolks

1. Sift cornstarch, sugar and salt into a 2 quart heavy pot or the top of a double boiler. Pour in the boiling water slowly, stirring with wooden spoon until completely blended. Cook over medium heat, stirring until thick and smooth. If mixture begins to stick on the bottom, remove it from the stove and lower the heat.

2. Pour the lemon juice in slowly, stirring constantly until thick and creamy. Beat egg yolks with a fork and add a bit of the hot mixture to them. This will prevent the yolks from curdling. Stir them into the pot with a wire whisk until smooth. Continue cooking, stirring with a wooden spoon until thick and creamy. Place a sheet of wax paper directly over the mixture and cool.

3. To Assemble: Slice each cake layer in half, creating 4 layers. Place the bottom layer on a cake plate. Spoon a third of the lemon filling over, bringing it all the way to the outer edges. Cover with a cake layer. Follow this procedure two more times, and cover with the top layer. Smooth any filling that has seeped out around the outside edges with a sharp knife. Cover tightly with plastic wrap and refrigerate overnight. Cover with Lemon Frosting.

Lemon Frosting

Yield: 2 Cups

1½ cups sifted 10X powdered confectioners sugar

¼ cup butter, softened

3 ounces cream cheese, softened

1 teaspoon grated lemon rind from Bearss lemon

2 tablespoons lemon juice from Bearss lemon

1-2 tablespoons coffee cream to smooth

1 lemon, sliced thin for decoration

1. Combine the sugar, butter, cream cheese and lemon rind and beat until smooth. Add the lemon juice and 1 tablespoon of cream. If too thick to spread, add more cream.

2. Cover the outside of the cake with the frosting. Slice a lemon thin and twist the rounds into pretzel shapes to decorate the top.

Follow the exit signs into Tampa and you will be on Bearss Avenue named for the fast growing, productive lemon prevalent to the area. This juicy, acidic fruit was originally discovered in the early 1950's as a seedling tree in the Bearss grove near Lutz, which is now a thriving suburb of Tampa. Tampa history lists the fruit as being a descendent of the "Sicily" lemon, which was planted in the late 1880's. The Bearss bears in abundance from July through December and has more flavor and tartness than the Meyer lemon, making it suitable for most recipes and a favorite choice for strong lemonade.

Bearss Buttermilk Ices

Yield: 5 Cups

2 cups granulated sugar

Grated rind of ½ Bearss lemon

½ cup Bearss lemon juice, strained

1 quart buttermilk, preferably not low fat

1. Mix in the order given above and freeze in an airtight container.

Avgholemono Soup

This Byzantine heirloom recipe, which has been a favorite since the sixth century, takes on a new dimension with Florida's Meyer lemon.

2 quarts rich chicken broth

¼ cup raw white long grain rice

3 whole eggs

¼ cup Meyer lemon juice

Salt and a touch of white pepper to taste

1. Heat broth to the boiling point. Add rice. Stir. Cover. Reduce heat to low and cook 20 minutes.

2. Beat eggs until frothy. Beat in lemon juice. Slowly add a little hot broth, stirring constantly. Continue adding hot broth until mixture is smooth. Slowly pour into the remaining broth in the pot with the rice.

3. Simmer slowly, stirring, for no longer than 3 minutes. Do not allow soup to boil or the eggs will curdle. Taste for salt and pepper and serve immediately.

Note: The rice may be cooked in the soup in advance and the egg-lemon mixture added directly before serving.

The prolific Ponderosa lemon that fertilizes itself grows to grapefruit sized proportions. The blossoms that begin its cycle of growth have such an intense fragrance they overpower the other citrus. This giant fruit produces a superior flavor for juicing or cooking, and the bright yellow skin livens up soups and desserts as a garnish. It is said that Florida is the largest producer of winter squash. The Butternut squash is the sweetest, lending itself particularly well to soup. Sweet Dumpling Butternut squash is the ultimate of ultimatums. Combined with orange blossom honey and finished with grated Ponderosa lemon peel, it always has snowbirds from the north begging for more.

Butternut Squash Soup

Yield: Approximately 2 cups

2 pounds "Sweet Dumpling" butternut squash to equal 1 cup cooked squash pulp

1 cup chicken broth

½ teaspoon coriander

½ teaspoon cinnamon

¼ teaspoon allspice

1 tablespoon orange blossom honey

⅛ teaspoon white pepper

Salt to taste

¼ cup coffee cream

¼ cup grated Ponderosa lemon peel

1. Slice the top off the squash ¼ from the stem. Scoop out the seeds. Place in a microwavable dish with water to cover the bottom. Microwave 3 minutes per pound. Put into a blender or food processor. Add coriander, cinnamon, allspice, honey, white pepper and salt to taste.

2. Stir in chicken broth. Pour into a blender and blend on high until puréed. Return to the pot. Stir in the coffee cream. Taste for seasoning.

3. Grate the lemon peel.

4. Spoon the soup into bowls and sprinkle the grated lemon over the top.

Note: This soup is good hot or cold. Chopped candied ginger may also be sprinkled across the top.

Victor's Gift

Victor and his family tended the citrus grove adjacent to our property. When we replanted after a devastating freeze, he offered to prune and fertilize our new fledglings. Within three years, his magical touch produced Hamlin, Valencia, Temple, Ambersweet, Page, Blood Seedless and Navel oranges. Each bore its own kind, unique in appearance and flavor, like children from the same family. Seven varieties of tangerines and tangelos, four varieties of grapefruit, oval and round kumquats, Persian and Key limes, and Ponderosa, Bearss and Meyer lemons grew strong and proud in perfectly symmetrical rows.

The demise of the second tree in the first row for no apparent reason left Victor visibly shaken. One of his 'babies' had not reached maturity. Shortly afterward, I noticed three sticks protruding where the tree once stood. One year later, strange vertical leaves sprouted on three thin trunks. No fruit. The second year produced bushy growth of the same leaves. No fruit. The third year gave birth to a species of green fruit on one branch only. Before the fruit ripened, the thin branch broke in half from the weight of whatever had taken it over. The fourth year we tied the branch to the others, which were still not producing anything other than leaves. The green giants ripened into Meyer lemons, more flavorful than any of the others in the grove. This year, the twigs have matured into a strange apparition of a wild triplicate of thin trunks holding branches that flail in every direction. Each branch is burdened to the ground with differently shaped fruit ready to ripen. The rope that ties them together and the wooden V-shaped forks propped against the trunks only serve to heighten everyone's curiosity about the outcome of Victor's gift.

Lemon Curd

Yield: 2 Cups

1 cup less 2 tablespoons Meyer lemon juice

Yellow skin of ¼ lemon (no white), cut into strips

8 tablespoons unsalted butter, cut into pieces

⅛ teaspoon salt

1 cup granulated sugar

4 jumbo graded egg yolks

1. Sterilize 2 (½-pint) jam jars and set aside.

2. Strain lemon juice into a non-reactive heavy pot or top of double boiler. Add strips of yellow rind.

3. Stir in butter and salt and cook over low heat until butter has melted and mixture is hot.

4. Stir the sugar into the egg yolks. This is an important step for the mixture to coagulate properly.

5. Stir some of the hot mixture into the sugar-egg yolks before adding them to the lemon mixture. Cook over medium-low heat, stirring constantly, until it thickens enough to coat a spoon. (Approximately 7 minutes.)

6. Remove from heat. Strain and fill jam jars, or cool to room temperature. Pour into a glass container to refrigerate up to one week.

Citrus Cheesecake Brownies

Yield: Approximately 32 Squares

Cheese Filling:

12 ounces softened cream cheese

⅔ cup granulated sugar

2 jumbo graded eggs, or 3 large

2 tablespoons lemon juice

2 tablespoons orange juice

1 tablespoon vanilla extract

½ cup all-purpose flour

1. Combine cream cheese and sugar and beat with an electric mixer until smooth. Add eggs, lemon and orange juice. Scrape the sides and bottom of the bowl and beat again to incorporate. Add vanilla and continue beating until thickened. Set aside.

The Brownies:

9 ounces semi-sweet chocolate

6 tablespoons butter

1 cup plus 2 tablespoons unsweetened cocoa

1 teaspoon baking powder

¼ teaspoon salt

1 cup plus 2 tablespoons granulated sugar

3 eggs

2 teaspoons vanilla extract

¾ cup finely-chopped (not ground) pecans

12x10x2-inch baking pan, or a size closest to it

1. Preheat oven to 350°F.

2. Melt chocolate chips and butter over low heat until chips soften. Remove from heat and stir. Cool 5 minutes.

3. Sift together the flour, cocoa, baking powder and salt.

4. Combine sugar, eggs and vanilla and beat with an electric mixer until well-blended and slightly thickened, approximately 5 minutes.

5. Beat in chocolate mixture. Add flour. Scrape sides and bottom. Beat on medium speed until mixture is smooth. Stir in pecans.

6. Spread ½ the chocolate mixture into the pan. Carefully spoon reserved cream cheese mixture over. Spoon the other half of the chocolate mixture over. Bake 30 minutes, or until a toothpick inserted in the center comes out slightly wet. Results will be moist and fudgie. For a firmer brownie, bake another 5 minutes.

7. Cool completely. Refrigerate until cold before cutting into squares.

We do not spray our fruit trees, so it is safe to eat the skins. If you do not have access to private citrus, use organic lemons.

Lemon Liqueur

(known in Italy as Limoncello)

Yield: 3 cups

2 cups vodka

½ cup Ponderosa, Bearss or Meyer lemon peel

1 cup granulated sugar

¾ cup bottled drinking water

1. Pour the alcohol into a clean glass bottle. Reserve the empty vodka bottle. Insert thin strips of the yellow skin of the lemons, being careful not to include the white, which is bitter. Close the bottle tightly and allow the flavors to incorporate together 2 weeks or longer.

2. Make simple sugar syrup: Combine the sugar and water in a stainless steel pot, stirring to incorporate. Bring to a boil, stirring constantly. Boil 2 minutes. Remove from the heat and cool to room temperature.

3. Add the syrup to the alcohol-lemon mixture. Leave in a cool place 2 weeks.

4. Strain and discard the lemon peels and pour the flavored liqueur into the reserved vodka bottle. Let the mixture rest another 2 weeks before drinking. Serve very cold from the refrigerator as an after dinner cordial.

Note: This is an extremely rich drink. Serve sparingly.

Plum Pudding

Yield: 8 Servings

1 pound Granny Smith apples
1½ cups plain toasted or stale breadcrumbs
1 teaspoon ground Allspice
¼ teaspoon salt
1 cup firmly packed dark brown sugar
8 ounces golden or dark raisins

4 ounces currants
6-7 ounces thinly sliced toasted almonds
4 ounces pine nuts
2 tablespoons honey
2 tablespoons lemon juice
Grated rind of 1 lemon
3 extra large eggs, beaten

1. Peel, core and chop apples.

2. Mix bread crumbs with allspice and salt. Add brown sugar, almonds, pine nuts, raisins and currants. Add apples.

3. Mix honey and lemon juice together and stir in to bread crumb mixture. Add grated lemon rind.

4. Beat eggs and mix in well.

5. Butter an eight cup mold or special mold made for English puddings (found in Gourmet shops). If you do not have a large enough container, divide the mixture into two four cup molds. Fill the mold(s), packing mixture tightly down. Cover with buttered cheesecloth or foil. Set mold in a pot with water reaching half-way up the sides. Bring water to a boil. Cover the pot. Boil rapidly for 3 hours. Check to make sure water does not evaporate, adding boiling water to the pot as it does.

6. Remove mold(s) from the water and allow to cool 30 minutes. Run a knife around the inside edges (Don't forget to run it around the inside tube as well). Invert pudding onto a plate.

7. Serve warm with Whiskey Sauce (recipe, page 52) on the side.

Limes

RECIPES:

Citrus Poppy Seed Salad

Lime Meringue Pie

Key Lime Pie

Key Lime Cheesecake

This is an excellent compliment to accompany or follow game and grilled fish.

Citrus Poppy Seed Salad

Yield: Approximately 1½ Cups to yield 4 salads

2 tablespoons Key lime juice (Persian for a stronger flavor)

⅓ cup Valencia orange juice

2 tablespoons poppy seeds

2 tablespoons orange blossom honey, or more to taste

½ teaspoon vanilla extract

½ teaspoon salt

½ cup mayonnaise

4 cups mixed lettuce leaves

2 tablespoons thinly sliced sugared ginger

½ pint blueberries

2 Valencia oranges, cut into segments

1 Ruby Red grapefruit, cut into segments

1. In a blender, combine lime, orange juice, poppy seeds, honey, sugar, vanilla, salt and mayonnaise. Blend on low speed until smooth. Refrigerate.

2. Toss lettuce with dressing. Divide onto 4 plates. Sprinkle the ginger and blueberries over. Place orange and grapefruit segments around.

Note: When fresh berries are out of season, substitute dried cranberries.

July: Just when the price of limes skyrockets in the grocery store, Nature delivers a "bumper crop" of Persian limes to our winter-bearing tree. Judging from the hundreds of minuscule green nuggets beginning to weigh down the branches of our lemon, lime, grapefruit, orange, tangerine and kumquat trees, next season will provide us with an abundance of citrus. By late October, they will become fully grown with their resplendent colors reflecting in the rays of the sun that has ripened them to juicy perfection.

Lime Meringue Pie

Yield: Approximately 8 Servings

Baked and cooled 9-inch pie crust

⅔ cup cornstarch

1½ cups granulated sugar

¼ teaspoon salt

3 cups boiling water

7 jumbo or 8 extra large egg yolks

¾ cup Persian lime juice

1. Sift the cornstarch with the sugar and salt into a 2-quart heavy pot or the top of a double boiler. Pour the boiling water in slowly, stirring with a wooden spoon until smooth, thick and creamy.

2. Beat the egg yolks with a whisk until blended. Slowly add some of the hot mixture to them. (This is an important technique to keep the eggs from 'scrambling'.) Stir mixture back into the pot and continue to cook, stirring constantly, until very thick. Stir in lime juice and continue stirring until mixture is thick and bubbly. Remove from the heat and cool completely. Do not refrigerate. Spoon into the baked pie shell and refrigerate until very cold.

Note: Lemon juice may be substituted for lime.

Meringue:

7 jumbo or 8 extra large egg whites

⅓ cup granulated sugar

1 tablespoon cornstarch

⅛ teaspoon salt

½ teaspoon cream of tartar

1. Sift together sugar, cornstarch and salt.

2. Beat egg whites in a bowl over simmering water until foamy with a hand electric mixer. Add cream of tartar. Add sugar mixture a tablespoon at a time, beating on high speed until thick and glossy, approximately 6-8 minutes.

3. Cover the entire top with the meringue, bringing it up into peaks with a spoon, or pipe rosettes with a fluted tube. Place under the broiler to brown.

Note: The word, 'meringue', is said to have come from the city of Meiringen in the Emmen Valley in Switzerland where crunchy egg white cookies filled with chocolate cream were served after festive dinners. Foreign guests who could not pronounce the original name, 'meiringerli', changed it to 'meringues'.

Our resident Bald Eagle soars over the citrus to the top of the highest tree in the adjoining woods. The sight of his wings, spread so proud and strong against the wind, causes us to raise our heads in awe. We watch his endeavor to bring food to his beloved, who sits on the single egg in their nest. The faithful eagle mates for life, taking another only upon the demise of the first. Like affluent humans, they have a second home on the water a short mile to the west, but theirs is not for recreation or ostentation, but safety, lest the other becomes endangered. When he completes his mission, we return to ours of picking the Key limes that have turned yellow before they fall to the ground.

Key Lime Pie

Yield: 8-10 Servings

2 8-ounce packages cream cheese, room temperature

6 extra large egg yolks

14.5 ounce can sweetened condensed milk

1 cup Key lime juice (Persian lime may be substituted)

6 extra large egg whites

¼ teaspoon cream of tartar

1 tablespoon granulated sugar

Pre-baked 9-inch pie crust

1. Preheat oven to 350°F.

2. Separate eggs, reserving whites covered tightly in the refrigerator. Beat cream cheese smooth. Add yolks, one at a time, beating well into the cream cheese. Continue beating on high speed 8 minutes. Slowly beat in sweetened condensed milk. Add lime juice in a very slow steady stream, beating until smooth and creamy.

3. Pour into a pre-baked pie crust. Bake 12 minutes. Cool to room temperature and refrigerate overnight or freeze.

4. Pour the egg whites into a mixing bowl and bring to room temperature or warmer. (Set the bowl into another bowl of hot water, being careful not to splash any water into the whites.) Beat with an electric beater on highest speed until frothy. Add cream of tartar and continue beating until very thick. Add sugar and beat until smooth. (10 seconds). Place under a broiler to brown. (Watch carefully not to burn.) Serve.

Key Lime Cheesecake

Yield: 12-16 Slices

32 ounces (4 8-ounce packages) cream cheese, softened to room temperature

1¼ cups granulated sugar

5 jumbo egg yolks, room temperature

2 teaspoons vanilla extract

¼ cup Key lime juice

7 tablespoons sour cream

3 tablespoons all-purpose flour

5 jumbo egg whites, room temperature or warmer

½ teaspoon cream of tartar

1 tablespoon granulated sugar

9-inch springform pan fitted with a crust

1. Preheat the oven to 450°F.

2. Beat the cream cheese on high speed of an electric mixer 10 seconds. Add the sugar and continue to beat until fluffy. Turn off mixer and scrape the sides and bottom of the bowl. Lower the speed to medium and add the egg yolks, one at a time, turning the mixer off after each yolk has been added to scrape the sides and bottom.

3. Add vanilla and Key lime juice on low speed. Add the sour cream. Add the flour. Scrape the sides and bottom and turn the mixer on high speed for a few seconds.

4. Beat the egg whites in a separate bowl on high speed until foamy. Add cream of tartar and beat until thick. Add sugar and continue beating until smooth.

5. Fold beaten whites into the cream cheese mixture and pour into the springform pan. Set the rack one-third from the bottom of the oven and bake the cake for 6 minutes, or until the top begins to turn color. Reduce heat immediately to 250°F and continue baking another 40 minutes. Turn off the oven and open the door to cool.

6. Refrigerate overnight, or freeze, tightly covered. Cover the top with Ganache Frosting (recipe, page 249) and slivers of lime peel.

Amaretto Lime Cheesecake:

Exchange the vanilla for 2 teaspoons almond extract or Amaretto liqueur and cover the top with Praline Topping (recipe, page 250) instead of the Ganache Frosting.

Oranges

RECIPES:

Parson Brown Waffles

Blender Sweet Crêpes

Hamlin Cheese Blintzes

Orange Butter

Orange Chiffon Cake

Orange Frosting

BSB Scrumptious Chocolate Cake

Chocolate Cream Cheese Frosting

Citrus Sunshine Cake

Valencia Spongecake

White Fruitcake

Hamlin Crème Brûlée

Glazed Orange or Lemon Rind

Tangerines in Syrup

Tangerine Compote

Orange County Orange Marmalade

Easy Orange Marmalade

Orange Liqueur Ices

Candied Carrots Sugar Free

Parson Brown Waffles

Yield: 4 Large Waffles

1½ cups all-purpose flour

2 teaspoons baking powder

1 teaspoon baking soda

3 teaspoons granulated sugar

½ teaspoon salt

2 egg whites, graded jumbo

2 egg yolks, graded jumbo

2 cups sour cream or vanilla yogurt

4 tablespoons melted butter

1 full teaspoon vanilla extract

3 tablespoons orange juice from Parson Brown Oranges

Optional: ¼ cup Florida pecan pieces

Optional: 1 cup sifted 10X powdered confectioners sugar

Maple syrup

Strawberries from Hillsborough (Plant City), Lake or Marion Counties.

1. Mix together the flour, baking powder, baking soda, sugar and salt.

2. Beat egg whites to a thick foamy stage, but not where peaks form.

3. Mix together egg yolks, sour cream (yogurt), melted butter, vanilla and orange juice.

4. Mix wet ingredients with dry ingredients until just blended.

5. Fold in egg whites. Cover bowl and let stand 15 minutes. Optional: Fold in nuts. Spoon batter on to the center of a waffle maker that has been preheated. (A Belgian waffle maker creates the perfect shape and size.) Close the cover tightly and cook until the light goes off, signifying the waffle is done. Serve with powdered sugar, maple syrup and fruit on the side.

6. Note: These can be made in advance and heated in a 200°F. oven. They also freeze beautifully, but nothing compares to the aroma of fresh waffles being baked.

Note: For a heavier waffle, do not separate eggs.

Blender Crêpes

Yield: Approximately 15-18 Crêpes, 6-7 inches in diameter

2 tablespoons melted butter	½ teaspoon granulated sugar
2 extra large eggs	¼ teaspoon salt
⅔ cup cold milk	¼ teaspoon vanilla extract
½ cup cold water	1 cup all-purpose flour

1. Crack eggs into a blender. Blend on medium speed 10 seconds. Add milk, water, sugar, salt and vanilla. Cover and blend on high 10 seconds. Add the flour. Blend on medium speed. Scrape sides. Blend again. Add the melted butter and blend on high 10 seconds. Refrigerate several hours or overnight.

2. Directly before cooking, blend again for a few seconds on high speed. Pour mixture into a cup with a pour spout. Heat a non-stick frying pan or crêpe pan (no larger than 6-7 inches inside diameter) over medium heat. Pour in enough batter to cover the bottom, and, as it begins to stick, immediately pour the extra batter back into the cup, leaving a thin layer in the pan. Allow the batter to set, and then cut around the edge where you have poured out the excess. Cook on one side until slightly light brown. This should take about 1 minute. . If the underside appears too raw, turn over and cook no longer than 5 seconds, or the crêpe will harden.

3. Set crêpes onto wax paper to cool, stacking them when they reach room temperature. Crêpes may be made in the morning. Extra crêpes may be frozen for a later date.

4. Roll up with Orange Butter (recipe, page 68) or fill with Hamlin Cheese Blintzes (recipe, page 68) or Lime Meringue Pie Filling (recipe, page 62) to serve immediately, or serve with Citrus Sauce (recipe, page 256) as an elegant dessert.

5. To make dinner crêpes, eliminate sugar and vanilla.

Note: Do not overcook crêpes or they will become crisp and break when filling.

Note: These crêpes may be served unfilled with Citrus Sauce (recipe, page 256) for a spectacular dessert.

Hamlin Cheese Blintzes (roll-ups)

Yield: 15-18 Crêpes

Blender Sweet Crêpes (recipe, page 67)

8 ounces farmer's cheese or mascarpone or ricotta cheese

8 ounces cream cheese

2 extra large egg yolks

1 teaspoon double fold vanilla extract (or, 2 teaspoons single fold)

1 tablespoon juice from the Hamlin orange

¼ teaspoon salt

1 tablespoon sugar

½ teaspoon cinnamon

⅛ teaspoon nutmeg

Melted unsalted butter to just cover the pan

2 cups sour cream or Crème Fraîche (recipe, page 31)

1 quart fresh Lake or Hillsborough County blueberries or strawberries served on the side

1. Make crêpes.

2. Beat cheeses together until smooth. Add egg yolks. Add vanilla, orange juice, salt, sugar, cinnamon and nutmeg and beat smooth. Spoon 2 tablespoons of the mixture ⅓rd from the edge of the uncooked side of each crêpe. Roll the edge over the filling and continue rolling until the crêpe is a cylindrical shape with the filling secure inside. Place on a baking sheet flap side down. Refrigerate or freeze until ready to cook.

3. Fry flap side down in a small amount of unsalted butter over medium heat until golden brown. Turn and brown the other side. Or, place on a greased baking sheet. Brush tops with melted butter and bake at 350°F until very hot.

4. Serve with sour cream or Crème Fraîche and fresh blueberries, or canned blueberry pie filling, if berries are not in season. If you are a yogurt fan, serve blueberry yogurt on the side.

Orange Butter

Approximately 1 Cup

1 cup unsalted butter, softened

⅓ cup orange marmalade

1 tablespoon grated orange peel

Optional: 1 tablespoon orange liqueur

1. Beat the butter with the marmalade. Stir in the grated orange peel (and liqueur).

Note: This should be made several hours in advance for the flavors to settle.

Orange Chiffon Cake

8-10 Slices

2¼ cups sifted all-purpose flour

1½ cups granulated sugar

1 tablespoon baking powder

1 teaspoon salt

½ cup vegetable oil

5 jumbo graded egg yolks

1 teaspoon finely-grated Valencia orange peel

¾ cup Valencia orange juice

2 teaspoons vanilla

8 jumbo graded egg whites

½ teaspoon cream of tartar

1 tablespoon granulated sugar

1. Preheat oven to 325°F.

2. Sift together the dry ingredients into a large mixing bowl.

3. Beat in the egg yolks, orange peel, orange juice and vanilla.

4. Beat egg whites to the foamy stage. Add cream of tartar and continue beating until very thick. Add sugar and beat until incorporated.

5. Pour the mixture into a 10-inch tube pan.

6. Bake 65 minutes, or until cake springs back when pressed on the top with your finger. Turn upside down on 3 inverted cups to cool.

7. Serve plain or Cover the top and sides with Orange Frosting.

Orange Frosting

Yield:1½ cups

½ cup sifted 10X powdered confectioners sugar

¼ cup orange marmalade

¼ cup Valencia orange juice

1. Beat ingredients together, adding the orange juice in a slow, steady stream.

2. Cover the top of the cake, spooning an ample amount of excess to drip down the sides.

BSB Scrumptious Chocolate Cake

Yield: 9-inch layer cake

1¾ cups all-purpose flour

½ teaspoon baking soda

1 full teaspoon baking powder

¼ teaspoon salt

¾ cup unsweetened cocoa

¼ pound unsalted butter, softened

1 cup granulated sugar

⅔ cup dark brown sugar

4 extra large eggs, separated

⅓ cup mayonnaise

1 full tablespoon vanilla extract

2 tablespoons juice from the sweet navel orange

1¼ cups 4% whole milk

2 9-inch cake pans

1. Preheat oven to 350°F. Rub butter over the bottoms and sides of 2 9-inch cake pans. Cut parchment paper to fit the bottoms. Set the oven rack ⅓ from the bottom.
2. Sift flour, baking soda, baking powder, salt and cocoa together. Set aside.
3. Cream butter for a few seconds on highest speed of an electric mixer. Slowly add sugars and continue beating until mixture is white and fluffy, scraping around sides with a spatula several times.
4. Reduce speed to medium. Beat in egg yolks. Scrape sides with a rubber spatula. Beat in mayonnaise, vanilla and orange juice.
5. Beat in flour mixture. Beat in milk, 2 tablespoons at a time.
6. Beat egg whites until just thick but not forming peaks. Fold into chocolate mixture.
7. Spoon mixture into the cake pans and set into the oven. Reduce temperature immediately to 325°. Bake 35 minutes, or until a toothpick comes out almost clean with some chocolate residue. Turn upside down immediately onto a rack to cool.
8. Fill the layers and cover the top and sides with Chocolate Cream Cheese Frosting. Do not refrigerate.

*Note: Convection oven: Preheat oven to 330°F. Bake 25 minutes. If cake is not done, reduce temperature to 315*F. and bake another 5 minutes.*

Chocolate Cream Cheese Frosting

To fill and frost 2 - 9 inch layers

1 (pounds (6 cups) 10X powdered sugar

¾ cup unsweetened cocoa powder

½ pound unsalted butter, softened

11 ounces cream cheese, softened
 (8 ounce and 3 ounce packages)

1 tablespoon vanilla extract

2 ounces sweet chocolate

1. Sift the sugar and cocoa into a bowl with the butter, cream cheese and vanilla.
2. Beat mixture until thick and smooth. Fill and frost cake. Shave chocolate over the top to finish.

Citrus Sunshine Cake

Yield: 10-12 Servings

8 jumbo graded egg yolks, room temperature

1⅓ cups granulated sugar

⅓ cup water

2 tablespoons vanilla extract

3 tablespoons Parson Brown Orange juice or Muscott Honey Tangerine juice

1 tablespoon Meyer lemon juice

1¼ cups all-purpose sifted flour

8 jumbo graded egg whites, room temperature or warmer

1 teaspoon cream of tartar

1 tablespoon granulated sugar

1. Preheat oven to 350°F.

2. Separate eggs, putting the yolks in the bowl of an electric mixer with the sugar. Reserve whites in a warm place. Beat yolks and sugar 1 minute on medium speed.

3. Combine the water, vanilla, orange and lemon juice in a small pot and heat to the boiling point. (Microwave 1 minute.) Add the hot liquid, drop by drop, into the yolk mixture, beating constantly on medium speed. Turn speed to high and beat 10 minutes, or until very thick and light in color.

4. Fold the flour in by hand with a spatula. Set aside.

5. Beat the egg whites on the highest speed of an electric mixer until foamy. Add the cream of tartar and continue beating until very thick. Add 1 tablespoon granulated sugar and continue to beat until smooth. Fold the whites into the yolk batter, being careful not to "break them down" by stirring too much.

6. Spoon batter loosely into a 9-inch ungreased tube pan. Do not smooth it down. Place the pan on a rack one-third from the bottom of the oven and bake 15 minutes at 350°F. Reduce temperature to 325°F. and bake another 40 minutes.

7. Turn the cake pan upside down on three cups or individual soufflé dishes turned upside down to cool. (This is necessary because the center of the cake will have risen above the sides.) When completely cool, remove the bottom and sides with a sharp knife.

Note: Aside from fruit pies, this cake was the only dessert my Grandmother made. It was her pride and joy and, because she was not very proficient in the kitchen, it took her all day to prepare. When the cake was placed in her oven, everyone was told to leave the house so that no slamming of doors or sudden jarring would cause her cake to fall. She called it her "Sunshine Cake," but I suspect the original recipe came from The Boston School Cookbook, published in 1896 and reprinted twice after in 1897. The (new, revised edition) published in 1936, was a fixture on her pantry counter until she gave it to me in 1963.

The Valencia orange is the backbone of the Florida citrus industry. Juicy and packed with vitamins, it is perfect for eating, juicing or incorporating into recipes. The Rohde Red Valencia orange has greater color and a milder flavor. It is available from March through May and is my choice for this cake.

Valencia Sponge Cake

Yield: Approximately 40 (2-inch) Squares

⅓ cup plus 2 tablespoons juice from Red Valencia oranges

⅓ cup Grand Marnier or Triple Sec liqueur

8 jumbo graded egg yolks, room temperature

8 jumbo graded egg whites, room temperature

1 cup granulated sugar

1 tablespoon vanilla extract

Grated rind of 1 Red Valencia orange

2½ cups sifted all-purpose flour

Pinch of salt

¼ teaspoon cream of tartar

4 tablespoons granulated sugar

10.5x14.75x2.25-inch baking dish, buttered and floured

1. Preheat oven 350°F.

2. Squeeze orange juice and refrigerate several hours, or until you can see the separation of the water on top and the juice on the bottom. Pour off as much water as possible and measure the juice to equal ⅓ cup. Combine with the Grand Marnier.

3. Separate the eggs. Combine the yolks with the sugar in a bowl set over a pot of simmering water and beat on highest speed with an electric beater 5 minutes. Scrape sides of bowl several times. Continue beating until mixture is very thick and pale yellow. This will take approximately 10 minutes.

4. Remove from heat and add the vanilla, grated orange rind and orange juice mixture. Stir in the flour with a spatula.

5. Beat egg whites with the salt until foamy on highest speed. Add cream of tartar and continue beating until thick. Sprinkle in sugar and beat until soft peaks form. Do not over-beat.

6. Fold beaten whites into batter.

7. Spoon into baking dish. Set on a rack one-third from the bottom of the oven. Bake 30 minutes, or until a toothpick comes out clean.

8. Cover the top with Orange Frosting. (recipe, page 69)

White Fruitcake

Yield: 2 9x4 tube cakes or 4 8x3½x2½ disposable loaf pans

8 ounces glacé colored cherries

8 ounces glacé colored pineapple

4 ounces dried apricots

7 ounces golden raisins

2 cups dark rum

6 ounces sugar glazed ginger, soaked 10 minutes in warm water to cover

2½ cups cake flour, measured after sifting 3x

2 teaspoons baking powder

½ teaspoon salt

1 cup butter (½ pound)

2 cups granulated sugar

6 jumbo graded egg yolks

1 tablespoon Bearss lemon juice

1 tablespoon Valencia orange juice

1 tablespoon Sunburst tangerine juice

3 ounces blanched, slivered almonds

3 ounces coarsely-chopped Florida pecans

6 egg whites, graded Jumbo

½ teaspoon cream of tartar

1 tablespoon granulated sugar

1 9x4-inch or 2 8x2½-inch tube pans with permanent bottoms, or

4 8x3½-inchx2½-inch disposable loaf pans

Grand Marnier or Amaretto liqueur

1. Cut cherries into quarters. Slice pineapple and apricots into small pieces and combine in a bowl with the raisins and rum.

2. Cover ginger with water to soften 10 minutes. Slice ginger into thin strips and add to the fruit mixture.

3. Combine the flour with the baking powder and salt and sift three times.

4. Cream butter and sugar on high speed of an electric mixer until white and fluffy. Add egg yolks, one at a time on medium speed, beating well after each addition. Scrape sides and bottom of bowl. Add lemon, orange and tangerine juice. Add flour on low speed, scraping sides several times.

5. Stir fruit mixture into the batter. Stir in almonds and pecans.

6. Beat egg whites until foamy. Add cream of tartar and continue beating on high speed until thick. Add sugar and beat until thick peaks form. Fold into the batter in 3rds.

7. Preheat oven to 275°F.

8. Grease the tube pan well with vegetable oil. (This is not necessary for disposable pans.) Spoon the cake mixture in loosely, and tap the bottom of the pan(s) several times on the counter top to incorporate it evenly.

9. Place the pan(s) in another pan with water 2-inches deep. Bake the cake 4 hours, or until a wooden skewer inserted comes out dry. If cakes are baked in disposable pans, timing will change to 2½ hours. Turn the pan(s) upside down until the cake has cooled. If baked in aluminum loaf pans, this is not necessary.

10. Remove the tube cakes from their pan(s).Leave the disposable pans intact. Wrap the tube cakes in a double layer of cheesecloth and set in a tightly closed container. Brush the cakes with Grand Marnier (for an orange flavor, or Amaretto (for an almond flavor) every week for a minimum of 4 weeks. Let the cakes age another 2-3 weeks before serving for optimum flavor.

Note: The best quality glacé fruit comes from Paradise, Inc®, Plant City, Florida.

Hamlin Crème Brûlée

Yield: Approximately 8 Servings

1 pint heavy cream (2 cups)

1 pint coffee cream (2 cups)

5 jumbo graded egg yolks

⅓ cup granulated sugar

2 teaspoons vanilla

1 quart baking dish, 2-inches deep (8x8x2-inch)

2 tablespoons finely grated orange peel

¼ cup granulated or natural brown sugar

1. Preheat oven to 350°F.

2. Combine the creams with the sugar in a saucepan and heat to lukewarm, stirring.

3. Separate eggs, reserving the whites for Pecan Meringue Cookies (recipe, page 120) or Strawberry Fluff: A Diet Dessert (recipe, page 31). Stir yolks until smooth in a bowl. Slowly pour in warm cream mixture, whisking (or beating with an electric mixer) until smooth. Add vanilla and grated orange peel.

4. Pour into the baking dish and place into a pan with hot water that reaches half-way up the sides. Set on a rack ⅓ from the bottom of the oven and bake 45-50 minutes, or until loosely set when a knife is inserted.

5. Remove from water bath immediately. Cool to room temperature.

6. Cover with sugar and place under the broiler to brown. Serve warm or refrigerate until very cold.

7. This recipe may be baked in 8 - ½ cup soufflé dishes. Timing will change to 20-22 minutes.

Note: Serve plain or with Citrus Sauce (recipe page 256) or fresh berries on the side.

Candied Carrots Sugar Free

Yield: 4-6 Servings

1 pound baby carrots

2 teaspoons finely chopped fresh ginger

¼ cup Blood Red or Valencia orange juice

2 tablespoons butter or butter substitute

½ teaspoon salt

½ packet Splenda®

1. Combine ingredients. Bring to a boil in a covered pot. Reduce heat to medium-low. Cook 10 minutes. Turn off heat for flavors to blend.

It's ten o'clock on a cold night in January that is becoming increasingly colder each hour. The weather man predicts freezing temperatures throughout Central and North Florida, but we will not know the extent of the freeze until it actually comes through. Wind factor is as essential to the survival of our grove as the temperature. If the wind is strong enough, it will blow the cold air through quickly. If the air is still, and the temperature drops to twenty-eight degrees or lower and lasts four or more hours, it can be disastrous. Our neighbor, Bill, who has fifty acres of citrus, just telephoned to advise us we must cover our plants and turn on the water of our "scaffold branch irrigation" to save the trees. Each tree has its own water pipe that ends in the scaffold branches, and a sprayer to spew water over the scaffold limbs. If the leaves freeze, the base and root of the tree will survive. The running water that gives off heat will keep the temperature at thirty-two degrees. Bill also advised that we pick as much fruit as possible immediately, and strip the trees in the morning after the freeze. And, so, we don our heavy jackets, scarves and gloves and head into the cold of the night to get the job done.

Hart's Grove

Key Lime	Persian Lime	Robinson Tangerine	Valencia Orange	Page Orange
Key Lime	Ambersweet Orange	Valencia Orange	Valencia Orange	Temple Orange
Key Lime	Dancy Tangerine	Valencia Orange	Valencia Orange	Oval Kumquat
Minneola Tangelo	Dancy Tangerine	Valencia Orange	Satsuma Tangerine	Oval Kumquat
Minneola Tangelo	Dancy Tangerine	Rio Red Grapefruit	Oval Kumquat	Murcott Tangerine
Orlando Tangelo	Red Valencia Orange	Hamlin Orange	Red Valencia Orange	Page Orange
Valencia Orange	Red Valencia Orange	Hamlin Orange	Sunburst Tangerine	Round Kumquat
Valencia Orange	Marsh White Grapefruit	Ruby Red Grapefruit	Meyer Lemon	Round Kumquat
Ponkan Tangerine	Marsh White Grapefruit	Ruby Red Grapefruit	Meyer Lemon	Blood Seedless Orange
Ruby Red Grapefruit	Parson Brown Orange	Red Navel Orange	Orlando Tangelo	Bearss Lemon
Hamlin Orange	Parson Brown Orange	Fallglo Tangerine	Orlando Tangelo	Ponderosa Lemon
Victor's Potpourri	Blood Orange	Blood Orange	King Orange	Pink Seedless Grapefruit
Oval Kumquat	Navel Orange	Navel Orange	Valencia Orange	Pink Seedless Grapefruit

The Dancy tangerine, Navel and Red Navel oranges, and Ruby Red grapefruit grown in Central Florida are almost seedless. Both are treasures of sweet juice and thin skin that lend themselves to marvelous jams. They are at their best in December until the end of January, and the Ruby Red grapefruit bears from October through May, allowing me to cook up a storm for Christmas presents to send to northern friends and family.

Glazed Orange or Lemon Rind

Yield: Approximately 1 Cup

Use the Red Navel orange, if possible. It is easy to peel and its deep, rich color will give a beautiful presentation to any dessert. It is available from November through January, although we pick them from our trees until the end of February.

5 Red Navel oranges or 3 Meyer lemons, or a combination	1¼ cups granulated sugar
	½ cup water
A vegetable peeler or small sharp serrated edge knife	1 tablespoon vanilla extract

1. Peel or cut the rind away, being careful not to cut through to the white pith underneath. Slice into thin (julienne) strips. Simmer in water to cover for 10 minutes, or until tender. Pour off water and dry the strips on paper toweling.

2. Combine the sugar and water and bring to a boil in a small saucepan. Continue boiling until mixture thickens to the point where it "spins a thread" when lifted from the pan with a spoon. If you have a candy thermometer, the temperature will show 230°F.

3. Stir in the vanilla. Stir in the julienne strips. Leave them in the syrup 45 minutes, stirring occasionally. Remove from syrup with tongs to decorate cakes.

Note: May be made in advance and refrigerated in the syrup up to one week.

Tangerines in Syrup

Yield: 8 Servings

8 sweet tangerines (Murcott or Honeybell)   1½ cups sugar

1 cup water   ½ cup water

1. Peel the tangerines, cutting away all white under the rind.
2. Slice the skin of 4 of the tangerines into thin strips. Boil 3 minutes in 1 cup water. Strain off water.
3. Boil the remaining sugar and water 5 minutes, or mixture spins a thread. Watch carefully so it does not bubble over the top of the pot. Lower heat if mixture bubbles up and continue to boil until thickened. Add the tangerines. Cook approximately 5 minutes over medium-low heat, stirring often. Remove to a serving bowl.
4. Sprinkle the strips over and cover all with the sugar syrup. Refrigerate several hours.
5. Serve as a dessert alone or with fruit sherbet.

Tangerine Compote

6 Servings

6 tangerines   ⅓ cup tangerine juice

6 Florida finger bananas, or 3 large, firm   1 tablespoon vanilla
 bananas   ⅓ cup dark brown sugar

¼ teaspoon mace   1 tablespoon cinnamon

½ cup packed dark brown sugar

1. Preheat oven to 350°F.
2. Peel the tangerines and separate the segments. Set aside.
3. Thinly slice the skin of 2 tangerines and toss with the segments.
4. Peel and slice the bananas into halves, lengthwise. Slice the large ones in half again. Place in a shallow baking dish, inside part down. Cover with the tangerine segments.
5. Combine the mace, brown sugar, tangerine juice and vanilla in a saucepan. Cook over low heat, stirring, until smooth. Pour over the fruit. Mix the brown sugar with the cinnamon and sprinkle over the fruit.
6. Bake 15 minutes. Serve warm or refrigerate until cold.

Fresh pineapple chunks may be served with this dessert.

Orange County Orange Marmalade

Yield: 6 Cups

1 pound Valencia oranges (2-3)

1 pound Hamlin oranges (2-3)

4 cups filtered water

6-7 cups granulated sugar, depending on the sweetness of the oranges

Non-reactive pot

1. Wash and cut the oranges into quarters. Combine with the water in a non-reactive pot. Bring to a boil. Lower heat to medium-high. Cover the pot and boil 15 minutes. Remove from heat and let stand 2 hours or longer.

2. Strain and return liquid to the pot.

3. Cut the fruit into tiny pieces by hand (not food processor), being careful to remove all seeds. Measure amount. You should have 6 cups total. Combine with the liquid in the pot. Add 6 cups sugar (or more, if oranges are not as sweet as you expected).

4. Boil over high heat, uncovered, 30 minutes. Lower heat to medium-high and continue to gently boil 1½ hours, or until marmalade thickens. Stir every 10 minutes.

5. Skim off all the foam from the top and fill sterilized jars according to directions.

The following is not a recipe, but an easy measuring device for the cook to follow.

Easy Orange Marmalade

1½ cups cold water per cup of oranges   1 cup granulated sugar per cup of oranges

1. Wash oranges. Cut off stem ends. Cut into halves and remove seeds. Slice very thin before chopping fine or pulverizing in a food processor.

2. Add cold water. Cover and let stand in a cool place overnight.

3. Pour into a non-reactive heavy pot and cook slowly over low heat 2 hours. Remove from heat and let stand overnight again in a cool place.

4. Add 1 cup granulated sugar per each cup fruit. Return to heat and cook 20-30 minutes over medium-low heat, stirring often. Lower heat if mixture begins to boil too quickly or stick to the bottom of the pot. When the sugar causes the fruit to become very thick, the marmalade is done.

5. Pour into sterilized jars and seal.

Orange Liqueur Ices

Yield: Approximately 3 Cups

¾ cup water

⅔ cup granulated sugar

½ cup orange juice

1 teaspoon grated lemon rind

2 tablespoons grated navel orange rind

¼ cup Triple Sec or Cointreau or Grand Marnier

2 egg whites

⅛ teaspoon cream of tartar

1 teaspoon granulated sugar

1. Bring the water to a boil with the sugar. Add orange juice, lemon rind and orange extract (or orange rind) and stir, cooking 30 seconds. Remove from heat. Stir in liqueur. Strain into a bowl. Cool.

2. Beat egg whites until frothy. Add cream of tartar and sugar. Beat until thickened but not stiff. Fold into mixture. Freeze.

3. To serve: Scoop into saucer champagne or Margarita glasses and decorate with mint leaves.

Corn

It seems redundant to equate the survival of our endangered species of animals, birds and fish with the multitude of small farms being sold to developers for unfathomable profits that could never be realized by these farmers during several lifetimes.

And, who can blame them?

People who till the soil are a benevolent specie. Most have solid values and religious sincerity because they work with the humane and against the cruel forces of nature that reward or punish them at will. Most never realize material wealth unless they make lucky investments or sell off the land. These are the folk who vote in our presidents and send their sons to far-away lands in order to uphold the principles and freedom of America.

And, yes. They are endangered.

RECIPES:

Zellwood Dip

Zesty Zellwood Marinade

Lake County Corn Pudding

Corn and Eggplant Appetizer

Corn and Shrimp Chowder

Lowfat Creamy Corn Chowder

Corn and Pepper Salsa

Corn Relish

Corn Salad

Pancotto with Corn

Southern Corn Bread

Cream-Style Corn Bread

Jalapeño Corn Bread

Corn Bread Dressing

Corn Fritters

Corn Pancakes

Creamed Corn with Bacon

Corncakes for Crab or Shrimp

Baked Corn and Potatoes

Chili Butter for Corn on the Cob

Zellwood Corn Industry

Signs along the road advertise, "Best Corn" and "Fresh Picked Corn". The word, "Zellwood", is blatantly missing. The huge flatbed trucks filled to the sky with mountains of fresh corn that parked each year on Highway 441 have been replaced with wood tables stacked with corn from somewhere else. Zellwood's annual corn festival has become a small country fair rather than its former celebration of harvest. A few private corn farms in the area still produce, but names, such as Jorgensen, who were synonymous with the sweet yellow, white and parti-color corn since they first drained the marshlands north of Lake Apopka in the 1940s, have disappeared. Growers, such as Long and Scott, who are not contiguous to the Lake, still produce for the festival and sell to a smattering of flatbed vendors on Highway 441. The earthen dikes that were built to expose the highly productive muck soil produced three crops each year but polluted not only Lake Apopka but the entire Harris Chain of Lakes, which has been our significant water resource. The St. John's River Water Management District promises restoration of polluted Lake Apopka, little Lake Beauclair, tiny Lake Carlton, Lake Dora, Lake Eustis, Lake Griffin and Little and Big Lake Harris. Although the lakes are beginning to recover, it could take twenty years or longer to bring them back to their original state. The excess storm water that was pumped into the lake carried high levels of phosphorus. This over-fertilized the lakes, killing healthy aquatic plants and game fish. Poor tiny Lake Carlton was the first to suffer the wash off from Lake Apopka, with Lake Beauclair taking the second serious hit. Since the land was returned to Lake Apopka in hopes of reclamation, the growers had few choices for pursuing their livelihood. Some simply sold the land and retired or sought other means of employment. Others picked up and moved to the Everglades regions of Okeechobee and Belle Glade, west of Palm Beach. A greater number have gone further south to Homestead and South Bay where the industry is most prolific. The corn we purchase in the supermarkets comes mainly from the huge crops produced in Homestead.

Although modern techniques have created improved varieties that maintain their sweetness and flavor longer, the sugar present in corn still begins its inevitable conversion to starch the moment the ear is picked. The longer corn sits, the more flavor and moisture is lost. Although the old dictate, "never pick corn until the water is boiling", may no longer be true, thanks to new sugar enhanced, super-sweet varieties, too much heat, long refrigeration and improper storage by supermarkets degrade the flavor and quality ultimately purchased by most folks living in large cities. Freshly picked corn contains vitamins C, A and B1, which diminish shortly after picking. The true corn connoisseur will find a U-Pick field while the water is heating on the stove.

It is not necessary to elaborate on the truism that the best way to enjoy corn is to simply boil it and chomp it off its ear. It can also be employed in endless recipes from breakfast to dessert, which makes it one of our most versatile vegetables.

Choosing Fresh Corn

The husk should be green. The corn should be without blemish. Pull the husk down. Fresh corn has white silk with green and yellow highlights. If dark, return the corn to the place where it was purchased.

Removing the Kernels

For cream-style: Cut the kernels down the center with the sharp tip of a knife. Then, scrape the cob with the back of the knife instead of the blade. This will leave the skin behind while extracting the juices. Don't press too hard or the skin will come also. For recipes calling for whole kernels of corn, drop the ears into boiling water. Cover the pot. When the water returns to a full boil, cook 2 minutes. Remove. Cool. Set the cobs in a shallow bowl to slice off the kernels to salvage the juice.

To Freeze

Husk the ears. Plunge into boiling water. When water returns to the bubbling stage, boil 2 minutes. Cool in ice water. Drain. Cut kernels from the cob and transfer to airtight plastic bags or containers. Freeze immediately. Frozen kernels will retain their quality for three months.

To Grill

Husk the ears. Remove the silk. Melt 1 teaspoon butter with 1 teaspoon water to brush on each ear. Close the husk. Wrap tightly in foil and throw them into the white coals for a super flavor. Grill 20-25 minutes. Opinionated corn aficionados claim this method steams the corn rather than grilling it, and advocate husking the ears to cook on the grill, basting often.

Zellwood Dip

Yield: Approximately 2 Cups

4 ears Florida parti-color (confetti) sweet corn

1 clove garlic, crushed

¼ cup olive oil

1 15-ounce can black beans

1 tablespoon Florida State Seminoles® hot sauce

1 teaspoon ground oregano

1 teaspoon white balsamic vinegar

Small red onion, cut up

1 teaspoon salt

1. Preheat oven to 400°F.

2. Cut corn from the cob and toss with crushed garlic and olive oil. Remove to a shallow pan with the kernels separated. Roast 10 minutes. Reset oven to broil and broil until corn begins to turn light brown. Remove to a food processor.

3   Add remaining ingredients and process until smooth and creamy. Spoon into a serving bowl. Refrigerate overnight for the flavors to "marry".

4. Serve with tortilla chips as an hors d'oeuvre.

Zesty Zellwood Marinade

Yield: Approximately 3 Cups

6 ears cooked yellow or 'confetti' sweet corn

2 tablespoons white balsamic vinegar

6 tablespoons Seasoned Garlic Oil (recipe page 246)

½ teaspoon black pepper

½ teaspoon salt, or more to taste

1. Cook corn and remove kernels to a bowl.

2. Combine remaining ingredients and marinate kernels several hours for a cold corn relish.

Note: The mixture of vinegar, seasoned oil, pepper and salt may also be heated and brushed on the cooked whole ears of corn instead of butter.

Lake County Corn Pudding

Yield: 6 Servings

2 cups cooked corn kernels, yellow, parti-color or white

¼ cup granulated sugar

2 tablespoons all-purpose flour

1 teaspoon salt

Pinch white pepper

4 extra large eggs, lightly beaten

1 cup coffee cream

1 cup whole milk

3 tablespoons melted butter

Nutmeg to sprinkle over the top

1½ quart soufflé or baking dish

1. Preheat oven to 350°F.

2. Combine sugar, flour, salt and pepper. Beat eggs lightly and stir into the flour mixture with a wire whisk. Whisk in cream and milk until smooth. Whisk in melted butter. Stir in corn.

3. Melt the butter and cover the bottom and sides of a soufflé or baking dish. Spoon in pudding. Sprinkle the top lightly with nutmeg. Bake 55-60 minutes, or until a knife inserted comes out "clean".

Corn and Eggplant Appetizer

Yield: Approximately 2½ Cups

1 cup diced eggplant

1 cup cooked corn kernels

1 celery rib

6 black Kalamata Greek olives, pitted

1 tablespoon capers, chopped coarse

1 small onion, diced fine

2 tablespoons extra virgin Italian olive oil

1 teaspoon white vinegar

1 tablespoon granulated sugar

½ teaspoon salt

½ teaspoon black pepper

1. Unless the eggplant(s) are very small, peel the purple skin. Dice into small squares. Combine with the cooked corn kernels.

2. Chop the celery and slice the olives in halves. Add them with the capers to the corn mixture.

3. Cook the onion in the olive oil in a small pan until the onion is soft but not colored. Add to the corn mixture.

4. Add the vinegar, sugar, salt and pepper and mix well. Refrigerate several hours or overnight.

5. Serve as an appetizer with crackers or tortilla chips, or as a relish with chicken, fish, or lamb.

Corn and Shrimp Chowder

Yield: Approximately 10 Cups

4 cups cooked yellow corn kernels (5-6 large
   ears)

2 cups water

2½ cups organic vegetable broth

1 cup dry white wine

2 dried bay leaves

4 ounces hard spicy sausage, such as the
   Spanish chorizo or Italian pepperoni

3 tablespoons unsalted butter

2 pounds large shrimp (16-20 to the pound)

1 teaspoon coriander

1 teaspoon cumin

¾ cup heavy cream

Salt and pepper to taste

1. Cook corn and cut off kernels. Set aside.

2. Peel, de-vein and refrigerate the shrimp, saving the shells.

3   Combine the shells, water, vegetable broth, wine and bay leaves in a pot. Bring to a boil. Lower heat to simmer and cook 20 minutes. Remove from the stove and cool to room temperature. Strain into another pot.

4. Slice the sausage very thin and add it to the strained liquid.

5. Melt the butter in a skillet and sauté the shrimp over medium heat until pink on both sides. Do not overcook. Add to the strained soup.

6. Stir the coriander and cumin into the soup and bring all to the boiling point but do not boil or the shrimp will become tough. Remove from the heat and stir in the cream. Taste for salt and pepper.

Note: Steps 1-3 may be done in advance. Do not add the shrimp and cream until ready to serve.

The combination of fresh ginger and bay leaf gives this chowder a lingering tangy flavor that is pungent but softer than the addition of hot peppers. The chopped red tomato, green scallions and yellow corn create a lovely color presentation in the white soup.

Lowfat Creamy Corn Chowder

Quick and Easy

Yield: 8 Cups

4 cups (5-6 ears) cooked corn kernels

2 cups vegetable broth (I use organic)

2 tablespoons finely diced ginger

1 cup diced red onion

1 dried bay leaf (2, if freshly picked from the tree)

1 teaspoon salt

¼ teaspoon black pepper

3 tablespoons all-purpose flour mixed with ⅓ cup cool water

2 cups fat free half-and-half

Seeded and coarsely chopped plum tomatoes to top each serving

Chopped chives or scallion greens to top each serving

1. Combine the vegetable broth, ginger, onion, bay leaf, salt and pepper in a pot and bring to a boil. Reduce heat to medium. Cover and boil gently 10 minutes. Stir in the corn.

2. Combine the flour with the water and stir into the soup. Slowly stir in the half-and-half, cooking until soup has thickened.

3. Ladle into bowls and sprinkle the chopped tomatoes and chives (scallion greens) on top.

Corn and Pepper Salsa

Yield: Approximately 2 Cups

2 large yellow bell peppers

2 large red bell peppers

2 banana hot peppers, chopped fine, or
½ ounce bottled, chopped

1 teaspoon powdered fennel

1 teaspoon powdered cumin

2 tablespoons lime juice

¼ cup chopped basil leaves, or 2 tablespoons
dried basil

1 cup cooked parti-colored corn kernels

Salt and black pepper to taste

1. Place the peppers on a baking sheet or piece of foil half-way down from the heat under the broiler. Broil until blackened. Turn to the second side and blacken. Continue turning until blackened all over. The chili peppers will take a shorter time. Remove them when done.

2. When peppers are blackened, transfer them to a plastic bag. Close the bag tightly so no air will escape for 5 minutes. Remove the peppers. The skins will peel off easily. (Wear plastic gloves when peeling hot peppers so they will not burn your skin.)

3. Remove the seeds and transfer to a food processor. Pulse several times until they are in tiny pieces but not puréed. Transfer to a bowl.

4. Add the fennel, cumin, lime juice, basil and corn, and toss. Add salt and pepper to taste. Refrigerate several hours or overnight. Serve with tortilla or potato chips.

Corn Relish

Yield: Approximately 8 Cups

4 cups uncooked corn (approximately 6 large ears)

3 green tomatoes

2 green bell peppers

4 red bell peppers

1 cup granulated sugar

1 tablespoon salt

3 Florida sweet onions

2 cups apple cider vinegar

1 teaspoon turmeric powder

1 tablespoon dry mustard

1 tablespoon celery seed

1. Cut corn from cob.

2. Plunge tomatoes into boiling water for 20 seconds. Remove skin and seeds.

3 Cut peppers into halves and remove seeds. Chop all fine by hand.

4. Place in a large pot. Add sugar, salt, onions, vinegar, turmeric, dry mustard and celery seed. Cook 20 minutes. Cool. Fill and seal sterilized jars according to directions.

Corn Salad

Yield: 6 Servings

6 ears parti-color corn, cooked and kernels sliced off cobs

1 small purple onion, minced

1 yellow bell pepper, seeded and chopped into small squares

2 tablespoons extra virgin olive oil

1 teaspoon salt

¼ teaspoon black pepper

¼ teaspoon ground cumin

¼ teaspoon ground coriander

Chopped cilantro leaves

1. Combine ingredients. Refrigerate several hours or overnight. Serve as an accompaniment to fish or chicken, or over a lettuce leaf as a salad. Sprinkle chopped cilantro leaves over the top.

Pancotto with Corn

Half Italian-half American: totally fun, delicious and different

Yield: 4 Servings

8 thin slices slightly stale Italian bread

Cold water to cover

2 cloves garlic, minced

1 cup cooked corn kernels

¼ cup extra virgin olive oil

1 pound Italian plum tomatoes, seeded and chopped

½ cup water

¼ cup grated Pecorino or Romano cheese

Salt and a pinch of white pepper to taste

Optional: 2 tablespoons heavy cream

1. Cut the bread into thin slices. Pour water over just to cover. Remove immediately and squeeze out the water.

2. Combine the garlic, corn kernels and olive oil in a small soup pot. Crumble the bread into it. Stir in the chopped tomatoes and water and bring to a boil. Reduce heat to low. Cook 10 minutes, stirring constantly. Stir in the grated cheese. Add salt and a pinch of white pepper to taste.

3. Spoon into individual bowls and swirl in the heavy cream to serve.

Southern Corn Bread

Yield: 9-inch square pan

2 cups yellow cornmeal

1 cup all-purpose flour

2 teaspoons baking powder

1 teaspoon salt

2 extra large graded eggs, beaten

1½ cups whole milk

3 tablespoons melted butter or liquid bacon drippings

1. Preheat oven to 375°F.

2. Sift the cornmeal, flour, baking powder and salt together.

3 Beat the eggs and stir into the cornmeal mixture alternately with the milk.

4. Stir in the melted butter or bacon drippings.

5. Pour into a greased 9-inch square pan that has been heated in the oven. Bake approximately 45 minutes, or until a toothpick inserted in the center comes out dry.

Cream-Style Corn Bread

Yield: Approximately 6 Servings

2 tablespoons butter

3 extra large eggs, beaten

½ cup vegetable oil

1 cup sour cream

2 cups cooked corn kernels

1 cup self-rising cornmeal

1. Preheat oven to 350°F.

2. Melt butter in an iron skillet. Combine remaining ingredients and pour into the hot skillet with the butter.

3. Set skillet into the oven to bake 20-30 minutes, or until set. Slice into wedges to serve.

Note: This is a typical southern recipe originally made with bacon grease instead of butter.

Jalapeño Corn Bread

Yield: Approximately 10 Slices

1 cup yellow cornmeal

½ teaspoon soda

2 teaspoons baking powder

½ teaspoon salt

½ cup vegetable oil

2 extra large eggs, beaten

1 cup sour cream

1 cup Cheddar cheese of choice

2 cups cooked corn kernels

1 onion, minced

2 jalapeño peppers, seeded and chopped fine
(or 4 ounces canned)

1. Preheat oven to 400°F.

2. Combine cornmeal, soda, baking powder, salt and vegetable oil. Beat eggs and stir in. Stir in sour cream, cheese, corn and minced onion. Stir in peppers.

3. Spoon into a greased baking dish or jellyroll pan (cookie sheet with sides). Bake 20-30 minute. If the top browns too quickly, lower oven temperature to 375°F. Cool slightly before cutting into squares.

Note: If you desire thicker squares, bake in a smaller, deeper baking dish for a longer time, or until a toothpick inserted comes out dry.

Corn Bread Dressing

Yield: Approximately 8 Cups

2 cups crumbled Jalapeño or Southern Corn
  Bread (recipes, page 91)

2 cups toasted French bread, coarsely crumbled

4 tablespoons melted butter

2 ribs celery, chopped

1 Florida sweet onion, chopped

4 extra large graded eggs, beaten

1 teaspoon salt

2½-3 cups hot chicken broth

1 tablespoon butter to grease a 13x9x2-inch pan

1. Preheat oven to 325°F.

2. Combine crumbled corn bread and toasted bread in a large bowl. Toss with the melted butter, celery, onion, beaten eggs and salt. Pour the broth in slowly, tossing with two forks to keep the mixture from becoming a pudding. Continue adding broth until the mixture is no longer dry.

3   Grease the pan and spoon the mixture in evenly. Set the pan into a larger pan with water on the bottom.

4. Bake, covered with foil, 45 minutes. Uncover and bake another 15 minutes.

Note: Chopped ham, Italian sausage, pine nuts, pecans, or any variety of other ingredients can be added to this simple version of Corn Bread Dressing.

Corn Fritters

Yield: 6 Fritters

1 cup cooked corn kernels

2 tablespoons melted butter

1 tablespoon granulated sugar

½ cup self-rising flour

½ teaspoon salt

Pinch of white pepper

2 beaten jumbo graded eggs

½ cup coffee cream

1. Combine ingredients. Heat a non-stick or greased griddle or shallow skillet. Drop by spoonfuls as large or small as you wish. Do not crowd pan. Cook on both sides until brown. Serve at once or reheat in a 325°F. oven directly before serving.

Corn Pancakes

Yield: 12-14 Pancakes

2 cups cooked corn kernels (4 ears)

1½ cups buttermilk

3 extra large eggs

1 teaspoon vanilla extract

1 tablespoon sugar

1 teaspoon salt

2 tablespoons melted butter

1 cup yellow cornmeal

¼ cup all-purpose flour

2 teaspoons baking powder

6 tablespoons unsalted butter (approximately)

Sour cream

1. Purée ½ cup of the kernels with ½ cup of the buttermilk in the blender on high speed. Add the rest of the buttermilk, eggs, vanilla, sugar and salt and blend on high speed 1 minute. Add the melted butter and blend another 20 seconds.

2. Combine the cornmeal, flour and baking powder. Stir in the blended mixture. Stir in the remaining corn kernels.

3 Melt butter to just cover the bottom of a 5-inch nonstick pan. Pour in ¼ cup of the batter and cook over medium heat until little holes appear across the top. Turn and cook until the second side has browned. As each pancake is cooked, set it into a 200°F. oven to stay warm.

4. Serve with sour cream on the side.

Creamed Corn with Bacon

Yield: 6 Servings

Cooked kernels from 3 large ears fresh corn
 (2½-3 cups)

6 slices thick-sliced bacon, cut into ¼-inch pieces

4 tablespoons butter

1 Florida sweet onion, minced

1 tablespoon all-purpose flour

1 cup coffee cream

Pinch of Cayenne pepper or white pepper

½ teaspoon minced tarragon leaves,
 or ¼ teaspoon dried tarragon

Salt and pepper to taste

1. Cook corn in boiling water no longer than 5 minutes. Cut off kernels and reserve.

2. Cook bacon crisp. Dice into approximately ¼-inch pieces.

3 Melt butter in a pot. Cook minced onion until soft but not colored.

4. Stir in flour and cream. Add Cayenne and tarragon. Taste for seasoning.

5. Add salt and pepper.

Corncakes for Crab or Shrimp

Yield: Approximately 30 pancakes 3 inches in diameter

1½ cups freshly cooked white or parti-color corn kernels (3 ears)

⅓ cup all-purpose flour, sifted

⅓ cup white cornmeal

½ teaspoon salt

Pinch of white pepper

2 extra large eggs

2 extra large egg yolks

½ cup whole milk or fat-free half-and-half

4 tablespoons melted unsalted butter or butter substitute cooking compatible

Optional: 2 tablespoons finely chopped fresh cilantro leaves

Crème Fraîche (recipe, page 31) to top

1 pound cooked Blue crab meat or tiny shrimp

1. Place corn kernels into a food processor. With an on-off motion, chop coarse.

2. Combine flour and cornmeal in a bowl. Add salt and white pepper.

3 Whisk in the eggs and egg yolks.

4. Whisk in the milk (half-and-half) and, finally, the melted butter.

5. Stir in the chopped cilantro leaves.

6. Heat a non-stick shallow skillet or griddle to medium. Spoon the batter into the pan by tablespoons. Cook approximately 2 minutes, or until slightly browned. Turn the pancakes over with a spatula and cook the other side. Remove to wax paper to cool.

7. Pile crab or shrimp on each pancake and serve one or two per person on salad plates. Top with a dollop of Crème Fraîche. Decorate with cilantro leaves and lemon wedges. These corncakes freeze beautifully to reheat at 200°F.

Note: These corncakes were originally designed as an accompaniment to caviar. Decrease the size by dropping them into the pan by spoonfuls to top with Crème Fraîche, minced onion and caviar of your choice (expense account).

Baked Corn and Potatoes

Yield: Approximately 4 Cups

4 ears corn

6 new red or white potatoes

1 small onion, sliced thin

Optional: 1 red or green bell pepper, seeds removed and sliced

2 tablespoons melted butter

4 tablespoons olive oil

Salt and pepper

1. Preheat oven to 425°F.

2. Husk corn. Break ears in half. Slice potatoes in half. Peel and slice onion. Remove seeds from pepper and slice.

3 Set into a shallow casserole. Melt butter with the oil and brush the corn, potatoes, onions and pepper. Sprinkle lightly with salt and pepper.

4. Roast, uncovered, 15 minutes, or until potatoes are brown on the outside and soft within.

Chili Butter for Corn on the Cob

Yield: Enough for 4 or more Ears of Corn

¼ pound butter, softened

2 teaspoons chili powder

¼ teaspoon ground cumin

¼ teaspoon ground coriander

1 tablespoon lemon juice

1. Mash butter with a fork, working in the remaining ingredients. Allow mixture to marinate several hours or overnight.

2. Spread on cooked corn to serve.

Mushrooms

The Portobello is best when brushed lightly with oil infused with garlic and quickly grilled or sautéed.

RECIPES:

Mushroom Rolls

Mixed Mushroom Soup

Mushrooms Stuffed with Ham

Portobello Pâté Toasts

Portobello Bruschetta

Grilled Portobello Mushrooms
and Plum Tomatoes

Portobello Spinach Salad
with Curried Eggs

Mushroom Soufflé

Duxelles with Shrimp

Portobello Mushroom Veggi-Burger

Portobello Garlic Potatoes

Portobello Pâté

Mushroom and Liver Pâté

Mushrooms, Sun-Dried Tomatoes
and Goat Cheese Rigatoni

Mushroom Smothered Asparagus

Mushrooms

Central Florida's Mushroom Farms:

The local mushroom facility in Zellwood originally owned by Terry Farms was acquired a few years ago by the California based national company, Monterey. Monterey's only other plant in Florida is the Quincy/Modern farm outside Tallahassee in North Florida. Both facilities are completely enclosed for optimal environmental control. Zellwood alone yields approximately seventeen million pounds of American whites and three million five hundred pounds of Portobello and Baby Bella mushrooms, for a whopping wholesale market that nets over twenty million dollars each year. Local folk can visit their little guard house to purchase odd sizes sold in paper bags for a fraction of the price of the supermarkets. It doesn't matter that they're not uniform in size or that some are better quality than others. They're fresh and fun to buy direct from the farm.

The marriage of fresh mushrooms with other vegetables and herbs is an ultimate culinary experience. Sodium, cholesterol and fat-free, they are also low in calories. It would seem that the mushroom triumphs as the most versatile vegetable grown.

The American white mushroom and large Portobello should be handled differently from each other. The white mushroom may be peeled and eaten raw in salads. The Portobello is rather dry and tasteless until it is cooked. The American white is more versatile and less delicate than the Portobello, lending itself to dressings, stews and sauces. Even cooked to death, it will still be palatable.

The Portobello is best when brushed lightly with oil infused with garlic and quickly grilled or sautéed. Overcooking will result in loss of texture with the juices running off in a brown stream from a mushroom that has become unpleasantly soft. After browning on both sides, it may be sliced for warm salads or as accompaniment to an entrée. Grilled, sliced, and set over chopped plum tomatoes mixed with minced basil, scallion greens and garlic oil on toasted French bread, it becomes a gourmet meal all by itself. The flavor and texture of the grilled Portobello mimes that of beef, making it possible to create faux hamburgers and filets for a vegetarian treat. The Baby Bella has a firmer texture, which allows it to pinch hit for both varieties. All three mushrooms lend themselves to being filled with seafood, vegetables and cheese.

Purchase mushrooms firm to the touch without blemish. If the caps are "slimy" or the stems "rubbery", return them to the store. An old mushroom is like a bad bottle of wine. Absolutely nothing can restore its flavor or texture.

Raw mushrooms do not freeze well. The large Portobello should not be frozen at all, cooked or uncooked. The American white survives best. Freeze only those that are very white and firm without blemish. Remove stems and lightly peel the caps with a small sharp knife or pull off the outer skin with your fingers. Do not rinse in water. Arrange caps on a baking sheet and freeze. When frozen, place into airtight bags or boxes. Cook without defrosting.

Mushroom Rolls

Yield: 24 to yield 50 pieces

1 pound large white mushrooms
1 large Bermuda onion
¼ pound butter or butter substitute
½ teaspoon salt
¼ teaspoon black pepper

Pinch of nutmeg
20 ounce loaf soft, sliced white bread, crusted and rolled thin
½ cup butter or butter substitute

1. Remove mushroom stems and peel caps with a small sharp knife. Do not wash.

2. Slice mushrooms and onions and cook together over high heat in ¼ cup butter 5 minutes. Add salt, pepper and nutmeg to taste. Drain off water in a strainer. Cool to room temperature.

3. Remove to a food processor and process on low to create tiny pieces.

4. Crust and roll each slice of bread thin. Trim the edges. Spoon a tablespoon of the mushroom mixture on the center of each piece of bread. Brush melted butter along the inside edges and fold one flap over the mushrooms and the other flap over the first to create a cylinder. Brush all over with the melted butter. Trim the edges with a sharp knife. Cut into halves and set on a greased or parchment covered baking sheet, flap side down.

5. Preheat oven to 375°F. Bake 25 minutes, or until very brown.

6. Optional: Cook the mushroom-onion in 4 tablespoons extra virgin olive oil instead of butter with 1 crushed garlic clove. Add 1 tablespoon minced fresh basil leaves to the food processor after the mushroom-onion has been cooked. This will create a different taste sensation.

Note: These freeze beautifully. Double or triple the recipe. Place rolls in a single layer on baking sheets and freeze, uncovered. Transfer the frozen rolls with a spatula and pile into airtight containers. When ready to use, separate onto a baking sheet to defrost. These may remain frozen several months.

Mixed Mushroom Soup

Yield: 4-6 Servings

1 pound potatoes, peeled and sliced	2 cloves minced garlic
2½ cups condensed chicken broth	1 tablespoon minced ginger
1¼ cups water	½ teaspoon ground coriander
2 pounds mixed Portobello and American white mushrooms	Optional: ¼ cup coffee cream
	Salt and pepper to taste
3 slices thick cut bacon	Parmesan Garlic Croutons (recipe, page 247)

1. Cook the cubed potatoes until very soft in the chicken broth and water. Cool and purée in a blender.

2. Remove and discard the stems from the Portobellos. Trim and keep the stems from the American white. Cut the mushrooms into cubes.

3. Cut the bacon into cubes and cook with the garlic and ginger and cook over medium-low heat. Add the mushrooms and cook over low heat until soft. Add potato mixture, and coriander.

4. Cook over low heat, covered, 15 minutes. Stir in cream. Add salt and pepper to taste. Serve topped with Parmesan Garlic Croutons.

Mushrooms Stuffed with Ham

Yield: 8 Stuffed Caps

8 American white mushroom caps	¼ cup finely chopped smoked ham or prosciutto
1 shallot, minced	¼ cup unflavored bread crumbs
8 stems, minced	2 tablespoons butter
2 tablespoons butter	½ cup seasoned bread crumbs
1 teaspoon Dijon mustard	

1. Peel caps. Remove and chop stems.

2. Cook minced shallot and minced stems in butter until soft. Stir in mustard. Stir in ham and unflavored bread crumbs. Fill caps.

3. Melt butter and toss with seasoned bread crumbs. Spoon a bit on each cap. Set under the broiler to brown. Serve as an hors d'oeuvre or accompaniment to fowl.

Portobello Pâté Toasts

Yield: 2 Cups Pâté to cover 8-10 Toasts

.85 pound Portobello mushrooms (¾ pound with stems removed)

1 roasted red pepper, skinned and sliced into thin strips

1 roasted yellow pepper, skinned and sliced into thin strips

1 large sweet Florida onion, minced

3 cloves garlic, minced

⅓ cup extra virgin olive oil

1 teaspoon salt, or to taste

½ teaspoon black pepper, or to taste

½ cup pitted black olives

1 tablespoon chopped canned chilies

1 teaspoon red balsamic vinegar

French baguette, sliced and toasted on one side only

Chopped plum tomatoes and basil leaves for decoration

1. Peel mushrooms and remove stems. Clean spongy surface with paper toweling.

2. Place the peppers on a piece of foil on the center rack under the broiler. Broil on all sides until blackened. Remove to a plastic bag and let stand 10 minutes. Remove core and seeds. Skin and slice into thin strips.

3. Cook the onion and garlic in oil over a low fire until soft. Add the sliced mushrooms and cook over medium heat until done. Mushrooms will absorb the oil, but mixture will not burn. Turn and brown the other side. Add salt and pepper.

4. Put the mushroom-garlic mixture into a food processor with the olives, chilies and vinegar. Turn on-off until mixture is thick and chunky. Taste for seasoning and add more chilies, if you like spice.

5. Toast the bread on 1 side only. Spread a layer of the mushroom mixture on the untoasted side. Place on a baking sheet and bake in a 350°F. preheated oven for approximately 5 minutes, or until hot. Set the pepper strips across the top, alternating color. Serve as an appetizer or intermezzo on a plate decorated with seeded, chopped plum tomatoes and basil leaves.

Note: Steps 1-4 can be done a day in advance.

Portobello Bruschetta

A first course winner!

Yield: 4 Servings

3 large Portobello mushroom caps (6-7 ounces)

2 tablespoons Seasoned Garlic Oil, (recipe, page 246)

4 large plum tomatoes

2 or more tablespoons finely-chopped fresh basil leaves

2 or more tablespoons finely-chopped scallion greens

1 tablespoon white balsamic vinegar

⅓ cup Seasoned Olive Oil, or ⅓ cup extra virgin olive oil mixed with 1 large clove garlic

½ teaspoon salt, or to taste

¼ teaspoon freshly ground black pepper, or to taste

4 slices Italian bread, cut ¼-inch thick

1. Peel the mushrooms and remove the stems. Brush with seasoned oil and place on a grill or barbecue over a medium flame until brown on one side. Brush the other side and brown. These mushrooms cook very quickly. They should be firm, not limp. Cool and slice rather thick. Sprinkle lightly with salt and set aside.

2. Slice the tomatoes into halves and remove the seeds. Cut into small squares and transfer to a bowl.

3. Mince the basil and scallion greens and add them to the tomatoes.

4. Stir in the balsamic vinegar, seasoned oil, salt and pepper.

5. Slice bread ¼-inch thick. Toast under the broiler on one side. Set untoasted side up on individual plates. Spoon the tomato mixture on top. Set the hot mushroom strips over each. Serve immediately.

Grilled Portobello Mushrooms and Plum Tomatoes

Yield: 6-8 Servings

4 large plum tomatoes, seeds removed and sliced into thick strips

½ cup chopped scallion greens

1 tablespoon chopped mint leaves

1 tablespoon chopped oregano leaves

1 tablespoon chopped basil leaves

2 tablespoons white balsamic vinegar

1 teaspoon red balsamic vinegar

¼ cup extra virgin olive oil

1 large clove garlic, crushed

1 teaspoon salt

Freshly ground black pepper

1 clove garlic, crushed

¼ cup olive oil

2 large Portobello mushrooms, 6-7 ounces total with stems

1. Slice tomatoes in half. Remove seeds and slice into thick strips. Combine with chopped scallion greens, mint, oregano and basil. Refrigerate. Combine vinegars with olive oil and crushed garlic and pour over tomato mixture. Add salt and grind in pepper. Place mixture in the refrigerator to marinate 1 hour or longer.

3. Remove mushroom stems and peel the outer layer from the caps. Rub clean with paper toweling. Do not rinse.

4. Combine garlic with olive oil. Brush mushroom caps. Place on a grill with the underside of the mushroom facing upward. Brush caps again while underside is cooking. The underside will cook very fast. Do not overcook. The Portobello loses texture when overcooked. Remove from grill. Cool slightly and slice into thick strips.

5. Spoon the tomato mixture across a serving plate. Place the sliced mushrooms on both sides of the tomatoes to serve.

Note: The mushrooms may be cooked in a non-stick pan. Combine olive oil with crushed garlic over high heat. Cook as above.

Portobello Spinach Salad with Curried Eggs

Yield: 6 Servings

Eggs:

4 extra large or jumbo graded eggs, hard-boiled

½ teaspoon Madras curry powder

1 tablespoon plus 1 teaspoon extra virgin olive oil

¼ teaspoon salt

1. Boil eggs. Cool to room temperature. Peel and slice into halves lengthwise.

2. Mix together curry, olive oil and salt. Set the eggs around the outside of a platter and spoon the curry mixture over. Refrigerate.

Mushrooms:

6 ounces Portobello mushroom caps (Approximately 3 mushrooms)

¼ cup balsamic white vinegar

¼ cup water

3 cloves garlic, peeled and split

½ teaspoon salt

⅛ teaspoon black pepper

1. Remove stems and thin outer dark skin of mushroom caps.

2. Combining remaining ingredients and bring to a boil. Lower heat to medium. Cover and boil gently 1 minute. Add mushrooms and cook 5 more minutes, removing cover to spoon sauce over several times. Drain, reserving garlic. Slice mushrooms into thin strips and create an inner circle around the eggs. Chop the cooked garlic and sprinkle over the mushroom strips. Refrigerate.

Spinach Salad:

3 tablespoons extra virgin olive oil

1 tablespoon balsamic white vinegar

Salt and pepper to taste

3 cups pre-washed baby spinach leaves

2 plum tomatoes, cut into strips to match the mushrooms

1. Whip the oil and vinegar together and add salt and pepper. Toss with the greens. Serve in the center of the platter with tomato strips set on top.

Mushroom Soufflé

Yield: 6 Servings

1 tablespoon unsalted butter

1 small shallot, minced

1 teaspoon all-purpose flour

½ cup coffee cream

4 egg yolks

1 pound puréed American white mushrooms

Pinch of white pepper

¼ teaspoon grated nutmeg

4 egg whites

¼ teaspoon cream of tartar

1 quart soufflé or baking dish

Unsalted butter to rub around soufflé dish

1. Preheat oven to 350°F.

2. Melt butter in a small saucepan. Add shallots and cook over low heat until soft. Stir in flour and coffee cream and cook over low heat until thick and smooth.

3. Beat egg yolks smooth. Stir a bit of the cream mixture into the yolks and then the yolks into the saucepan. Stir until hot and smooth.

4. Purée mushrooms in a food processor and add to saucepan. Stir in white pepper and nutmeg. Remove from heat.

5. Beat egg whites with an electric beater until foamy. Add cream of tartar and beat on highest speed until very thick. Fold into mushroom mixture.

6. Rub butter around the inside of soufflé dish. Spoon in mixture and bake on lowest rack 30 minutes, or until puffed and brown. Serve as a side vegetable or first course.

Duxelles with Shrimp

Yield: 4 Servings

Duxelles:

1 pound American white mushrooms

1 shallot, minced

3 tablespoons butter

1 tablespoon extra virgin olive oil

1 teaspoon minced thyme leaves, ½ teaspoon dried

Salt and pepper to taste

1. Clean and chop mushrooms with stems. Mince shallots. Cook in butter and oil over low heat until soft. Stir in thyme, salt and pepper. Set aside.

Note: Duxelles is the French name for sautéed mushrooms and onions. It is the base for many French sauces.

Shrimp:

1 pound extra large shrimp, cleaned, back vein removed, tails left on

2 tablespoons butter

2 tablespoons white wine

1 tablespoon minced cilantro leaves

1 large Ponderosa lemon, sliced on the round

1. Remove shells and dark vein along the backs of the shrimp. Leave the tails intact.

2. Cook the shrimp in the butter over medium heat until pink on one side. Add the wine and cilantro and cook until pink on the other side. Do not overcook. Arrange on a serving platter in lines with tails all facing in the same direction. Spoon duxelles around. Set sliced lemon in a circle around the outside of the platter. Serve with white rice.

Portobello Mushroom Veggi-Burgers

Yield: 4 Servings

1 cup red balsamic vinegar, aged 8 years or longer

⅓ cup extra virgin olive oil

1 large garlic clove, minced or grated

1 tablespoon minced basil leaves

8 medium size Portobello mushrooms, 3-inches in diameter

1 green zucchini squash, approximately 2-inches in diameter

2 large yellow crookneck squash, approximately 2-inches in diameter

1 red, yellow, or green bell pepper, halved and seeded

Salt and freshly ground black pepper

8 slices soy (vegetarian) pepper jack or Cheddar cheese

Optional: Thin sliced red onion

Italian white bread

1. Bring balsamic vinegar to a boil. Reduce heat to medium and boil gently until mixture thickens. (Approximately 10 minutes.) Set aside.

2. Combine oil, minced garlic and basil.

3. Remove stems from mushrooms. Wipe mushrooms clean with damp paper towels. Dry completely. Trim rough edges.

4. Slice zucchini and crookneck squash into rounds, approximately ¼-inch thick. Cut bell pepper in half and remove seeds.

5. Brush squash with the oil mixture and grill or broil on both sides until browned. Brush Portobellos with the oil mixture and grill or broil on both sides. Grill or broil red pepper on both sides and cut into thin strips. Do not overcook vegetables or mushrooms.

6. Toast Italian bread slices on one side. Brush the untoasted side with the oil mixture. Set each on a plate and keep warm.

7. Turn four mushroom caps open side up on the bread. Sprinkle with salt and grind black pepper over. Stack grilled green squash slices on each. Set a slice of cheese over. Set grilled yellow squash on top. Set a few strips of pepper over. Repeat. Set a thin slice of onion over, if you like. Cover with remaining mushroom caps for an open "burger", or toast four more pieces of bread to top.

8. Drizzle remaining oil and balsamic vinegar syrup in irregular thin lines over.

Note: This giant burger can be cut into four sections to pick up. Otherwise, accompany it with a fork and knife.

Portobello Garlic Potatoes

Yield: 4 Servings

1 large Portobello mushroom

2 pounds Idaho potatoes

1 teaspoon salt

4 tablespoons butter

½ cup warm milk

1 teaspoon salt

1 large clove garlic, crushed or grated

⅛ teaspoon red pepper flakes

1. Peel the mushroom. Remove stem. Wipe mushroom clean with paper toweling. Brush with olive oil. Brown on both sides on a griddle, grill, or in a non-stick pan. Slice into thin strips and set aside.

2. Peel and quarter the potatoes. Cover with water. Add 1 teaspoon salt and bring to a boil. Boil, covered, until potatoes are very soft. Pour off water.

3. Push the potatoes through a strainer, or mash fine with a potato masher. Add butter and gradually stir in milk while mashing. Add salt, garlic and pepper flakes. Fold in mushroom strips. Taste for seasoning.

Portobello Pâté

Yield: 2 Cups

12 ounces Portobello mushroom caps, stems removed

1 tablespoon minced Italian dried porcini

1 medium onion

¼ cup Seasoned Garlic Oil (recipe, page 246), or ¼ cup extra virgin olive oil mixed with 2 cloves crushed garlic

1 teaspoon salt

½ teaspoon black pepper

⅛ teaspoon white pepper

1 teaspoon Herbes de Provence (gourmet stores) or 1 teaspoon Italian herb seasoning

2 tablespoons port wine

2 tablespoons brandy

1. Combine mushrooms and onion in a food processor. Purée. Add oil and garlic and purée again. Add salt , peppers and Herbes de Provence and turn machine on-off quickly.

2. Cook in a skillet over low heat 10 minutes.

3. Add port and brandy. Lower heat to simmer and cook another 5 minutes. Cool to room temperature.

4. Refrigerate overnight or several days.

5. Spread a thin layer on toast points to serve.

Mushroom and Liver Pâté

Yield: 6-8 Servings

1 pound fresh chicken livers or livers from young ducklings or hens

4 tablespoons butter, chicken fat or duck fat

1 large onion, sliced thin

1 clove garlic, minced

¼ pound American white mushrooms, sliced

4 hard-boiled eggs

1 teaspoon salt

¼ teaspoon black pepper

⅛ teaspoon nutmeg

2 tablespoons brandy or cognac (optional)

1. Wash livers, removing any fat and connective tissue.

2. Melt the butter. Add the onion, garlic and mushrooms and cook until soft but not colored. Add the livers. Cook slowly, turning often, until livers are cooked through, but very soft. (Overcooked livers become bitter.) Cool slightly.

3. Boil eggs. Peel and combine with the cooked liver mixture.

4. Add salt, pepper and nutmeg to taste. Add brandy. Chop fine or put into a food processor to purée.

5. Spoon into a crock or form a mound to serve with crackers or thin toast points.

Note: Make a day in advance for the flavors to settle.

Mushrooms, Sun-Dried Tomatoes and Goat Cheese Rigatoni

Yield: 6 Servings

2 pounds American white mushrooms

8 ounces sun-dried tomatoes

1 ounce vodka

⅓ cup extra virgin olive oil

1 cup cilantro leaves, before chopping

1 teaspoon salt

½ teaspoon white pepper

Optional: 1 whole head garlic

1 tablespoon extra virgin olive oil

1 pound rigatoni, ziti or penne pasta

8 ounces goat cheese

1. Peel and slice mushrooms into ⅑-inch thickness.

2. Rinse tomatoes several times under cold, running water in a strainer or colander. Slice thin and soak in the vodka 15 minutes.

3. Remove tomatoes from the vodka and combine with the oil and mushrooms in a deep skillet. Cook, stirring over high heat, 5 minutes. Add the vodka, cilantro, salt and pepper and continue cooking over high heat until moisture has absorbed. Remove from heat.

4. If you are a garlic aficionado, combine the whole head with 1 tablespoon extra virgin olive oil on a double layer of aluminum foil. Close the foil over and place in a preheated 250°F oven. Bake 35-40 minutes, or until the garlic has become very soft within the cloves. Cool and push the garlic out of the cloves. Mash or leave intact and stir into the mushroom mixture.

5. Cook the rigatoni in boiling water until done but still firm (al dente). Drain and toss with the mushroom mixture. Divide into 6 portions.

6. Cut the goat cheese into small pieces and sprinkle over the rigatoni to serve.

Mushroom Smothered Asparagus

Yield: 2 Servings. May be doubled or tripled.

8-10 thick asparagus spears

Salt and freshly ground black pepper

1 tablespoon lemon juice

½ pound thinly sliced large white mushrooms

2 tablespoons butter

Thin slices Provolone cheese to cover asparagus

1. Cut asparagus spears approximately ⅓ from the bottom, or where the color changes from pale to deep green. With a vegetable peeler, lightly peel off the shoots and a very thin layer of the outside of each spear. Set in a row in a skillet with water barely to cover. Bring to a boil. Cover. Boil 1 minute only, or until just tender. Drain immediately and remove to a shallow baking dish or individual heat-proof plates. Sprinkle with salt and pepper. Toss with the lemon juice. Set aside in a warm place.

2. Slice the mushrooms thin and sauté in the butter until done. Cover the asparagus spears, pouring the juice from the skillet over.

3. Cover the mushrooms with Provolone. Place under a hot broiler until brown and bubbly. Serve at once.

Pecans

Although pecans are more abundant in the Pan Handle, there is a smattering of this delicious gift of nature within Central Florida.

RECIPES:

Sugared Pecans

Hot Stuff Pecans

Cinnamon Sugared Pecans

Pecan Bourbon Pie with Bourbon Sauce

5-Layer Florida Pecan Torte

Orange County Pecan Pie

Chocolate Pecan Truffles

Pecan Rum Balls

Pecan Meringue Cookies

Individual Pecan Chocolate Soufflés

Apple-Cranberry-Pecan Bread

Zucotto

Chocolate Angel Food Mousse-Cake

Sugared Pecans

Yield: 1 pound

4 tablespoons melted butter
3 tablespoons white corn syrup
½ cup granulated sugar

2 teaspoons cinnamon
1 pound pecan halves

1. Preheat oven to 200°F.
2. Melt the butter with the corn syrup. Add the sugar and cinnamon and stir. Remove from heat.
3. Place the nuts into a plastic bag and pour in the sugar mixture. Close the bag tightly and toss the nuts and sugar mixture together.
4. Set in a single layer on a baking sheet covered with parchment paper. Bake 45-50 minutes, or until the sugar has solidified on the nuts. Remove nuts to paper toweling to dry.

Hot Stuff Pecans

Yield: 1 Pound

1 pound pecan halves
2 tablespoons melted butter
¼ cup Worcestershire sauce

1 teaspoon ketchup
1 teaspoon (or to taste) Florida State Seminoles® Hot Sauce

1. Preheat oven to 300°F.
2. Combine butter, Worcestershire sauce, ketchup and hot sauce in a plastic bag. Add the pecans. Close the bag tightly and shake until all are coated.
3. Spread pecans in a single layer on a baking sheet covered with parchment paper.
4. Bake 30 minutes, turning nuts over after 15 minutes.
5. Remove nuts to paper toweling to dry. Sprinkle with salt.

Note: Several delicious Florida hot sauces are available locally or through the internet. One of these is Harry's Florida State Seminoles® Hot Sauce, made with cayenne pepper in a bottle decorated with team colors and logo. Another is Sam McGees®, which incorporates Florida oranges with Florida Datil peppers.

Cinnamon Sugared Pecans

Yield: 2 pounds

2 tablespoons cinnamon
2 cups granulated sugar
2 pounds large pecan halves

2 jumbo egg whites
3 tablespoons light corn syrup

1. Preheat oven to 250°F.
2. Combine cinnamon and sugar in a jumbo plastic bag. Add pecans and shake to incorporate.
3. Beat egg whites with a whisk until frothy. Stir in corn syrup.
4. Pour the syrup mixture into the bag with the pecans and shake to cover the nuts. Spread in a single layer onto several baking sheets.
5. Bake 1 hour, or until the sugar has hardened and the nuts are fairly dry. Remove nuts to paper toweling to cool.

Note: These make fabulous Christmas presents.

Pecan Bourbon Pie with Bourbon Sauce

A Southern favorite for the holidays.

Yield: This rich pie will serve 10

1 baked Short Pie Crust (recipe, page 266)

3 extra large graded eggs

½ cup granulated sugar

1 cup dark Karo® syrup

Pinch of salt

2 teaspoons vanilla extract

1 tablespoon Valencia orange juice

2 tablespoons bourbon whiskey

¼ cup unsalted, melted butter

1 tablespoon all-purpose flour

2 cups pecan pieces

1 cup pecan halves

1. Preheat oven to 425°F.

2. Beat eggs with sugar on highest speed of an electric mixer until thick and light in color, approximately 6 minutes. Reduce speed to low and beat in Karo® syrup, salt, vanilla, orange juice, bourbon and butter. Add flour. Fold in the pecan pieces by hand. Spoon mixture into the pre-baked crust. Place the pecan halves around the top in a pretty design.

3. Bake 10 minutes at 425°F. Reduce oven temperature to 350°F. and bake 35 minutes more. Serve at room temperature or refrigerate until very cold.

4. Accompany with Bourbon Sauce on the side.

Note: For a lighter pie, exchange the dark Karo® syrup for light.

Bourbon Sauce:
Yield: 2 Cups

1½ cups whole milk

5 tablespoons granulated sugar

Pinch of salt

3 extra large graded egg yolks

2 tablespoons, or more, bourbon whiskey

1. Bring the milk, 3 tablespoons of the sugar and salt to a boil in a small saucepan, stirring constantly.

2. Whisk yolks with remaining 2 tablespoons sugar in a bowl. Slowly beat the hot mixture into the yolks. Pour the yolk mixture back into the saucepan and stir over low heat until the custard coats a spoon. Stir in the bourbon and cook 1 minute longer. Do not allow mixture to boil. Cover and refrigerate.

5-Layer Florida Pecan Torte

Yield: Approximately 16 Slices

5 jumbo graded eggs

½ cup granulated sugar

2 teaspoons vanilla extract

2 tablespoons tangerine juice
(preferably Murcott honey tangerine)

1 cup all-purpose flour

¼ teaspoon salt

Bottoms of 10-inch cake pans

3 tablespoons unsalted butter, melted

Parchment paper

1. Preheat oven to 345°F.

2. Set a large bowl over a pot of simmering water. Add eggs, sugar, vanilla and tangerine juice and beat with a hand-held electric mixer on highest speed for about 10 minutes, scraping the sides often, until mixture is white and mousse-like. Remove from the heat and beat another 5 minutes.

3. Sift together flour and salt and fold into the egg mixture.

4. Turn cake pans (or springform pans or, even a pizza pan) upside down. Brush with melted butter. Cut parchment paper the size of the bottoms and press over the butter to adhere. Brush butter over the paper. Cover with the batter no more than ⅜-inch deep, leaving ⅑-inch space around the edges for batter to spread.

5. Bake about 10 minutes, or until golden. Turn upside down immediately onto wax paper and carefully remove the parchment paper. Generally, you can use the same paper for several layers, repeating step 4. The batter should yield 5 layers. Allow them to rest several hours before filling, or freeze for a later date.

6. Fill and cover with Pecan Filling and Frosting.

Pecan Filling and Frosting:
Yield: 4 Cups

6 ounces semi-sweet chocolate

1½ pints heavy cream

½ cup granulated sugar

1 tablespoon vanilla

2 cups toasted, finely chopped pecans

1. Melt chocolate, adding ¼ cup of the cream to smooth. Remove from the heat to cool.

2. Beat the remaining cream with the sugar and vanilla until thick. Fold in the cooled chocolate and 1 cup of the nuts.

3. Fill the layers. Cut around the edges to conform the size of the layers. Cover the top and sides. Sprinkle remaining nuts over the top.

Orange County Pecan Pie

Yield: 9-inch Pie

3 jumbo graded eggs

1 cup light corn syrup

½ cup granulated sugar

2 tablespoons orange juice from Hamlin or Valencia orange

1 tablespoon vanilla

2 cups coarsely chopped roasted pecans

Pecan Crust (recipe, page 257)

Pecan halves to top

1. Preheat oven 350°F.

2. Beat eggs. Beat in corn syrup, sugar, juice and vanilla.

3. Sprinkle pecans over unbaked pie shell. Pour filling over. Set as many pecan halves as you please, open side down, over the top.

4. Bake 45-50 minutes, or until pie is light brown and the center still slightly soft. Cool on a rack.

Chocolate Pecan Truffles

Yield: Approximately 25 Truffles

8 ounces semisweet chocolate

6 tablespoons unsalted butter

¼ cup bourbon whiskey

1 tablespoon strong liquid coffee (not instant)

½ cup ground pecans

½ cup unsweetened cocoa

½ cup granulated sugar

1. Cut the semisweet chocolate and butter into small pieces and melt together with the bourbon and coffee in the top of a double boiler or in a bowl set over simmering water.

2. Spoon into a shallow pan and refrigerate 1 hour.

3. Remove the chocolate mixture 1 teaspoon at a time from the refrigerator to roll into balls. Dip each into the nuts and place on a cookie sheet that has been covered with parchment or wax paper. Refrigerate until very cold.

4. Combine the cocoa and sugar in a bowl and roll the truffles until well coated, returning them to the cookie sheet.

5. Remove balls to an airtight container and refrigerate or freeze.

6. To serve: Set each truffle in little paper or foil candy cups.

Pecan Rum Balls

Yield: Approximately 34 Pieces

1 cup vanilla wafers

8 ounces (2 cups) pecans

8 ounces (2 cups) ground pecans

2 tablespoons unsweetened cocoa powder

Pinch of salt

3 tablespoons rum or bourbon whiskey

3 tablespoons light corn syrup (Karo®)

10X confectioners powdered sugar

1. Grind the wafers in a food processor. Remove to a bowl.

2. Grind the all the pecans in a food processor. Separate them into two containers. Combine half with the wafers.

3. Add the cocoa, salt, liquor and corn syrup.

4. Form into small balls the size of walnuts, rinsing your hands frequently to make rolling easier.

5. Dip balls, one at a time, in cool water, shaking off excess, and roll in reserved ground pecans, pressing nuts in to coat heavily.

6. Store in an airtight container several days or weeks to gather the flavors together. They may also be frozen.

7. To serve: Roll in confectioners sugar.

Note: 1 tablespoon vanilla may be substituted for the rum.

Pecan Meringue Cookies

Yield: Approximately 48 Cookies

½ cup sugar

2 tablespoons cornstarch

6 extra large egg whites, room temperature

¼ teaspoon cream of tartar

8 ounces finely-chopped pecans

Pastry bag fitted with a medium-size star tube

1. Preheat oven to 200°F. Set the rack one-third from the bottom.

2. Line baking sheets with parchment paper.

3. Combine the sugar with the cornstarch.

4. Beat egg whites with an electric mixer on highest speed 30 seconds until foamy. Add cream of tartar and beat until soft peaks form. Add the sugar mixture, 1 tablespoon at a time. Beat until whites are very stiff and shiny, 4-6 minutes.

5. Stir in finely-chopped pecans.

6. Fill the pastry bag with the mixture and, in one movement, pipe three circles on top of each other, bringing each to a point in the center. Create even rows of meringue circles one-half inch apart on the parchment.

7. Bake meringues 3 hours without opening the oven door. Turn off oven. Leave meringues inside closed oven overnight. Store in an airtight container.

Note: Chocolate or raspberry powder may be sprinkled over the tops of the meringue cookies before baking.

Individual Pecan Chocolate Soufflés without Flour

Yield: 6 Individual ¾ Cup Soufflés

Prepare the Soufflé Dishes:

1 cup ground pecans

2 tablespoons unsalted butter

Soufflé dishes that hold ¾ cup liquid

1. Grind pecans fine in a food processor. Melt the butter and coat the bottom and sides of the soufflé dishes. Press the pecans into the butter. Place into the refrigerator or freezer until very cold.

Prepare the Soufflé:

4 ounces good quality semi-sweet chocolate

½ cup heavy cream

1 tablespoon vanilla extract

3 jumbo graded egg yolks

5 jumbo graded egg whites brought to room temperature or warmer

¼ teaspoon cream of tartar

⅓ cup granulated sugar

Powdered 10X confectioners sugar for dusting

1. Melt the chocolate and cream over low heat. When chocolate is soft, stir well with a wooden spoon and then a wire whisk until smooth and thick. Add the vanilla and stir again.

2. Pour a little of the chocolate mixture into the egg yolks and stir. Add to the chocolate in the pot and cook, stirring, over low heat until very thick. Remove from the heat and cover tightly.

Finish and Bake:

1. Preheat oven to 425°F and set rack on lowest level.

2. Beat egg whites on highest speed of an electric mixer until foamy. Add the cream of tartar and continue to beat until very thick. Add the sugar and beat until smooth. (About 10 seconds.)

3. Fold the whites and soufflé dishes, running your finger around the rim of each to create a narrow indention. Place into the oven immediately.

4. Bake 6 minutes. Reduce oven temperature to 400°F and bake another 2½ minutes, or until the soufflés have risen and are firm on top. Remove from the oven immediately. Sprinkle lightly with sifted powdered sugar and serve immediately with Vanilla Sauce (recipe, page 257) on the side.

Note: Do not allow soufflé to stand after folding in the whites. Bake and serve immediately.

Apple-Cranberry-Pecan Bread

Yield:9½ X 5½ inch loaf

2 cups sifted all-purpose flour
¼ teaspoon salt
1 scant teaspoon baking soda
½ teaspoon baking powder
½ teaspoon cinnamon
½ cup butter
1 cup granulated sugar

1 extra large egg
1 cup chopped, pared Granny Smith apples
  (2 medium sized)
¼ cup dried cranberries
¼ cup chopped pecans
½ cup whole 4% milk

1. Preheat oven to 350°.

2. Sift flour, baking soda, baking powder, salt and cinnamon. Set aside.

3. Cream butter and sugar on high speed of an electric mixer until white and fluffy.

4. Add egg on medium speed, beating until light.

5. Peel and chop apples with the cranberries and pecans in a food processor. Add to the batter.

6. Add the milk in thirds, alternating with the flour mixture.

7. Stir the batter with a spatula until evenly combined.

8. Spoon into a greased loaf pan. Bake 45 minutes to 1 hour, or until a toothpick comes out "clean".

9. Serve warm or freeze. Defrost and reheat, covered tightly in foil, for ½ hour at 250°.

Zucotto

Yield: 8 Servings

Loaf pound cake, purchased at bakery

½ cup brandy mixed with 2 tablespoons Amaretto liqueur

1 quart high quality vanilla ice cream

4 ounces Paradise® glacéed red cherries, cut up

4 ounces Paradise® glacéed green cherries, cut up

4 ounces Paradise® glacéed yellow pineapple, cut up

6 ounces semi-sweet chocolate

1 pint heavy cream for whipping, divided

2 tablespoons granulated sugar

2 cups large pecan halves

1. Line a stainless bowl or deep mold with cheesecloth, hanging it over the edges for easy removal later.

2. Slice the cake into ¼ inch pieces. Brush lightly with the brandy mixture. Line the sides of the mold.

3. Bring the ice cream to the soft stage and stir in the glacéed fruit and remaining brandy mixture. Spoon into the mold, leaving a large hole in the center. Freeze 1 hour, covered.

4. Set chocolate on a large plate over simmering water. Place a cover over and allow it to melt without stirring. Remove from heat to cool slightly.

5. Whip ½ pint of the cream thick. Stir in chocolate. Fill the center of the mold. Set cake slices over the top. Cover tightly and freeze several hours or overnight.

6. Remove from freezer and pull the Zucotto out of the mold by the cheesecloth. Turn upside down so cake will be on the bottom.

7. Beat remaining cream with the sugar until very thick. Cover the Zucotto, smoothing the cream with a knife. Insert pecan halves in rows from top to bottom. Serve.

Note: This holiday dessert may be frozen several weeks. Cream and pecans should be added directly before serving.

Chocolate Angel Food Mousse-Cake

Yield: 12 or more servings

16 ounces semi-sweet chocolate or chocolate chips

3 extra large egg yolks

2 pints heavy cream

1 tablespoon vanilla extract

8-inch angel food cake, homemade or store-bought

1 pint heavy cream to cover and decorate the cake

2 tablespoons granulated sugar

2 cups ground toasted pecans

9x3-inch springform pan

1. Melt the chocolate with ½ cup heavy cream in a saucepan over low heat until melted. Stir. Separate eggs, saving whites in an airtight container in the refrigerator for another use. Add a bit of the chocolate mixture to the yolks before stirring them into the hot chocolate in the pan. Cook, stirring, over a low fire until mixture becomes very hot. Remove from heat and cool to room temperature.

2. Beat 1½ cups heavy cream until very thick. Fold into the chocolate mixture.

3. Break the angel food cake into 2-inch irregular pieces in a large bowl. Using a spatula, fold in chocolate mixture. Pile loosely into the springform pan and refrigerate or freeze at least 24 hours.

4. Beat 1 pint heavy cream with the sugar until very thick. Remove the sides of the springform and place cake on a platter. Cover the top and sides with cream. Insert a fluted tube into a pastry bag and fill with remaining cream. Pipe rosettes around the top. Sprinkle heavily with ground pecans.

Fish

This "River of Currents," as the Spanish called it in the sixteenth century, flows South to North from Vero Beach through narrow canals and lakes until it reaches Jacksonville and the Atlantic Ocean. Alligators, turtles and river otters lazily bask along the shores of the creeks and canals where Audubon once captured rare birds on canvas in the 1830s.

RECICPES:

Blackened Redfish

Gingered Red Fish or Bass

Grilled Redfish

Capt. Hammond's Grilled Redfish

Grilled Fish with Citrus Curry Sauce

Brackish Fish Stew

Grilled Bass with Tofu and Avocado Sauce

Bass with Lime Glaze

Honey Glazed Sorrento Onions

Herbal Baked Bass

*Poached Largemouth Bass
with Caper Sauce*

Cold Caper Sauce

Fish - Bass and Redfish

Our friend, Bill, navigates his 1929 Chris Craft triple upswept, "Wave", gracefully through the water as we move south upstream in a parade of forty-eight "Woodies", or antique boats. We are not on the Nile. This is Central Florida's St. John's River. Don't ask me why it flows south upstream and north downstream. If you explain a thousand times why this "River of Currents", as the Spanish called it in the sixteenth century, flows south to north from Vero Beach through narrow canals and lakes until it reaches Jacksonville and the Atlantic Ocean, I still will not understand. What I do understand is that it's a little slice of heaven! Alligators, turtles and river otters lazily bask along the shores of the creeks and canals where Audubon once captured rare birds on canvas in the 1830s while living on his plantation by Lake Dexter. Hundreds of buoys designating blue crab traps bob in the water. Every mile marker is a nest for a mama and papa osprey oblivious to us kicking up wakes as we move from Jacksonville to Sanford. As the river narrows at the end of Lake George, we change our speed to neutral to observe the "No Wake" and "Manatee Zones". The river takes a sharp turn at Marker 26, and someone informs us this was the place where the steamships, "Fannie Dugan" and "City of Jacksonville" collided in 1890.

It is our seventh sojourn to this celebration of nature. Trailing our boats in a caravan, we cruise north from Palatka down the river past marker #24, turning east just south of Green Cove Springs Bridge on the way to Palma Cove and into the Six-Mile Creek to our favorite restaurant, Outback Crab Shack. Signs on the dock advertise, "No Shirt - No Shoes - No Problem", and servers wearing green T-shirts bearing the caption, "Free beer tomorrow", dash between the wooden, umbrella-covered picnic tables carrying pitchers filled with varieties of draft beer and trays piled high with fresh seafood.

The Redfish that come from the tributaries of the St. John's River are a unique specie that emit a pleasurable sensation all their own. Heavier with a more pronounced flavor than the bass, they are similar although not as strong of flavor as the ocean swordfish. Most people who catch these fish just sprinkle them with salt and pepper to toss on an outside grill. I like to rub the outside with my recipe for "Chain of Lakes Seasoning" (recipe, page 245) before brushing with citrus juice and butter or butter substitute for a spectacular repast.

Blackened Redfish

Yield: 2 Servings

2 Redfish fillets, boned and skinned

Salt to sprinkle

1 tablespoon Chain of Lakes Seasoning

1 tablespoon Persian lime juice

1 tablespoon Ruby Red grapefruit juice

1 tablespoon Hamlin orange juice

2-3 tablespoons melted butter or butter substitute

Citrus Butter (recipe, page 255)

1. Skin the redfish fillets in the following manner: Insert the point of a knife under the wide end of the fillet and carefully cut away the skin, being careful not to cut into the flesh. Then, insert the back end of the knife under the skin and pull the skin down towards the narrow end with your other hand. If the fish is fresh, the skin should peel away easily. If it doesn't, the fish may have been frozen or held on ice for too long a time.

2. Sprinkle fillets with salt and rub Chain of Lakes seasoning over. Combine citrus juices and cover the fillets. Set aside 15 minutes.

3. Remove fillets from citrus juices and brush heavily with butter or butter substitute. Set over white charcoal or low heat of a gas grill. When just browned on one side, turn fish over. Brush again with butter or butter substitute. Cook until flesh separates with a fork. Do not overcook, but do not eat this fish rare or pink because it will have a tallow flavor within.

4. Set fillets on a plate and spoon Citrus Butter on top.

Notes on freezing fish fillets: Most fish purchased in supermarkets have already been frozen and thawed to place in the case. Never refreeze fish. To freeze fresh fish, place the cleaned fish into a plastic bag larger than the fish itself and add enough water for the fish to lie in. Close the bag tightly and freeze with the whole fish or fillets lying flat in the water. Fish that is air-frozen will lose texture and become dry. It's logical that anything that swims in water should be stored in water.

Gingered Red Fish or Bass

Yield: 4 Servings

4 red fish or bass fillets, skinned and boned

4 tablespoons (½ stick) butter

1 teaspoon finely diced fresh ginger

1 teaspoon white horseradish

A little salt and pepper

1½ cups unflavored bread crumbs

4 tablespoons vegetable oil

1. Wash and dry fish fillets.

2. Melt butter. Stir in ginger and simmer over very low heat 2 minutes. Remove from heat. Stir in horseradish and salt and pepper. Coat the fillets with the mixture and dip into the bread crumbs, pushing them in to adhere.

3. Heat vegetable oil in a shallow skillet and cook fillets until browned and done to your liking. Bass take less time to cook than Redfish. Do not overcook.

The seagrass flats of the Indian River Lagoon in the Titusville area can reward the amateur fisherman with a trophy sized redfish. These lovely fish that are best simply grilled with citrus or blackened Cajun style never venture out of the lagoon, but remain in the shallow grass flats, even when the water seems too shallow to hold the largest that can weigh over thirty pounds and have grown over forty inches long.

Grilled Redfish

Yield: 2 Servings

2 filleted, boned and skinned Redfish

1 tablespoon Key lime juice

1 tablespoon Dancy Tangerine juice

1 tablespoon Ruby Red grapefruit juice

Salt and pepper to sprinkle

1 sweet Vidalia or Sorrento onion, coarsely chopped

1 small yellow or orange bell pepper (½ cup coarsely chopped)

2 tablespoons clarified unsalted butter

2 seeded and coarsely chopped plum tomatoes

1 tablespoon 2 Guys® or Hurricane Bay® hot sauce

2 tablespoons clarified unsalted butter to brush the fish

1. Combine the fruit juices and marinate the fish 30 minutes. Remove from the marinade and sprinkle with salt and pepper. Reserve the marinade.

2. Sauté the onion and pepper until soft in 4 tablespoons clarified butter. Add the chopped tomatoes and Florida hot sauce.

3. Pat the fillets dry. If you like, sprinkle with a little salt and pepper. Brush with butter and place on a grill over medium heat of gas or charcoal or wood. Cook until lightly colored on one side. Turn. Brush with butter. Cook until colored on the other side. Do not overcook.

4. Bring the marinade to a boil and brush the fillets well before serving.

5. Serve with a green vegetable and freshly sliced tangerine and grapefruit.

Note: Texas and Louisiana hot sauces, Move Over! We have our own sensational sauces brewed in our peninsula we call Florida. Florida Gourmet Foods in Deland (1-800-243-3877) manufactures Hurricane Bay and Island Grove sauces to enhance fish, fowl and game. An outfit called 2 Guys manufactures a Louisiana type jalapeño hot sauce that will 'knock your socks off'.

Ease into any creek off the Intercoastal waterway during the last hours of incoming and outgoing tides and you will be promised a king's ransom of Redfish and Flounder just for throwing your hook into the water. There are many charter boats to choose from, but the best known captain in the area, Jim Hammond (904-757-7550), will take two people for $250 for four hours or $350 all day for an excursion from Jacksonville in-shore for Trout in the flats close to deep water and Snook and Redfish in the creeks that can weigh up to ten pounds. The following is his recipe for Grilled Redfish. The secret might be the sauce made with half a bottle of beer leaving the other half for the cook to enjoy while the fish grills to perfection.

Capt. Hammond's Grilled Redfish

Yield: 2 Servings

2 fillets of Redfish, scales and skin left on
½ bottle of beer, not light
2 garlic cloves, crushed or shaved

1 small Florida sweet onion, minced fine
3 tablespoons butter

1. Clean and bone fillets, leaving skin and scales intact.

2. Combine remaining ingredients in a saucepan and cook over low heat 5 minutes or longer.

3. Sprinkle fish with salt and pepper. Brush heavily with the butter mixture and set over a gas grill or white coals. Cook on one side. Brush heavily again and turn fish over to cook on the other. Because of the skin and scales, the fish will curl up around the edges and the juices will remain within for a truly delicious country culinary experience.

If I didn't know better, I would swear the earth is flat as I watch the massive red fire ball we call Sun begin to disappear over the west edge of Lake Dora. By eight o'clock, the semi-darkness of evening's dusk will play host to hungry mosquitoes and swarming gnats. The old alligator that has considered our shore home for twenty years floats lazily with only his gigantic head above water without awareness that he is part of this tapestry. Further out, there is a lingering boat with its occupant still hopeful of catching a large bass or netting a dinner of tilapia. The absolute quietude is interrupted only by the occasional call of a blue heron or squawk of a Broad-winged or Red-tailed Hawk in pursuit of a slow-moving squirrel on shore.

Our Lake Dora is connected to Lake Eustis on the north through the Dora Canal and to Lake Apopka to the south through the Apopka Beauclair Canal. Twenty years ago the nine lakes that comprise the Harris Chain were fertile entities for some of the best bass fishing in Florida. Lake Eustis, which is connected to Big Lake Harris through the mile long Dead River and Lake Griffin through Haines Creek, is the home of the famous "Gator Hole", a deep sink hole at the end of a natural canal leading off the main lake. This is the "secret paradise" of Lake County folk's "Fish Tales" retold by the light of campfires and on the Eustis City and Buzzard Beach public ramps on the lake. And, an hour south of Lake County, savvy fishermen cast their lines into Little Lake Conway and Lake Tohopekaliga (known as Lake Toho) to bring home trophy sized bass that practically jump into their boats.

Grilled Fish with Citrus Curry Sauce

Yield: 2 or more Servings

2 fillets cut from redfish, bass, or another firm
    fish

Salt and pepper

½ cup Murcott Honey or Dancy Tangerine juice

½ cup Orlando or Honeybell (Minneola)
    Tangelo juice

1 tablespoon finely chopped fresh ginger

1 large garlic clove, finely chopped

1 teaspoon ground cumin

1 teaspoon ground coriander

1 teaspoon Madras curry powder

½ cup chopped red onion

1 tablespoon extra virgin olive oil

2 tablespoons melted butter

1. Sprinkle salt and pepper lightly on both sides of the fillets.

2. In a glass dish, combine the tangerine and tangelo juices with the ginger, garlic, cumin, coriander and curry. Add the chopped onion and olive oil and place the fish in to marinate several hours.

3. Remove the fish to grill skin side down over white coals or medium gas heat. Brush the flesh with the melted butter before turning the fillets over.

4. Pour the marinade into a small saucepan and bring to a boil, stirring. Remove the fillets to 2 plates and pour the marinade over. Accompany with boiled red potatoes and fresh asparagus. Set tangerine and tangelo segments around the plate.

Brackish Fish Stew

Yield: 6 Servings

10 pounds combined whole Redfish, Bass, Trout, or other firm fish from brackish tributaries of St. John's River

Salt and pepper

¼ pound melted butter

3 cups fish broth, or bottled clam juice

1 cup white wine

1 cup seeded and diced plum tomatoes

1 large onion, diced

1 rib celery, diced

1 clove garlic, minced

A few threads saffron, or 1 teaspoon turmeric

1 teaspoon coriander powder

Pinch of red pepper flakes

2-3 sage leaves or ½ teaspoon dried sage

10-ounce package frozen lima beans

2 sweet potatoes, peeled and cut into small chunks

Thickly sliced French bread, toasted and rubbed with garlic

1. Make fish broth by boiling the heads in water or half white wine and water to cover. Onion, celery, salt and pepper may be added. Strain. Bottled clam juice may be substituted.

2. Bone and skin the fish. Cut into large pieces. Sprinkle with salt and pepper. Brush with melted butter.

3. Combine remaining ingredients, reserving the bread. Bring to a boil. Add the fish. Cover and boil gently 15-20 minutes, or until fish is tender. Add more salt and pepper to taste.

4. Toast the bread. Rub with garlic and brush with remaining butter. Set in large soup bowls and ladle the stew over.

The marriage of fish fillets with seasoned tofu accompanied by citrus and avocado will provide a happy occasion for all who join in the feast. Change the proportions of spices to suit the tastes of your guests. You may substitute my recipe for Seasoned Garlic Oil for the garlic and peanut oil listed. Do not omit the sesame oil.

Grilled Bass with Tofu and Avocado Sauce

Yield: 4 Servings

Avocado Sauce:

1 ripe but firm Florida large green avocado

Juice from 1 Persian lime

2 tablespoons chopped cilantro leaves

2 tablespoons chopped scallion greens

1 Ruby Red grapefruit, peeled and sectioned

Salt and a pinch of white pepper to taste

1. Mash the avocado but do not purée. Stir in lime juice. Combine remaining ingredients and stir in. Taste for salt and pepper. Leave the avocado mixture fairly mild to temper the spices in the tofu. Set aside.

The Tofu:

4 ounces firm tofu, drained and dried on paper toweling

Salt and black pepper to sprinkle

1-2 cloves garlic, minced

1 tablespoon peeled and minced ginger

2 tablespoons sesame oil

2 tablespoons peanut oil

Pinch of red pepper flakes

1 teaspoon cumin powder

1 tablespoon coriander powder

1 teaspoon soy or Tamari sauce

1 ripe but still firm plantain or 4 Florida finger bananas

¼ cup sesame seeds

6 ounce can chopped mild or hot chili peppers

1. Slice the tofu across into pieces approximately ¼-inch thick. Before separating, slice into 2 or 3 strips, depending on the width of the tofu. Then, cut the strips into triangles. Sprinkle with salt and pepper.

2. Combine the garlic, ginger, sesame and peanut oil in a shallow non-stick skillet. Add a touch of red pepper flakes, cumin and coriander. Fry the tofu pieces quickly on both sides until brown. Remove from the skillet to a plate.

3. Add the soy sauce to the skillet. Slice the plantain (bananas) rather thick and cook over medium heat in the soy until browned on both sides. Add sesame seeds and chilies. Spoon over the tofu and cover with plastic wrap to keep warm.

(Continued)

GRILLED BASS WITH TOFU AND AVOCADO SAUCE *(Continued)*

The Bass:

4 fillets of small Largemouth Bass   Salt and black pepper to sprinkle

1. Return the skillet to medium-high heat. Add more oil if necessary to lightly cover the bottom.
2. Salt and pepper the bass fillets and cook on both sides until just browned. Do not overcook. Set fillets on four plates. Set tofu slices on the plate. Spoon the sauce from the tofu over the fish.
3. Spoon avocado sauce around the outside edge of the plate or next to the fish.

Largemouth Bass are members of the Black Bass family. They are also called Florida bass, Green bass, Bigmouth, Bucketmouth, Oswego and Green Trout. They are the largest members of the Sunfish family. The meat is white, flaky, and low in oil content. The bass pulled out of our Chain of Lakes are delicious broiled, pan fried or battered and deep fried. This fish is white, flaky, and tender, with a mild flavor. The larger bass found in the brackish waters are best more highly seasoned and baked to remove the stronger weedy taste.

Because bass have a zillion tiny bones, the easiest method of cooking the smaller fish is to leave it whole for the flesh to be removed easily. The fish must be thoroughly cleaned before cooking. Cut off the fins. Scrape off scales from the tail towards the head. Wash the fish under cold water. Insert a sharp point of a knife in the anal vent and slit the belly open to the head. Remove entrails. Open and clean the blood from the backbone. Wash the cavity well. Larger bass can be filleted more easily. Set the whole fish on a flat, firm surface. Cut off the head and cut along the back to behind the dorsal fin and then through the body to the tail with a sharp knife. Hold the fish by its tail as you slice down the side of the backbone and remove the flesh from the rib cage. Cut off the tail. Insert the point of a knife under the skin by the tail and then, holding the knife on a slant, separate the skin from the flesh from the tail to the head. It should pull away easily if the fish is fresh. Repeat the process for the other side.

Cooking Chart for Baked Whole Fish: Preheat oven to 400°F.

1½ pound fish	15 minutes
3 pound fish	25 minutes
5-6 pound fish	40 minutes
7-8 pound fish	45 minutes

Bass with Lime Glaze

Yield: 4 Servings

4 Chain of Lakes bass fillets, skinned and boned

Salt and pepper to sprinkle

¼ cup Key lime juice

2 garlic cloves, crushed

1 teaspoon cumin

6 ounce can chopped mild green chili peppers

2 tablespoons finely chopped cilantro leaves

2 tablespoons flat leaf parsley

2 tablespoons orange blossom honey

3 tablespoons extra virgin olive oil

3 tablespoons unsalted butter

1. Wash and dry fillets. Sprinkle with salt and pepper.

2. Combine lime juice, crushed garlic, cumin, chili peppers, cilantro, parsley and honey in a blender. Remove to a saucepan and cook over low heat 5 minutes.

3. Melt olive oil with butter in a shallow skillet. Brown fillets on both sides. Add sauce. Cover pan and simmer over low heat until fish flakes with a fork.

Note: Serve with Honey Glazed Sorrento onions.

Honey Glazed Sorrento Onions

Yield: 6 Servings

6 sweet large Sorrento onions

¼ cup butter, melted

¼ teaspoon salt

Tiny pinch white pepper

¼ cup orange blossom honey

1. Preheat oven to 350°F.

2. Peel onions and cut a small hole in the in the top. Place in a shallow baking dish.

3. Combine butter, salt, pepper and honey in a small pan and cook, stirring, over low heat until mixture is smooth. Pour the mixture over the onions. Bake approximately 30 minutes, or until glazed.

Note: The onions can be filled with spinach, mashed potatoes or squash. Cut a circle into the centers three-quarters to the bottom before baking. Chop centers fine. Sauté in a little butter until soft and add to vegetables. Fill onions with vegetable the last 15 minutes.

Herbal Baked Bass

Yield: Approximately 6 Servings

6-7 pound Largemouth Bass, head and tail intact, gills and scales removed

¼ cup olive oil

Salt and black pepper

2 fresh rosemary sprigs

8 fresh basil leaves

2 garlic cloves, peeled and sliced

2 tablespoons lemon juice

¼ cup light dry sherry

Kosher salt and black pepper

Paprika

2 slices black or green pimento filled olives for the eyes

6 long, narrow pimento or roasted red pepper strips for garnish

Handful of watercress for garnish

12 cherry tomatoes for garnish

1. Preheat oven to 400°F.

2. Cut fish open along its belly to its backbone. Remove gills and scales and wash the inside. Carefully make a slit along both sides of the bone at the tail section. (Most fishmongers will do this for you.)

3. Lay a large piece of heavy aluminum foil on a flat cookie sheet. Brush the foil with oil. If the fish is too large for the foil, lay another piece of foil overlapping the first.

4. Sprinkle the fish cavity with salt and pepper. Insert the rosemary, basil and garlic evenly from heat to tail. Brush the cavity with lemon juice and sherry, adding more, if necessary, to moisten the flesh well.

5. Close the cavity of the fish. Lightly sprinkle kosher salt and pepper over the skin and head on both sides. Brush well with olive oil. Sprinkle with Paprika. Bring up the edges of the foil, tent style. Lay the fish flat and fold the edges of the foil over each other, being careful not to touch the top of the fish. Fold the ends of the foil tightly together.

6. Place in the preheated oven and bake 6-7 minutes per pound. Open the foil and pull a bit of skin up and insert a fork. If the flesh separates easily and is white in color, the fish is done. Do not overcook or fish will take on a rubbery consistency.

7. Carefully slide the fish away from the foil on to a large platter with two spatulas. Remove eyes with a small, sharp knife and place a black or green olive into each socket. Encircle the olives with a narrow strip of pimento. Place 4 pimento strips across for decoration. Arrange watercress and grape tomatoes across one side of the platter and boiled red potatoes and broccoli florets on the other.

Note: This recipe was created for Craig Claiborne, Food Editor of The New York Times and author of 19 cookbooks, when he had dinner at our home. He featured it in his column on March 3, 1982, and later in his book, Southern Cooking, published in 1987. For a spectacular presentation, the whole fish was surrounded by giant shrimp (8-10 per pound), steamed in beer with Old Bay® Seasoning.

"The biggest fish he ever caught were those that got away."

Eugene Field

Best kept secret fishing holes in Mount Dora are three tiny land-locked spring fed lakes. Lake Saunders, East Crooked Lake and Loch Levin hoard enough bass to keep the worms dancing at the end of every young Tom Sawyer's fishing pole. A friend of ours tells the tale of casting six times and catching five fish with his son. "Set out at four o'clock in the morning before the sun rises and wait for the reeds to move. Bait your hook with a purple worm in the morning and rapella jigging minnows in the afternoon."

Poached Largemouth Bass with Caper Sauce

Equipment: Fish poacher or deep skillet with cover

Yield: 6 Servings

6 pound bass fillet, skin left intact

Kosher salt and freshly ground black pepper to sprinkle

2 cups dry white wine

2 cups water

1 tablespoon minced fresh dill or 1½ teaspoons dried dill

Juice of 1 Persian lime

2-inch piece ginger, peeled and sliced

1 Florida sweet onion

Leaves and top cut from whole stalk celery

1 clove garlic, split

¼ teaspoon mustard seed

Optional: 1 pound large shrimp (26-30 per pound)

1. Clean and scale bass, slitting from the head to the tail along the belly. Sprinkle bass lightly with salt and pepper and set aside.

2. Reserving shrimp for later, combine remaining ingredients in the poacher and bring to a boil. Boil 1 minute. Set bass into broth flesh side up. Cover. Steam 2 minutes over high heat. Lower heat to medium. Ladle broth over. Cover again and steam 7 minutes more. Ladle broth over again. Cover and steam about 6 minutes longer, or until fish flakes with a fork. Do not overcook. Cooking time should be approximately 15 minutes in total.

3. Remove fish from poacher. For a glorious feast, add 1 pound large (26-30) shrimp to the broth and bring to a boil. Cook 1 minute only. Remove shrimp from poacher.

4. Strain broth into a saucepan to serve as gravy or as the base for Caper Sauce (recipe, page 139).

5. Carefully remove skin from fish with a sharp knife. It should slide off easily. Set fish on a warm platter.

(Continued)

POACHED LARGEMOUTH BASS WITH CAPER SAUCE *(Continued)*

6. Remove shells and veins from the shrimp and set around the fish. Or, let your guests peel their own shrimp. Ladle some of the broth over and cover with plastic wrap to keep warm. Make Caper Sauce.

Hot Caper Sauce:
Yield: Approximately 2½ Cups

2 tablespoons unsalted butter
2 tablespoons all-purpose flour
2½ cups strained broth from the poached fish
¼ cup heavy cream

½ cup tiny capers
¼ cup chopped fresh dill
Salt and pepper to taste

1. Melt unsalted butter in a saucepan over low heat. Stir in flour. Slowly stir in broth, cooking until mixture thickens slightly and becomes smooth. Stir in cream. Mixture will continue to thicken. Do not allow it to boil. Stir in capers and chopped dill. Pour ½ cup over the fish and serve remaining sauce on the side. Decorate with tiny red tomatoes for color.

Note: The fish may also be served cold with Cold Caper Sauce.

Cold Caper Sauce

Yield: 2 Cups

1 cup sour cream, regular or fat-free
1 cup mayonnaise
2 tablespoons chopped fresh dill
2 tablespoons chopped cilantro leaves

1 tablespoon white horseradish
½ cup tiny capers
Salt and pepper to taste

1. Combine the ingredients and refrigerate several hours. Spoon ½ cup over the fish and serve remaining sauce on the side. Decorate with tiny red tomatoes for color.

RECIPES:

Pecan Tilapia for Two

Sautéed Tilapia with
Fried Zucchini Blossoms

Tilapia Stuffed with Crab Meat

Tilapia in Turmeric Sauce with Fennel

Nutsy Buds Sautéed Tilapia

A Fish in Thyme

Fillet of Tilapia Muscadine

Blackened Tilapia with Spicy Sauce

Tilapia, Redear or Bluegill Mornay

Tilapia: The Fish of the Bible

A new fish, known as the Nile Perch, achieved instant popularity in restaurants and home kitchens when it invaded the canals and lakes of Florida. Actually, this new fish is one of the oldest edible fish known to mankind. Tilapia, the mild little freshwater fish with white, firm flesh, is said to have been "St Peter's Fish" of the Bible. It is widely believed to have been the fish in the Sea of Galilee that was multiplied by Jesus to feed the masses of hungry people - a miracle that taught the apostles to have faith.

The common name, Tilapia, refers to several species of fish belonging to the Cichlid family native to Africa and the Middle East. Raised by the Egyptians over 4,500 years ago for food, it is the second most widely cultured fish in the world next to the Carp. Reportedly more than one billion pounds of Tilapia were raised last year in ponds, cages and rice fields. There are two explanations for their entry into the lakes of South and Central Florida. The first is conjecture that, after the fish was imported into South America, it was smuggled into south Florida for breeding in private ponds, but somehow wound up in the canals of Dade County. Documented facts, however, show that Auburn University imported them in 1959 for aquaculture research to study their spawning behavior and early life history, food habits and lower lethal temperature. During the sixties they were imported into Florida by the Florida Game and Freshwater Fish Commission as a biological control agent of nuisance aquatic plants and as a sport fish like the bass. Phosphate pits at the Pleasant Grove Research Station near Tampa were stocked. The experiment was a failure, but the Tilapia had already been promoted as a "superfish". Before the study was completed, the public gained access to the fish and began spreading it into the lakes, canals and private ponds throughout the state. It was so adaptable to fresh, saline and brackish waters, reproducing in abundance approximately every six months, that researchers feared it would harm some Florida ecosystems. The trade-off was that it created commercial and sport fishing in some lakes that would have been ecosystems with low yields. Surpassing bass in their ability to fight, they usually are brought in by nets.

Although Taiwan, Thailand and Indonesia supply a greater portion of the world with frozen fillets, most of ours in Central Florida arrive fresh from Costa Rica and Ecuador. These little fish are so hardy (and hearty) that they can be transported live to Oriental markets and restaurants, where they have become a favorite selection. Tilapia has absolutely no "fishy" odor or taste. It is so mild and sweet with such a lovely texture that it lends itself to a creativity all its own. It is equally fabulous sautéed in butter, creamed, curried, prepared with Oriental seasonings or spiced-up under a variety of sauces.

"Of all the world's enjoyments
that ever valued were,
there's none of our employments
with fishing can compare."
Thomas D'Urfey

Pecan Tilapia for Two

Yield: 2 servings

Handful of roasted pecan halves or pieces

1 tablespoon butter, melted

2 tilapia fillets, skinned and boned

Juice from 1 Persian lime

Salt to sprinkle

Touch of white pepper

¼ cup plain fine bread crumbs

1 small shallot, minced

3 tablespoons butter

¼ teaspoon Madras curry powder

¼ teaspoon ground coriander seed

1 seedless Florida navel orange, membranes removed and sectioned

Optional: chopped curly parsley or cilantro leaves

1. In a small pan, warm the pecans in the butter until coated. Keep warm in the pan.

2. Saturate the tilapia fillets in the lime juice and sprinkle salt over.

3. Add a touch of white pepper to the bread crumbs and coat the fillets. Set aside.

4. In a shallow, non-stick skillet, cook the shallot in the butter over low heat until soft. Stir in the curry powder and coriander. Add the fillets, turning the heat to medium. Cook less than 1 minute, or until browned on one side. Turn fillets over and cook until browned on the other.

5. Remove fillets to two plates. Cover with the nuts and set orange segments across the top or around the plate with chopped parsley or cilantro leaves for color.

Note: Crushed pecans may be substituted for the bread crumbs to coat the fillets.

Sautéed Tilapia with Fried Zucchini Blossoms

Tilapia fillets

Salt and pepper

Combined ratio of ¼ cup all-purpose flour to ¾ cup commercial seasoned bread crumbs

Half unsalted butter, half vegetable oil just to cover the bottom of a skillet

Lemon wedges on the side

1. Lightly salt and pepper the fillets.

2. Combine flour and bread crumbs in a plastic bag. Place the fillets in, one at a time, and coat well.

3. Heat butter and oil in a non-stick skillet. Cook the fish, uncovered, until browned on both sides. Serve with lemon wedges on the side. Accompany with quickly steamed fresh broccoli, spinach or cauliflower (Melt sharp Cheddar cheese, mozzarella or Gorgonzola over the cauliflower for extra flavor.) Serve freshly-baked French bread on the side.

Fried zucchini blossoms (Fiori Fritti) are considered a delicacy in fine restaurants throughout Italy. Usually, the blossom is delicately seasoned with salt, lightly battered, and quickly fried in a light vegetable oil to a golden color of crisp perfection. Some restaurants stuff them with herbs and bread crumbs, anchovy, or chopped prosciutto ham and Parmesan cheese. Anyone who has been privileged to eat these recounts the experience as memorable.

Zucchini is one of the easiest vegetables to grow. Left alone, the green zucchini grows to gargantuan proportions, necessitating two hands to lift the mature squash from the ground. The open flowers of the infant zucchini must be snatched at precisely the right time in their development. The blossoms are wide open early in the morning when the sun is high in the sky and the day still cool. The female flower is more desirable than the male because it has the tiny edible beginnings of the developing squash (French: "courgette") at the top of its stem.

Fried Zucchini Blossoms

Yield: 8 Flowers

8 female zucchini flowers, open	3 tablespoons extra virgin olive oil
¾ cup self-rising flour	4 or more tablespoons water
½ teaspoon salt	Optional: Bread crumbs, chopped anchovy, chopped smoked ham or cheese
⅛ teaspoon white pepper	
1 extra large egg, separated	Grape seed, vegetable, canola, peanut oil, or a combination of two or more

1. Wash flowers under cool, running water. Remove the internal pistils. Set stems in cold water until ready to cook.

2. Combine flour with salt and white pepper. Mix the egg yolk with the olive oil. Stir into the flour mixture. Stir the water in by tablespoons until the batter is quite thin. Let stand 45 minutes.

3. Beat the egg white until it reaches the thick stage, but not stiff. Stir it into the flour mixture.

4. Dry the flowers gently with paper toweling. Remove the stems, being careful not to bruise the flower. Remove any green leaves. If desired, insert a tiny piece of anchovy or chopped ham or cheese into the center.

5. Heat oil of your choice in a pot to deep fry.

6. Dip the flowers into the batter. Shake off excess. Fry until golden. Serve immediately.

Note: These cannot be made in advance and reheated, but must be prepared immediately upon serving.

Tilapia Stuffed with Crab Meat

Yield: 6 Servings

Béchamel Sauce:

2 tablespoons unsalted butter

1 shallot, minced

2 tablespoons flour

1 cup light cream

Salt and a pinch of white pepper to taste

1. Melt butter in a saucepan. Cook shallot until soft, but not colored. Stir in flour. Stir in cream, salt and pepper. Mixture will be very thick. Remove from heat.

Baking Sauce:

½ cup dry white wine

½ cup organic vegetable broth (Pacific®)

Juice from ½ Meyer lemon

1 tablespoon unsalted butter

2 large plum tomatoes, skinned, seeded and coarsely chopped

1. Combine ingredients and set aside.

Fish Stuffing:

6 fillets of Tilapia, boned and skinned

Salt and pepper

½ pound cooked Blue Crab meat, cleaned and flaked

1 shallot, minced

1 teaspoon parsley, minced

¼ teaspoon fresh tarragon leaves, minced

⅛ teaspoon white pepper

1 egg white, beaten to the foamy stage

¼ cup heavy cream

¼ cup fine unseasoned bread crumbs

1. Lightly salt and pepper the fillets and set them on a flat surface.
2. Mix the remaining ingredients together and let stand 10 minutes.
3. Spread the stuffing over one-half of each fillet. Fold the other half over the stuffing and place into a shallow baking pan. Cover with baking sauce.
4. Butter a piece of wax or parchment paper and set it on top of the fish.
5. Preheat oven to 350°F.
6. Bake fish 12-15 minutes, or until a fork inserted separates the flesh. Do not overcook.
7. Carefully remove the fish from the pan onto a serving platter.
8. Strain the broth from the pan and stir it into the Béchamel Sauce over medium heat until creamy. Pour over fish to serve.

Kumquats

Roast Duck

Venison Ragoût

Herbal Baked Fish

Crab in Filo Dough

Crab in Artichoke

Pecan Chocolate Soufflé

Table of Desserts

1. Citrus Sunshine Cake
2. Hamlin Crème Brûlée
3. Zucotto
4. Plant City Strawberri
5. Chocolate Angel Foo
   Mousse-cake
6. Berry-a-Trifle
7. BSB Scrumptious
   Chocolate Cake
8. Strawberry Pie

Tilapia in Turmeric Sauce with Fennel

Yield: 4 Servings

4 Tilapia fillets

¼ teaspoon salt

2 tablespoons unsalted butter

1 teaspoon flour

½ teaspoon turmeric (spice dept)

1 tablespoon chopped fresh tarragon, or 1 teaspoon dried

1 cup concentrated chicken broth

1 small fennel bulb, julienne into fine strips

⅓ cup heavy cream

1. Sprinkle the fillets with salt. Melt the butter in a skillet. Sauté quickly on both sides until brown but not overcooked. Remove the fillets from the pan to a warm platter.

2. Over low heat in the same skillet that the fish was cooked, stir in the flour. Add turmeric and tarragon. Add the chicken broth, a little at a time, stirring. Add the fennel strips and continue to cook until the sauce has thickened. Stir in the heavy cream. Spoon the sauce over the fillets and serve immediately.

Note: Tilapia is a delicate fish that cooks immediately on contact with heat. Do not overcook. Wide noodles tossed simply with chicken broth and a little butter or Corn Fritters (recipe, page 93) are good accompaniments.

August fourteenth, four o'clock in the afternoon: The temperature is ninety-eight degrees. Lake Dora shimmers like a huge slab of wet glass, beckoning the foolish to walk on its glistening surface. The dragonflies are as big as baby birds and swarming unmercifully through everything in their path. Their antagonist, the butterfly, gently kisses the open blossoms on shore, fluttering innocently from petal to petal. The giant heron that has adopted our dock stands transfixed without apparent worry that anyone will bother him, and my favorite local bird, the Anhinga ("Snakebird"), is erectly perched on top of my boat's hitching post with the late afternoon sunlight reflecting his outstretched wings as they dry. I wonder if this black waterbird with his protruding multi-feathered long tail and pointed yellow bill that spears fish before swallowing them head first, has just had his fill of tilapia, or if the brave little fish was too fast for him. The anhinga is a tireless hunter, flying through the water with only his head and long skinny neck maneuvering like a snake. But, because he lacks oil glands to waterproof himself, he eventually is too heavy to continue when his feathers become waterlogged. As soon as he dries off, he'll be off again in search of another meal.

Nutsy Buds Sautéed Tilapia

Quick, easy, crunchy and delicious!

Yield: 2 Servings

2 Tilapia fillets	2 medium egg whites
Salt to sprinkle	½ cup, or more, Betty Crocker® Potato Buds
A whiff of white pepper	1 tablespoon unsalted butter
1 medium egg yolk	1 tablespoon vegetable oil

1. Sprinkle fillets lightly with salt and a whiff of white pepper.
2. Beat the egg yolk and whites together. Dip the fillets in until very moist.
3. Cover the fillets lavishly with the potato buds. For a heavier batter, dip the fillets into the eggs a second time and coat with the buds again.
4. Sauté the fillets over medium heat, covered until brown on one side. Remove cover. Turn fillets over and brown the other side, tossing in extra almond slices to brown.

Note: An alternative choice to potato buds is to coat the fillets with crushed nuts of choice. One-half cup pulverized unsalted almonds or unsalted cashew nuts will create a very special recipe. Pulverize the nuts to the chunky stage in a food processor or simply place them in a plastic bag and crush them with a hammer or mallet.

A Fish in Thyme

Yield: 2 Servings

2 Tilapia fillets, skinned and boned	1 tablespoon all-purpose flour
Salt to sprinkle	¾ cup concentrated chicken broth, heated
1 tablespoon Bearss lemon juice	¼ teaspoon dried thyme, or 1 teaspoon minced thyme leaves
1 tablespoon butter or butter substitute	
¼ pound American white mushrooms, or 1 large portobello mushroom	1 teaspoon minced basil leaves
	1 teaspoon minced curly parsley
2 tablespoons butter or butter substitute	

1. Sprinkle the fillets lightly with salt. Cover with lemon juice.
2. Melt the butter in a shallow pan. Slice the mushrooms and sauté quickly over medium-high heat. Portobello mushrooms cook more quickly than the American white variety. Remove mushrooms from the pan and set aside.
3. Add 1 tablespoon butter. Stir in flour. Add hot broth slowly, stirring until smooth and thick. Place fish into the broth mixture. Add thyme and basil. Cover the pan and cook over medium heat approximately 6-8 minutes, or until the fish is white within and separates with a fork. Do not overcook.
4. Cover with minced parsley to serve.

This is a gentle recipe for these tender, delicate fish. It is based on the French school of cooking, rather than America's newer adventures with tangy, spicy overtones.

Fillet of Tilapia Muscadine

Yield: 4 Servings

1 cup or more Muscadine grapes
4 tilapia fillets, boned and skinned
Salt and pepper
2 tablespoons unsalted butter

1 shallot, minced
1 cup dry light sherry
½ cup water

1. Peel skins off grapes and remove seeds. Set aside.

2. Sprinkle the fillets with salt and pepper. Melt butter and mix with the shallot in a shallow skillet large enough to set the fish in touching each other but not overlapping.

3. Set the fillets on top of the shallot mixture. Pour in the wine and water and bring to a boil. Cover the skillet. Lower the heat to medium-low and cook the fillets no longer than five minutes.

4. Remove the fillets from the pan with a wide spatula so they will not break in half. Set aside, covered, to keep warm.

Béchamel Sauce:

1 tablespoon unsalted butter
1 tablespoon all-purpose flour
Liquid and shallots in which fillets cooked

½ cup half-and-half
2 tablespoons heavy cream
Salt and pepper to taste

1. Melt the butter. Stir in flour and gradually add the liquid and shallots from the fillets. Stir in the half-and-half and bring to a boil. Lower heat to medium and add the heavy cream, stirring until thick. Taste for salt and pepper.

2. Pour the sauce over the fillets. Sprinkle the grapes over and around the plate.

Blackened Tilapia with Spicy Sauce

!!!!Spice and more spice!!!!

Yield: 2 servings

2 Tilapia fillets
Juice of ½ lemon
1 tablespoon unsalted butter, melted

Chain of Lakes Seasoning (recipe, page 245)
Cast iron skillet

Sauce:

1 teaspoon chopped fresh oregano,
   or ½ teaspoon dried
⅛ teaspoon cumin powder
1 small onion, chopped fine
Optional: 1 clove minced garlic

14½ ounce can stewed tomatoes with spices of
   choice
Optional: 1 teaspoon seeded and minced
   jalapeño pepper (wear gloves to handle)
Red Bliss or new white potatoes

1. Squeeze lemon over fillets. Melt butter. Brush or dip the fillets with the melted butter. Rub Chain of Lakes' seasoning into the fish.

2. Heat the skillet over an outside gas or wood burning grill. The hotter the grill, the better the results. Do not cook this recipe inside. This is very important because this cooking method produces intense smoke.

3. Cook over high heat for a short time on one side. Turn fillets and cook on the other side. Be careful not to burn. Serve with sauce on the side.

Sauce:

1. Combine oregano, cumin, chopped onion, garlic and canned stewed tomatoes in a saucepan. Add minced jalapeño, if desired. Bring to a boil, stirring. Reduce heat to simmer and cook 15 minutes, or longer. Or, combine ingredients in a covered microwavable container. Microwave 1 minute on high. Stir. Microwave 1 minute longer for crunchy onions, 2 minutes for soft.

2. Boil small potatoes to accompany. May be made in advance.

The Sunfish family produces two lovely deep bodied specimens in the canals of Central Florida. The Redear Sunfish, or yellow bream known as "shellcracker" because it feeds on snails, is a rainbow of green-gold with orange or yellow flecks on its breast and bright red edges around its gill covers. The Bluegill is also a bream fish from the Sunfish family. Small in size than the Bass and Crappie, they both have white flaky, sweet-tasting meat and are known as "panfish". Recipes for Tilapia and other white fish are interchangeable with the Redear and Bluegill.

Tilapia, Redear or Bluegill Mornay

Yield: 4 servings

4 fillets of Tilapia, Redear or Bluegill

Salt and pepper

1 cup dry white wine, or to just cover fish

1 shallot, minced fine

3 tablespoons unsalted butter

3 tablespoons all-purpose flour

1½ cups half-and-half

½ cup grated Emmantaler Swiss cheese

4 tablespoons grated Parmesan cheese

1. Sprinkle the fillets with salt and pepper. Bring the wine to a boil with the shallot in a skillet. Add the fillets. As soon as the water returns to a boil, lower heat to medium. Cover the pan and poach the fillets just until the fish flakes with a fork. Remove the fillets to an ovenproof dish.

2. Melt the butter in a saucepan and stir in the flour.

3. Combine the half-and-half with 1 cup of the wine mixture and bring to a boil. Add it all at once to the butter and flour, stirring hard with a wire whisk and scraping the sides and bottom intermittently with a wooden spoon. Stir until it becomes a thick, smooth sauce. Remove from the heat.

4. Stir in the Swiss cheese and taste for salt and pepper.

5. Pour the sauce over the fish. Sprinkle the tops with Parmesan cheese. Place under the broiler to brown.

Fish - Cleaning and Filleting

Set the whole fish on a flat, firm surface.

1. Hold the fish by its tail and slice down the side of the backbone to remove the fish from its rib cage.

2. Cut off the head. Cut along the back to behind the dorsal fin, then through the body to the tail with a sharp knife.

3. Cut off the tail.

4. Insert the point of a knife under the skin by the tail and, holding the knife on a slant, separate the skin from the flesh, working from the tail to the head. It should pull away easily if the fish is fresh. Turn the fish over and repeat the process.

Crab

Anyone who has wrestled live Blue crabs might opt in the future to pay the price to purchase the meat already cooked and separated from their shells.

RECIPES:

Country Blue Crab Feast

Baked Crab

Crab and Shrimp in Filo (phyllo)

Crab au Gratin

Crab Puffs in Pâte à Choux
(Cream Puffs)

Crab Filled Artichokes

Crab Toasts

Light Crab Dip

Stuffed Mushroom Caps

Crab Meat Soufflé

Crab Stuffing for Fish

Crab Quiche

Tropical Crab Salad

Ginger Crab Crêpes

Deviled Crab Cakes

Crab Stir-Fry

Crab Florentine

Soft-Shell Crabs with Fried Caper Berries

Soft Shell Crabs with Spicy Seasoning

Soft Shell Crabs with Dipping Sauce

Getting Acquainted with Your Blue Crabs

Blue crab season is a serious celebration in Central Florida. Brackish Lake George on the south end of the St. John's River is fed by Juniper, Silver Glen Spring Run and Salt Springs creeks that discharge massive saline deposits from the west. The salty water influx creates a Mecca for Blue Crab, Bass and Speckled perch (Crappie) fishermen. Traps and nets are everywhere, making it necessary for boaters to zigzag carefully around to protect propellers. Another hazard is the lake itself, which, although the second largest freshwater lake in Florida, averages between six to ten feet deep in the center and less than five feet deep towards shore. I have crossed this lake many times with the Antique and Classic Boat Society (ACBS) and have experienced rough waters comparable to the ocean. It's necessary to pay close attention while crossing, lest your boat gets stuck on a sand bar. It isn't until the area narrows again in Dunn's and Cross Creeks that the depth abruptly changes to fifty feet.

Pros and amateurs both know the rules: Males crabs only. The female's legs are tipped bright reddish-orange, and its abdomen is dome shaped, whereas the abdomen of the male is elongated and its legs blue. Anyone who doesn't know the difference is subject to serious fines as well as ostracism by other crabbers.

In Palatka, crabbing reaches a frenzied crescendo Memorial Day weekend. The gourmet festival draws thousands of would-be trappers and celebrators who congregate to dance, imbibe and gorge themselves on the tiny crustacean.

Florida Blue crabs are caught and marketed in both the hard and soft-shell stages. During the summer months, hard-shell crabs may be purchased live or cooked in the shell. If you purchase the meat already cooked, there are three classifications of cooked crab: Jumbo Lump and Lump, which are the most expensive, Flaked or Special, which are small pieces of white meat from the body, and Claw, which is a beige tinged meat from the claws. Flaked and Claw must be carefully picked through for traces of shell and cartilage.

Anyone who has wrestled live Blue crabs might opt in the future to pay the price to purchase the meat already cooked and separated from their shells. A one-pound crab furnishes only two and a quarter ounces meat, which is only about a fourteen percent yield. The crab is also extremely perishable. Dead crabs are dangerous to consume and must be discarded.

Squeamish folk, like me, boil the blue crab before dismantling it. Seasoned crabbers are able to remove its carapace (top shell) while it is still alive. Immersing it in ice water several minutes, the chef waits for the crab to "fall asleep". He then grabs its legs on one side of its body, and using the sharp spines for leverage, pulls away the shell to instantly kill the crab. Once this is accomplished, he removes the "apron" and prepares the crab for cooking. The downside of this maneuver is the possibility the crab might awaken and get even with its captor before being sacrificed.

Instructions for Boiling

1 dozen live blue crabs   1 cup cider vinegar
1 bottle beer   ¼ cup Zatarin® or Old Bay® Seasoning mix

Outside The House: Follow these steps outside on the lawn or driveway next to a hose outlet:

1. Fill a cooler or bucket with water from the hose to cover the crabs. Add ½ cup or more Kosher salt. Drop the crabs into the bath for 10 minutes. Pour off the water. Cover the crabs again with fresh water and add salt. Leave the crabs to kick around for another ten minutes. If the water still appears muddy, repeat a third time. This will purge them of any toxic waste.

2. Pour off the water and carry the cooler into the kitchen.

3. Fill a lobster pot, large soup pot, or double boiler with water and bring to a boil. The lobster pot is best. The double boiler is second, and the soup pot third on my list of choices. Add the beer, vinegar and seasoning.

4. With a pair of barbecue type long tongs, drop crabs into the boiling water. This is no easy maneuver. These little creatures are fierce fighters. All legs and pinchers move at once in different directions to grab onto anything within reach. Often, it's each other's pinchers, making it possible to fling two or more at once into the pot. They also resist their ultimate destiny by holding on to the side of the pot. The worst scenario is allowing one's hand to come into contact with one of these tenacious pinchers!

5. Cover the pot and return the water to a full boil. Boil approximately 12-15 minutes, or until they turn bright orange-red. If any tone of green patches or mottled gray can be detected on the shells, they need to boil a few minutes longer. Remove crabs to the sink to drain and cool.

6. Outfit your hands with a pair of latex gloves, so the sharp shells will not cut your fingers.

7. Turn the crab over to expose its breast plate, or "apron". Insert a small, sharp knife in the crack at the back of the crab. The "apron" will easily pull off. You will see a covering that can range from light gray to black and fibrous threads on both sides. These spongy gills are known as "dead man's fingers". Remove them and the yellowish "mushy" center. (Some crab aficionados eat this reproductive structure, but I prefer to discard it.) Break off and discard the small pointy legs and small pinchers.

8. It will appear as though there isn't any meat in the shell, but it's tucked underneath. Let the hungry crack open the shells to find it themselves.

Country Blue Crab Feast

As many Blue crabs as you can eat

Shrimp, if you like

Bass, cleaned, boned, skinned and cut into large chunks

Corn on the cob, husked

Huge soup pot or steamer

Several bottles of regular beer (not light)

Heaps of peeled fresh garlic cloves and Cajun seasoning mix

Baby red potatoes

Polish sausage, hot or mild, grilled on the barbecue

Sweet Florida onions, cut into quarters, grilled on the barbecue

1. Wash the crabs as directed above. Leave the shrimp in their shells. Cut up the bass. Husk the corn. Bring beer to a boil with the garlic and Cajun seasoning. Toss in the crabs. Return to the boil. Add corn and potatoes. Cover the pot and boil 10 minutes. Add the shrimp. Cook another 5 minutes. Add the bass. Cook another 5 minutes, or until all are cooked.

2. While you are cooking the crabs, set the sausage and onions on a barbecue. Cover and cook over white coals or medium gas heat until browned. Slice the sausage into large pieces.

3. Serve with hammers and knives and lemon and seafood forks and picks.

Baked Crab

Yield: 4 Servings

2 cups cooked lump crab meat

2 extra large graded eggs, separated

⅓ cup sour cream

½ cup commercial bread stuffing mix

1 teaspoon Worcestershire sauce

Florida hot sauce to taste (Approximately 4 drops)

3 tablespoons clarified butter

½ cup crushed cornflake crumbs to top

1. Pick over the crab for cartilage and shells.

2. Combine egg yolks with sour cream and stuffing mix, stirring until smooth.

3. Stir in Worcestershire and hot sauce.

4. Beat egg whites until very thick and fold into the stuffing mixture.

5. Carefully fold in crab and spoon into a shallow baking dish or individual ramekins.

6. Preheat oven to 350°F.

7. Melt butter and toss with cornflake crumbs. Sprinkle over the crab mixture and bake 6-8 minutes, or until brown on top.

Crab and Shrimp in Filo (phyllo)

Yield: 12 Triangles

½ pound cooked lump crab meat

½ pound medium (26-30 per pound) raw shrimp

1 tablespoon lemon juice

4 tablespoons butter or butter substitute

4 tablespoons all-purpose flour

2 cups half-and-half

½ teaspoon salt

⅛ teaspoon white pepper

1 tablespoon minced tarragon leaves

1 tablespoon minced cilantro leaves

½ pound filo (phyllo) dough (Found in 1 pound packages in frozen food department)

½ cup melted, clarified butter

1. Pick over the crab for cartilage and shells. Set aside. Remove shells from shrimp and remove back veins. Toss shrimp with lemon juice.

2. Melt the butter and stir in the flour. Slowly stir in the half-and-half. Cook until thick and smooth over medium heat. Add salt, pepper, tarragon and cilantro. Taste for seasoning. If your sauce is too bland for your taste, add a pinch of Cayenne pepper or a touch of hot sauce. If you are a curry aficionado, add a spoonful of Madras curry. Add the shrimp-not the crab- and cook 1 minute only, stirring. Cool to room temperature, or refrigerate.

3. Defrost the filo dough. Remove half to use and return the other half to the freezer in a closed zip lock bag.

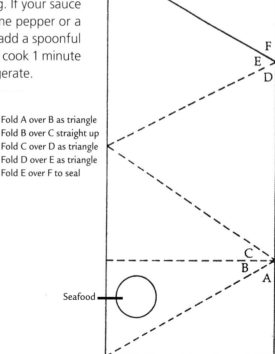

Fold A over B as triangle
Fold B over C straight up
Fold C over D as triangle
Fold D over E as triangle
Fold E over F to seal

Seafood

4. Open the dough and cut into 4 strips lengthwise. Using 2 strips for each triangle for thickness, spoon 2 or more tablespoons of the shrimp mixture onto the strip as shown in the diagram below. Spoon a bit of the reserved crab on top. Fold dough as you would a flag to create a triangle. Brush the surface with melted butter and place on a non-stick or parchment covered baking sheet. Refrigerate until ready to cook.

5. Preheat oven to 375°F.

6. Bake until dough is golden brown and crisp. (Approximately 20 minutes.)

Note: For best results, thaw dough directly before using. When it sits at room temperature or is exposed to the air for any length of time, the leaves dry out and tear into pieces instead of separating.

Crab au Gratin

Yield: 6 Servings

1 pound lump crab meat

2 tablespoons unsalted butter

2 tablespoons all-purpose flour

2 cups half-and-half (or 1 cup milk, 1 cup coffee cream)

Pinch of cayenne pepper

⅛ teaspoon grated nutmeg

1 teaspoon white horseradish

½ teaspoon Dijon mustard

Salt and pepper to taste

Optional: ¼ cup light dry sherry

1 cup freshly grated Gruyère or Parmesan cheese, or a combination to top

Wide egg noodles, cooked al dente and tossed with a little butter and canned chicken broth

1. Pick through crab meat to remove shells and cartilage.

2. Melt butter in a saucepan. Stir in flour. Warm milk (microwave 40 seconds) and stir in slowly until smooth and thick. Add cayenne, nutmeg, horseradish and mustard. Add salt and pepper to taste. Stir in sherry, if desired.

3. Cook noodles until opaque but not soft. Drain and toss with butter and broth and spoon into individual ramekins or a shallow casserole dish. Spoon crab meat across the top(s). Spoon sauce over crab meat. Sprinkle heavily with grated cheese. If noodles and sauce are hot, set under the broiler to brown. If they have cooled, bake 10 minutes at 350°F. Turn oven to broil and brown tops.

Note: There are no proportions for noodles with butter and broth. This dish may be extended with more or fewer noodles per person.

Crab Puffs in Pâte à Choux (Cream Puffs)

Yield: 20-24 Pieces

Pâte à Choux (recipe below)

1 cup coarsely-diced or flaked cooked blue crab meat

2 tablespoons butter

1 tablespoon Pernod liqueur

⅓ cup light cream

1 teaspoon chopped dill weed

¼ teaspoon white horseradish

Pinch white pepper

1. Preheat oven to 350°F.

2. Make Pâte à Choux, keeping puffs bite-sized. Set aside.

3. Melt the butter. Stir in the flour. Stir in the cream and Pernod. Add the dill, horseradish and pepper. Carefully fold in the crab.

4. Split and fill the puffs. Set puffs on a baking sheet and bake 6-8 minutes, or until very hot.

Pâte à Choux

Food processor method: quick and easy

Yield: Approximately 22-24 Puffs

1 cup water

¼ pound butter, cut up

¼ teaspoon salt

1 cup all-purpose flour

3 extra large eggs

1. Combine water, butter and salt in a small saucepan and bring to a rolling boil. Remove from the heat immediately and pour the flour in all at once, stirring quickly in a circular motion with a wooden spoon. Bring ingredients together into a large ball and place on a piece of wax paper to cool.

2. Place ball into a food processor with the steel blade. Turn on-off quickly to loosen dough. Add eggs all at once. Turn on 15 seconds. Turn off and scrape around bowl. Turn on and leave on 30 seconds.

3. Cover a baking sheet with parchment paper. Spoon batter ½-inch apart, creating small balls the size of walnuts. As you release the batter from the spoon, bring the centers up to a point.

4. Preheat oven to 350°F.

(Continued)

PÂTE à CHOUX *(Continued)*

5. Bake 20-25 minutes, or until puffed and light brown. Cool to room temperature before cutting into halves and filling.

6. To serve: Preheat oven to 350°F. Set crab puffs on a baking sheet and bake 10 minutes, or until very hot.

Note: These puffs keep several months in the freezer.

Variations: For cheese puffs: Add ¼ cup grated Parmesan cheese to the food processor at the same time as the eggs to fill with sharp Cheddar beaten with equal parts cream cheese and a touch of cayenne pepper. To serve: Bake puffs approximately 10 minutes in a preheated 350°F.

Croutons in soups: Use a demitasse spoon measure the size of the puffs. Reduce cook time to approximately 15 minutes. Garlic powder, minced cilantro or parsley may be added with the eggs for additional flavor. Luncheon Size: Double or triple the size and increase baking time to 35-40 minutes. For dessert puffs add ½ teaspoon sugar and ¼ teaspoon vanilla to the water. Fill with whipped cream or Pastry Cream (recipe, page) and top with chocolate sauce.

Crab Toasts

Yield: 12 Pieces

½ pound cooked crab meat

¾ cup mayonnaise

1 tablespoon white horseradish

¼ teaspoon Dijon mustard

1 teaspoon chopped dill weed

12 slices thin white bread

¾ cup cornflake crumbs

1. Pick through the crab meat for any shells or cartilage.

2. Combine the mayonnaise, horseradish, mustard and dill. Carefully stir in the crab meat.

3. Crust and cut circles into the bread slices with a cookie cutter or small glass. Toast the bread on one side only.

4. Spoon the crab meat mixture on the untoasted side. Sprinkle with cornflake crumbs and bake in a preheated 400°F. oven for 6-8 minutes, or until very hot. Pass on a tray decorated with parsley and cherry tomatoes.

Crab Filled Artichokes

Yield: 6 First Course Servings

6 fresh artichokes

1½ cups cooked lump crab meat

1 tablespoon lemon juice

2 tablespoons white horseradish

⅛ teaspoon dry mustard

1 teaspoon chopped dill weed

¼ teaspoon chopped parsley

½ cup mayonnaise

6 outside radicchio or Bibb lettuce leaves

Tiny capers for garnish

Olives for garnish

Chopped plum tomatoes for garnish

1. With a serrated edge knife, cut off stems so artichokes will stand straight. Cut off tops ⅓ from the top. Cut points off each leaf with a sharp scissors. Artichoke will now resemble a flower. Bring to a boil in water to cover with ½ lemon. Cover and boil gently until a leaf pulls away easily. Artichokes are tricky. Undercooked they are hard and inedible. Overcooked they fall apart. Remove from the water and turn upside down on paper toweling to drain and cool.

2. Carefully remove cactus centers with a small spoon, leaving the bottoms in tact. Refrigerate until very cold.

3. Gently spread the center of each artichoke open as far as possible.

4. Mix together the lemon juice, horseradish, mustard, dill weed, parsley and mayonnaise. Carefully fold in crab meat after picking through for shells and cartilage.

5. Fill the artichoke hearts with the mixture and set them on lettuce leaves. Sprinkle tiny capers over and decorate with olives and chopped tomatoes. Serve with Spicy Mayonnaise (recipe, page 260) on the side.

Note: This recipe will also fill twelve large canned artichoke hearts, if fresh whole artichokes are not available.

Light Crab Dip

Yield: Approximately 2 Cups

1 cup cooked crab meat

8 ounce package reduced fat cream cheese, softened

½ cup fat-free sour cream

2 tablespoons white horseradish

1 teaspoon Dijon mustard

2 tablespoons chopped cilantro leaves

½ teaspoon Meyer lemon juice

1. Pick over crab meat for shells and cartilage and set aside.

2. Combine remaining ingredients and mix until smooth. Carefully fold in crab meat. Pile loosely into a serving dish. Refrigerate until very cold.

3. Decorate the dip with paprika or chopped parsley for color. Serve surrounded by toast points or crackers.

Stuffed Mushroom Caps

Yield: 6 Servings

12 large white mushrooms

½ cup minced sweet Florida onions

3 tablespoons butter

1 teaspoon flour

2 tablespoons dry sherry

1 tablespoon finely-chopped parsley

Pinch white pepper

1 cup cooked crab meat, picked over for shells and cartilage

½ cup cornflake crumbs

4 tablespoons melted butter to sauté

4 tablespoons melted butter to coat caps

Baking sheet with sides

1. Remove the stems from the mushrooms and discard. Peel the thin outer layer from the caps and transfer to a buttered baking sheet.

2. Peel and mince the onion. Sauté it in the butter until soft. Stir in the flour, sherry, parsley and white pepper. Carefully fold in the crab meat.

3. Brush the round outer area of the caps with melted butter. Spoon the filling into the inside of the mushroom caps. Sprinkle the tops with cornflake crumbs and dot each with a small amount of melted butter. Bake in a preheated 350°F. oven 5 minutes, or, until the tops are browned.

Note: These may be made in the morning, refrigerated, and baked just before serving. Serve over several leaves of warm, wilted spinach or radicchio leaves as a first course. I was very young when I developed this recipe for Gourmet Magazine, published March, 1967.

Crab Meat Soufflé

Yield: 6 Servings as an Appetizer

1 cup cooked crab meat
3 tablespoons butter
¼ teaspoon Dijon mustard
⅛ teaspoon nutmeg
Optional: pinch of cayenne pepper
½ teaspoon white horseradish
1 tablespoon Meyer lemon juice

3 tablespoons all-purpose flour
1 cup warm milk (4 percent whole milk)
4 egg yolks
5 egg whites, room temperature or warmer
¼ teaspoon cream of tartar
1½ quart soufflé dish
1 tablespoon fine bread crumbs

1. Preheat oven to 375°F.

2. Melt the butter in a saucepan. Add mustard, nutmeg, pepper, horseradish and lemon juice. Stir until smooth over low heat. Remove from heat.

3. Stir in flour. Stir in ¼ cup of the milk until smooth. Return saucepan to medium-low heat. Slowly stir the remainder of the milk into the pan until mixture is thick and creamy.

4. Separate the eggs, discarding the last yolk, or saving it for another purpose. Stir a bit of the hot mixture into the yolks before adding them to the sauce. Stir until egg yolks are fully incorporated and mixture begins to bubble. Remove from the heat and cover.

5. Beat egg whites on the highest speed of an electric mixer until foamy. Add the cream of tartar and continue beating until very thick but not dry. Fold the sauce into the egg whites in thirds.

6. Carefully fold in the crab meat.

7. Grease the soufflé dish with butter. Sprinkle fine bread crumbs in and tip the dish around and upside down to "dust" the sides and bottom before tipping out extra crumbs.

8. Loosely spoon soufflé mixture into the dish. Run your finger around the outside edge to create a slight dent in the mixture.

9. Bake 30-35 minutes, or until the soufflé has risen and is browned on top. Serve immediately.

Crab Stuffing for Fish

Yield: Approximately 2 cups to stuff a 4-5 pound fish

Also may stuff 6 fillets

1½ cups cooked crab meat

4-5 pound whole fish, or 6 boned and skinned fillets

¼ cup unsalted butter (half a stick)

2 large shallots, minced

1 rib celery, minced

¼ pound white mushrooms, sliced thin

1 cup toasted white bread cubes, crusted

⅛ teaspoon nutmeg

½ teaspoon salt

⅛ teaspoon white pepper

Fine plain bread crumbs

1. Preheat oven to 350°F.

2. Pick over the crab for cartilage and shells and set aside.

3. Melt butter in a saucepan over medium heat. Add shallots, celery and mushrooms. Cook 1 minute. Stir in bread cubes and cook until they soften. Stir in nutmeg, salt and pepper. Carefully fold in crab meat. Cool.

4. Wash the inside of the whole fish and slit the sides to make room for the stuffing. Season with salt and pepper. Spoon in the crab stuffing and close the fish tightly. Salt and pepper the outside and brush with melted butter or oil. Sprinkle the outside with paprika and bake at 350°F. until done.

5. Or, lay fish fillets on a flat surface and spoon some of the mixture across the widest part. Fold tail over the stuffing and secure with a skewer. Brush with butter. Sprinkle with bread crumbs and bake until done.

Crab Quiche

Yield: 9-Inch Pie

½ pound (1 cup) cooked lump crab meat

¾ cup finely-chopped Swiss cheese

¾ cup finely-chopped Gruyère or Fontina cheese

¼ pound sliced white mushrooms, sautéed in
  1 tablespoon butter

4 extra large graded eggs

2 cups half-and-half (or 1 cup cream mixed with
  1 cup whole milk)

½ teaspoon salt

Pinch of white pepper

⅛ teaspoon nutmeg

2 tablespoons grated Parmesan or Romano
  cheese to sprinkle over the top.

9-inch pie crust, partially pre-baked but not
  browned

1. Preheat oven to 350°F.

2. Pick over crab meat for cartilage and shells.

3. Sprinkle chopped cheeses, mushrooms and crab meat over the bottom of the pie crust.

4. Beat eggs. Beat in half-and-half, salt, white pepper and nutmeg and pour over the cheese mixture. Sprinkle Parmesan or Romano over the top.

5. Bake 30 minutes, or until a knife inserted comes out clean.

Tropical Crab Salad

Yield: 4 Servings

2½ cups, or more, crab meat

1 yellow bell pepper

1 tablespoon chopped dill

1 tablespoon chopped fresh tarragon

1 rib celery, chopped

1 tablespoon Dijon mustard

Juice from 2 lemons

1 cup low fat mayonnaise

Chopped lettuce of choice

Seeded Muscadine grapes and sliced melon

1. Carefully remove crab meat in large pieces to a bowl and set aside.

2. Place the pepper on a piece of foil under the broiler, turning it over to brown on all sides. Remove it from the oven and close the foil to shut out the air. Let stand 10 minutes and peel off the skin. Slice the pepper into thin strips.

3. To make the dressing, combine the dill, tarragon, celery, mustard, lemon juice and mayonnaise. Taste for salt and pepper.

4. Chop the lettuce and toss it with a small amount of the dressing. Spoon the crab over and top with more dressing. Set the strips of broiled red pepper over. Surround with the grapes and melon.

Note: The grapes and melon may be exchanged for grapefruit sections and sliced avocado.

Ginger Crab Crêpes

Yield: Approximately 12 Crêpes

Recipe for Dinner Crêpes (recipe, page 67)

1 pound lump crab meat

4 tablespoons unsalted butter

2 shallots, minced

2 tablespoons minced ginger

½ pound sliced American white or fresh morel mushrooms

3 tablespoons all-purpose flour

3 tablespoons Pernod aperitif or Anise liqueur

2 cups organic vegetable broth

Salt and pepper to taste

Optional: Seeded and chopped plum tomatoes

Optional: Chopped cilantro leaves

1. Preheat oven to 350°F.

2. Pick over the crab for cartilage and shells.

3. Sauté the shallots, ginger and mushrooms in the butter. Stir in the flour. Stir in the Pernod. Add the vegetable broth a little at a time and cook, stirring with a wooden spoon and wire whisk until thick and smooth.

4. Place a good amount of crab in the center of the uncooked side of each crêpe. Spoon just enough sauce over to bind and fold one side of the crêpe over. Close the other side over, overlapping so the crab will not fall out during the cooking. Place flap side down on an oiled, sided cookie sheet. Brush each crêpe with a little butter.

5. Bake until very hot.

6. Place two crêpes on each plate or a heated platter and spoon some sauce over.

7. Sprinkle the chopped plum tomatoes and cilantro over the crêpes for color.

Note: 2 tablespoons Madras curry powder may be added to the sauce for curried crêpes. Exchange dry white wine for the Pernod.

Deviled Crab Cakes

Yield: 6 Cakes

1 pound(2 cups) cooked crab meat

½ cup mayonnaise, or more to bind

½ cup roughly crushed saltine crackers

½ teaspoon salt

⅛ teaspoon black pepper

⅛ teaspoon powdered ginger

⅛ teaspoon hot Hungarian paprika, or more to taste

2 teaspoons lemon juice

1 tablespoon white horseradish

4 tablespoons chopped yellow pepper

Vegetable spray

Fine noodles or angel hair pasta to accompany, if desired

Chopped cilantro leaves

Chopped chives or scallion greens

1. Pick through crab for shells and cartilage and set aside.

2. Combine mayonnaise, crushed saltines, salt, pepper, ginger, hot paprika, lemon juice, horseradish and chopped pepper. Carefully fold in crab meat.

3. Wash an empty tuna can, 3-inches in diameter. Fill the can to the top and turn upside down onto a hot griddle or non-stick shallow pan that has been sprayed with vegetable oil. Release the crab cake. Do this 5 more times. Cook the cakes over medium-high heat until very brown. Turn over carefully to brown on the other side. Or, set the griddle under the broiler rather than turning the cakes over to more easily keep their perfect shapes.

4. Sprinkle chopped cilantro over the tops. Decorate the outer edge of the plate with the chopped scallions.

Note: For a complete dinner, surround the crab cakes with angel hair pasta tossed in chicken broth flavored with salt and pepper to taste. Accompany with Citrus Poppy Seed Salad (recipe page 61).

Crab Stir-Fry

For Lovers Only

Yield: 2 Servings

1 cup or more cooked crab meat

2 tablespoons sesame oil

½ red onion, sliced thin

4-5 Baby Bella mushrooms, sliced thin

2 teaspoons finely chopped cilantro leaves

1 cup diced Jicama*, or 4 ounces whole water chestnuts

2 teaspoons Tamari (soy) sauce

1 tablespoon sweet rice wine

12 ounces fresh bean sprouts

Salt and pepper to taste

1. Heat the oil. Add the onion and mushrooms and simmer over low heat until soft.

2. Add cilantro, diced jicama, tamari and rice wine and stir over medium heat 3 minutes.

3. Stir in the sprouts and cook no longer than 1 minute, or until sprouts have gathered the flavors of the seasonings. Taste for salt and pepper.

4. Divide onto two plates and cover with the crab meat.

*Note: Jicama is sometimes called a Mexican potato. It is a crunchy root vegetable with a light brown skin and white flesh that has a pleasant, apple-like, nutty flavor. It is delicious raw in salads or as a vegetable to cut into strips for dips.

Crab Florentine

Yield: 4 Servings

3 cups cooked Blue crab meat

2 10-ounce packages frozen leaf spinach,
  or 1½ pounds fresh salad spinach

1 teaspoon salt

½ pound white mushrooms, coarsely cut

4 tablespoons butter

1 clove crushed garlic

½ teaspoon dried sage leaves

¼ cup white wine

Salt and pepper to taste

Tiny tomatoes, cherry or 'grape'

1. Wash the spinach and remove the stems. Bring to a boil in water to cover. Cook, stirring, until spinach is limp. Remove to a strainer and rinse with cold water. Toss with salt. Leave in the strainer to drain.

1. Pick over the crab meat for shells and cartilage.

2. Wilt the spinach in boiling water. Remove immediately. Drain off all water and chop. Toss with salt and set aside.

3. Cook the mushrooms in the butter, garlic and sage. Add the wine and bring to a boil. Taste for salt and pepper.

4. Toss the spinach with the mushroom mixture. Divide onto 4 plates. Top with the crab and surround with tiny tomatoes. Serve with lemon wedges on the side.

Soft-Shell Crabs with Fried Caper Berries

Yield: 4 Servings

8 small soft-shelled crabs, cleaned

2 cups low-fat buttermilk

1 teaspoon salt

1 teaspoon black pepper

Pinch of cayenne pepper or a splash of hot pepper sauce

⅛ cup (2 tablespoons) minced flat leaf (Italian) parsley leaves

2 cups fine, plain bread crumbs

6 tablespoons unsalted butter

2 tablespoons vegetable oil

1 tablespoon Worcestershire sauce

Optional: ½ cup slivered almonds

Lime wedges

1. Buy live soft shell crabs in season. (April-May) Have the fishmonger clean them.

2. Soak in buttermilk, refrigerated, 1 hour or longer.

3. Combine salt, pepper, cayenne and parsley with the bread crumbs.

4. Remove crabs from buttermilk, shaking off excess, and cover well with the seasoned crumbs.

5. Combine butter and oil in a skillet. Over medium heat, sauté crabs 5 minutes on one side, or until browned. Add the Worcestershire sauce. Add the almonds. Turn the crabs over and cook on the other side. Remove to a serving platter surrounded by lime wedges. Sprinkle with fried capers (recipe below) and serve Meyer Lemon Sauce on the side.

Fried Caper Berries

½ cup large caper berries (specialty food stores)

¼ cup white cornmeal

Strainer

Vegetable oil

Small deep fryer

1. Toss capers in cornmeal in a strainer set into a bowl. Lift up the strainer to shake off excess. Heat oil in a small deep fryer and plunge the strainer in for approximately 1 minute to create a crisp crust around each caper.

Soft Shell Crabs with Spicy Seasoning

Yield: 4 Crabs

4 soft shell crabs, cleaned

A sprinkling of Spicy Seasoning (recipe below)

1 egg, beaten with 1 teaspoon water

2 cups cracker crumbs

2 cloves garlic, minced

2 shallots, minced

½ pound white mushrooms, chopped coarse

¼ cup canola or vegetable oil

¼ cup dry white wine

1 tablespoon finely-chopped flatleaf parsley

Crème Fraîche (recipe, page 31)

Optional: Caviar of choice

Lemon or lime wedges

1. Wash the crabs well and sprinkle with the spicy seasoning. Rub lime juice into them with your fingers.

2. Dip crabs into the beaten egg. Coat with cracker crumbs. Dip into the egg again, and coat with cracker crumbs. Refrigerate until cold to make the batter adhere to the crabs.

3. Sauté the garlic, shallots and mushrooms in the oil over low heat until soft but not colored. Remove from the pan.

4. Set the crabs in the pan and brown on one side, covered. Remove the cover. Turn the crabs over and brown the other side. Remove to paper toweling to drain.

5. Add the wine to the pan. Bring to a boil, stirring. Transfer the crabs to individual plates or a platter and spoon the sauce over. Sprinkle with parsley and top each with a spoon of Crème Fraîche and a dollop of caviar. Serve lemon wedges on the side.

Spicy Seasoning:

½ teaspoon ground thyme

½ teaspoon ground oregano

¼ teaspoon black pepper

½ teaspoon hot Hungarian paprika or a pinch of cayenne pepper

½ teaspoon salt

¼ teaspoon garlic powder

½ teaspoon onion powder

1. Mix all together in a bottle or shaker. Keeps indefinitely.

Soft Shell Crabs with Dipping Sauce

These are contagious. The smaller crabs can be picked up as finger-food.
Serve them with ice cold beer and watch them disappear.

Yield: 12 Crabs

12 soft shell crabs, cleaned

1½ cups canola oil

½ cup peanut oil

4 eggs, beaten with 4 tablespoons milk

2 tablespoons chili powder

2 tablespoons ground cumin

1 tablespoon black pepper

1 teaspoon salt

1 teaspoon paprika

½ cup white cornmeal

½ cup all-purpose flour

And, for spicy hot, if you must: A pinch of Cayenne or red pepper flakes

1. Clean the crabs.

2. Heat the oil in a deep skillet or deep fryer to 375°F.

3. Beat the eggs with the milk.

4. Combine remaining ingredients in a bowl for seasoning.

5. Dip the crabs, one at a time in the egg mixture, and cover heavily with the seasoning. Drop them into the hot oil. Fry approximately 2 minutes on each side in a skillet, or 4 minutes total in a deep fryer. When they rise to the top, they should be done. Dry on paper toweling. Serve with Dipping Sauce (recipe below).

Note: Trim and peel white mushrooms (do not wash) to deep fry as above to accompany the crabs, or by themselves as hors d'oeuvre. The Florida finger banana is also fabulous cooked in this fashion. The bananas should be very firm.

Dipping Sauce:

1 cup mayonnaise

¼ teaspoon dry mustard

2 tablespoons minced parsley

1 clove crushed garlic

½ teaspoon onion powder

1 tablespoon minced dill pickle

1 tablespoon minced capers

1 tablespoon minced scallion greens

1. Combine ingredients several hours in advance for the flavors to incorporate. Serve hot or cold to accompany soft shell crabs.

Shrimp

Once you have tasted shrimp (or anything that swims or flies) brought directly from their natural home to yours, you will never again be satisfied with a substitute.

RECIPES:

Shrimp Rolls

Shrimp Faux Rémoulade

Cold Shrimp

Dirty Shrimp

Cajun Shrimp

Shrimp-Kebab

Grilled Shrimp and
Hot Sausage Kebabs

Caribbean Shrimp

Grilled Shrimp in
Sun-Dried Tomato-Garlic Sauce

Sautéed Shrimp

Oriental Style Shrimp

Alexa's Shrimp Margarita
with Confetti Rice

Pizza: Shrimp and Spinach
with Goat Cheese

Shrimp and Corn Salad

Shrimp Dijon

Shrimp in Avocado

Shrimp St. John's

Shrimp Rolls

Yield: Approximately 2 Dozen

1 pound tiny (55-60) shrimp, cooked, shelled and de-veined

20 ounce loaf soft, sliced white bread, crusted

½ cup mayonnaise

3 ounces cream cheese, softened to room temperature

1 teaspoon white horseradish

1 tablespoon finely-chopped dill

1 teaspoon finely-chopped capers

Mayonnaise or softened unsalted butter to hold bread together when filling

1. Cook and clean the shrimp.

2. Remove the crusts from the bread.

3. Combine the mayonnaise, cream cheese and horseradish, mixing until smooth. Stir in the dill and chopped capers. Fold in the shrimp.

4. Spoon a bit of the mixture across the center of each piece of bread. Fold 1 side of the bread across the filling. Spread a thin layer of mayonnaise or softened butter across the other side and fold it across the 1st to create an elongated roll. Turn flap-side down on a serving platter. Garnish with fresh dill or parsley. Cover tightly with plastic wrap and refrigerate until ready to serve.

Refrigerate fresh shrimp at a temperature of 32-38°F. Freeze no longer than 6 months at 0°F.

Shrimp Faux Rémoulade

Yield: 4-6 servings 1st course, 2-3 servings entrée

1 pound small shrimp (41-50 per pound)

Water to cover

1 cup mayonnaise

1 heaping teaspoon white horseradish

½ teaspoon Dijon mustard

½ teaspoon minced dill

1 teaspoon chopped capers

1 tablespoon chopped gherkins (sweet or dill pickles)

Chopped iceberg lettuce

1. Cover shrimp with water in a large pot. Bring to a boil. (Watch carefully or water will foam over the top creating a mess to clean up.) Reduce heat to medium and boil 1 minute. Remove from fire and cool 5 minutes. Pour off water and rinse shrimp in cold water. Peel and de-vein immediately. (Or, purchase shrimp cooked and cleaned. If shrimp are frozen, pour boiling water over them for a fresher flavor.) Refrigerate in a bowl, making sure all water has been poured off.

2. Make Rémoulade Sauce: Combine mayonnaise, horseradish, mustard, dill, capers and gherkins. Toss well with the shrimp and serve over chopped lettuce.

3. Decorate the plate with quartered tomatoes, olives, sliced hard boiled egg, or cold vegetables of your choice.

Note: Rémoulade recipe may be doubled to serve on the side.

Cold Shrimp

Directions for cooking large and jumbo shrimp

Large shrimp: 16-20 per pound
Water to cover

Juice from ½ lemon
Oriental Sauce, (recipe, page 261) Red Cocktail
Sauce (recipe, page 262)

1. Fill a large pot half-way with water. Bring to a boil and add the shrimp. When water returns to a full boil, stir so shrimp will cook evenly. Reduce heat to medium-high so water will not boil over the top. Boil gently 3 minutes.

2. Turn off the heat and allow shrimp to cool in the water 10 minutes.

3. Pour off the water and run cold water over the shrimp. While the shrimp are still warm, remove the shells, leaving the tail shell intact. (Shrimp appear larger when the tail shell is left on. It is proper for guests to hold the shrimp by its tail to dip into the sauce and eat, thus eliminating the need for cocktail forks and plates.)

4. Remove the dark vein by cutting a thin line down the back of the shrimp and rinsing it under cool water. Drain off any excess water and refrigerate, covered, several hours or overnight.

To Serve: Place shrimp in a bowl or on a round platter set into a bowl filled with ice. Or, place a freezer block covered with heavy aluminum foil in the bottom of the bowl.

Summer on the St. John's River is great fun, but don't forget to purchase a recreational saltwater fishing license to "shrimp" in the area of Green Cove Springs and Palatka. The shrimp run begins in July, reaches its peak in August, and continues through September. Early September is the best time to venture with nets cast into the shallow grassy flats because the shrimp are larger than those that run during the summer months.

The shrimp found in most supermarkets and seafood markets have been previously frozen, unless otherwise advertised. When handled correctly, they are more than acceptable. However, once you have tasted shrimp (or anything that swims or flies) brought directly from their natural home to yours, you will never again be satisfied with a substitute. These shrimp are most succulent quickly grilled over an open fire or simply boiled, with or without seasonings, and served in their shells to peel at the table. A favorite dinner feast in the south is "Dirty Shrimp". Although there are many variations of this recipe, the following will promise foolproof results.

Dirty Shrimp

Ingredients measured per pound of shrimp

½ pound margarine

½ pound or more large shrimp per person

1 tablespoon black pepper

½ teaspoon cayenne pepper

¼ teaspoon red pepper flakes

2 cloves garlic, peeled and mashed

1 pound of the largest shrimp available

1. Melt the margarine in a saucepan. Combine black pepper, cayenne, pepper flakes and mashed garlic. Cook over low heat at least 5 minutes. Pour into a bowl. This may be done in the morning or a day or two in advance for the flavors to incorporate together.

2. Remove heads from the shrimp. With a small, sharp knife, make a slit through the top of the shell (the shrimp's back) and wash out the dark vein under cool, running water. Dry the shrimp with paper toweling. Toss the shrimp into the margarine mixture to coat them well.

3. Preheat oven to 200°F.

4. Remove shrimp from the margarine mixture and set them into a shallow baking dish. Bake until shells are pink and flesh has turned opaque, approximately 20-25 minutes. Do not overcook.

5. Return margarine mixture to a saucepan and heat.

6. Pour margarine mixture into individual ramekins for dipping. Pile the shrimp on a platter. Accompany with white rice and a green salad.

Cajun Shrimp

Yield: 5 pounds jumbo shrimp

Approximately 2-3 shrimp per person hors d'oeuvres

6 tablespoons Cajun Seasoning

5 pounds jumbo shrimp (12 per pound)

½ cup Worcestershire sauce

6 ounces dark beer

6 large garlic cloves, minced

Handful chopped fresh parsley

2 tablespoons lemon juice

3 cups extra virgin olive oil

Cajun Seasoning:

1 tablespoon dried oregano

1 tablespoon dried thyme

2 tablespoons onion salt

2 tablespoons garlic powder

2 tablespoons black pepper

1 tablespoon Cayenne pepper

2 tablespoons paprika

1. Combine ingredients in a glass jar. Store indefinitely.

2. Slit each shrimp through its shell to remove back vein, but leave the shell on.

3. Combine remaining ingredients. Add Cajun Seasoning (to taste) and toss with the shrimp. Marinate in the refrigerator at least 1 hour.

4. Preheat oven to 375°F.

5. Spread shrimp out on a baking sheet and bake 15 minutes, or until done. Remove to paper toweling to drain.

Succulently sweet pink shrimp are fished from the grassy beds of the St. John's River near Palatka. You will rarely find them in the supermarket. Look for roadside stands with signs beckoning you to buy "fresh local shrimp".

When we journey by boat, we stay at the infamous Blair's Jungle Denn, a fish camp and fun experience located between Lake George and Lake Dexter. Blackwater Inn, located just east of the Astor Bridge, has an abundance of local atmosphere with plates heaped high with surprisingly sophisticated food at unsophisticated prices.

Shrimp Kebab

Yield: 4-6 Servings

½ pound bacon

2 pounds, or more, extra large shrimp (16-20 per pound)

2 cloves garlic, peeled and split

1 onion, diced

4 tablespoons curly leaf parsley, minced

4 tablespoons Tamari soy sauce

4 tablespoons dark brown sugar

1 tablespoon ground ginger

¼ teaspoon dry mustard

¼ cup extra virgin olive oil

Juice of 1 Bearss lemon

2 tablespoons light sherry

1. Cut bacon strips in half and set aside.

2. Remove shells from shrimp, leaving the tail shell in tact. With a sharp knife, make a slit along the back of the shrimp and remove the dark vein.

3. Combine remaining ingredients and marinate the shrimp several hours.

4. Remove garlic from the marinade. Wrap shrimp in bacon and put onto skewers alone or with cubes of fresh pineapple, mushrooms and bell peppers.

5. Set skewers on a barbecue, grill, or under a broiler. Baste frequently while cooking. Do not overcook.

Grilled Shrimp and Hot Sausage Kebabs

Yield: 4 Servings

12 jumbo shrimp (10-12 per pound)

Juice from 1 lemon

8 whole white mushrooms

½ pound spicy smoked sausage, sliced on the bias about 5⁄8-inch thick

½ teaspoon dried oregano

¼ teaspoon dried thyme

1 clove crushed garlic, or ½ teaspoon powdered

½ teaspoon black pepper

1 teaspoon paprika

4 tablespoons melted butter

1. Remove the shrimp shells, leaving the tail shells in tact. Devein the shrimp and toss them with the lemon juice.

2. Clean the mushrooms. Slice the sausage.

3. Combine oregano, thyme, garlic, pepper and paprika. Stir into the melted butter. Brush the shrimp and mushrooms with the herb-butter seasoning.

4. Alternate the shrimp, sausage and mushrooms on four skewers.

5. Grill over medium heat until done on both sides. Brush with oregano mixture during cooking.

Caribbean Shrimp

Yield: 2 Servings

8 jumbo shrimp

Juice from ½ lemon

3 tablespoons butter

1 small onion, minced

1 small pepper of choice, mild or hot, seeded and minced

1 clove garlic, minced

1 bay leaf

2 cups pineapple juice

1 tablespoon arrowroot

Canned or fresh pineapple chunks

1. Remove shells and veins from the backs of shrimp. Leave the shells on the tails. Toss in lemon juice and let stand 10 minutes.

2. Melt butter in a skillet. Cook shrimp quickly over medium heat. Remove from the pan and set aside.

3. Cook onion, pepper and garlic until soft with the bay leaf in the shrimp pan. Stir the pineapple juice into the arrowroot and add to the pan. Bring to a boil, stirring, but do not allow mixture to continue boiling. Stir in the pineapple chunks and shrimp and cook until very hot.

Serve with Banana Fritters (recipe, page 10).

Grilled Shrimp in Sun-Dried Tomato-Garlic Sauce

Yield: 4-6 Servings

24 jumbo shrimp, shelled, de-veined, tails left in tact

Extra virgin olive oil to brush shrimp

4 ounces sun-dried tomatoes

2 cups extra virgin olive oil

8 large cloves garlic

1 teaspoon salt

¼ teaspoon white pepper

¼ cup minced cilantro leaves

¼ cup minced basil leaves

¼ cup dry white wine

1. Clean shrimp, leaving tails in tact. Brush with oil and grill over white coals or gas just until they begin to turn color. Remove immediately and keep warm.

2. Soak tomatoes 15 minutes in warm water. Drain and cut into small pieces. Remove to a bowl and add 2 cups olive oil.

3. Peel and mince garlic. Add to sun-dried tomato mixture. Add salt, white pepper, cilantro and basil leaves. Remove to a saucepan. Stir in wine and cook over medium-low heat 15 minutes.

4. Boil rice or pasta until done to your liking. Stir shrimp into tomato mixture and spoon over rice or pasta to serve.

Sautéed Shrimp

Yield: 2 Servings

8 extra large shrimp from Lake George

4 tablespoons unsalted butter

2 cloves finely minced garlic

1 tablespoon Persian lime juice

¼ pound chopped Baby Bella mushrooms, cut into quarters

1 teaspoon chopped cilantro

1 teaspoon chopped tarragon

1. Clean and de-vein shrimp, leaving tails in tact.

2. Combine the butter with the garlic and simmer over very low heat 5 minutes.

3. Cook the chopped mushrooms in the butter mixture over medium heat 1 minute only.

4. Add the shrimp to the mushrooms and cook over medium heat until just done. Do not overcook. Toss with the lime juice, cilantro and tarragon and serve.

Oriental Style Shrimp

Yield: 4 Servings

1 pound large or jumbo shrimp

2 tablespoons butter

2 tablespoons olive oil

2 cloves garlic, crushed or shaved

1 teaspoon finely chopped ginger

2 ribs bok choy, cut into small squares

8 or more small scallion bulbs

1 small yellow pepper, cut into fine strips

8 ounce canned whole water chestnuts, cut into quarters

½ cup rice wine

Salt to taste

Sniff of white pepper

1. Peel and devein shrimp, leaving shell tails in tact.

2. Melt butter with oil in a skillet. Add garlic, ginger, bok choy, scallion bulbs, pepper strips and water chestnuts and cook over low heat 5 minutes. Stir in wine and cook another minute. This may be done in advance.

3. Directly before serving, add shrimp and cook over medium heat until done on both sides. Taste for salt and white pepper. A pinch of cayenne may be added, if desired.

Alexa's Shrimp Margarita with Confetti Rice

Yield: 2 Servings

1 pound extra large Jacksonville pink shrimp

4 tablespoons Clarified Butter (recipe, page 247)

1 tablespoon Persian lime juice

1 tablespoon cold butter

1 teaspoon all-purpose flour

Touch of red pepper flakes

5 ounces tequila whiskey

2 tablespoons Triple Sec liqueur

1. Remove shell and dark vein from shrimp. Lightly sprinkle them with salt and pepper. Heat clarified butter and sauté them on both sides until pink but a bit underdone. Toss in lime juice. Remove from heat and set aside.

2. Mix butter and flour together with a fork. Add just a touch of red pepper flakes.

3. Combine tequila and Triple Sec in a saucepan and bring to a boil. Lower heat to medium and stir in the butter mixture. Stir until mixture begins to thicken.

4. Return shrimp to medium-high heat. Pour the tequila mixture over and toss with the shrimp. Serve over Confetti Rice.

Confetti Rice

Yield: 2 Cups Rice

2 tablespoons extra virgin olive oil

2 tablespoons yellow bell pepper, cut into tiny cubes (confetti)

1 tablespoon green bell pepper, cut into tiny cubes (confetti)

1 link spicy turkey sausage, cooked, skinned and cut into tiny pieces (confetti)

1 cup water

½ cup long grain white rice

2 tablespoons scallion greens, cut into tiny pieces (confetti)

1. Cook the peppers in the oil over low heat until soft. Add cooked sausage. Add water. Bring to a boil over high heat. Stir in rice. Lower heat to medium. Cover the pot and cook approximately 15 minutes, or until rice is cooked through. Stir in scallion greens.

Pizza Topping(s)

2 (10-ounce) packages fresh salad spinach leaves

1 teaspoon salt

3 tablespoons Seasoned Garlic Oil (recipe, page 246), or ½ garlic clove crushed in 3 tablespoons oil

1 pound cooked shrimp (35-40 per pound)

½ cup commercial pizza sauce

14 ounce can diced tomatoes in mild green chilies

14 ounce can diced tomato with green pepper and onion

Optional: chopped cilantro leaves

Optional: ½ pound goat cheese, chopped coarse

1. Cook, shell and de-vein shrimp. Toss with pizza sauce. Set aside.

2. Bring 1 cup water only to a boil in a large pot. Stir in spinach and cook, 30 seconds, stirring constantly, until just wilted. Do not overcook. Drain and squeeze out all water. Toss with salt and garlic oil. Spread over baked pizza shell.

3. Spoon shrimp over spinach. Spoon diced tomatoes over shrimp.

4. Return to oven and bake 10 minutes, or until very hot.

5. Sprinkle with chunks of goat cheese at room temperature, and cut the pizza into squares to serve.

Note: Blue crab may be added or substituted.

Pizza: Shrimp and Spinach with Goat Cheese

Yield: Approximately 36 Squares

Crust:

1 package (¼ ounce) Fleischman's® Rapid Rise Yeast

½ teaspoon granulated sugar

2¼ cups lukewarm water

2 pounds, or, if you do not have a scale, 3 cups, semolina (hard wheat durum flour)

½ teaspoon salt

3 tablespoons olive oil

1 cup commercial pizza sauce

15x10-inch coated baking sheet with sides (jellyroll pan)

Dough hook method:

1. Combine yeast, sugar and water in a cup.

2. Weigh flour. Add salt. Pour into a mixer fitted with a dough hook.

3. Turn mixer on lowest speed and add the yeast mixture slowly until it forms a ball. If it appears dry, add more water. When dough forms into a ball, remove to a crockery or glass bowl that has been heavily rubbed with olive oil.

4. Pour remaining oil over ball and roll until completely covered. Cover bowl with a damp towel and let rise 15 minutes.

5. Preheat oven to 350°F.

6. Roll dough to size of baking sheet, overlapping sides. Brush with pizza sauce. Bake 20 minutes. Remove and cool slightly. Follow directions for Pizza topping.

Hand Method:

1. Work dough by hand to create a ball. Follow remaining instructions.

Shrimp and Corn Salad

Yield: 6 Servings

2 pounds small shrimp (50 per pound)
4 ears white Zellwood corn
1 large sweet Sorrento onion, chopped
½ cup chopped cilantro leaves

½ cup Key lime juice
2 Dancy tangerines, peeled and sectioned
1 cup sliced black olives
½ cup sliced green pimento olives

1. Cook and clean shrimp. Refrigerate until very cold.

2. Cook and remove kernels from corn. Toss with shrimp.

3. Peel and chop the onion. Toss with shrimp.

4. Toss in remaining ingredients.

5. Serve over lettuce leaves with warm rolls or garlic bread for lunch, appetizer or Sunday supper.

Shrimp Dijon

Yield: 4 Servings

24 large shrimp
2 tablespoons lemon juice
4 tablespoons clarified butter
2 tablespoons minced large leaf parsley
1 teaspoon Dijon mustard

½ teaspoon white pepper
¼ teaspoon ground ginger
¼ cup dry white wine
2 Navel oranges, peeled and cut into segments
½ pound Muscadine green grapes, seeds removed

1. Remove the shells and veins from the raw shrimp. Toss with the lemon juice.

2. Combine the butter, parsley, mustard, white pepper and ginger in a pan over medium-low heat. Add the shrimp. Cook just until shrimp have turned pink, turning them to cook on both sides. With tongs or a slotted spoon, remove only the shrimp to a warm serving platter.

3. Add the wine to the pan and bring to a boil, stirring. Add the orange segments and grapes and cook only until very hot.

4. Pour over the shrimp to serve.

Shrimp in Avocado

Yield: 4 Servings

1 pound small shrimp	1 tablespoon minced scallion greens
2 large Florida avocados	1 tablespoon minced cilantro leaves
½ cup sour cream	1 teaspoon chili powder
½ cup mayonnaise	½ teaspoon coriander
2 tablespoons lime juice	¼ teaspoon salt
Optional: 2 drops Florida hot sauce	Black peppercorns to grind over the top

1. Cook the shrimp. Remove the shells and veins and refrigerate several hours.

2. Cut the avocados in half and remove the pits, leaving the skins on. Scoop out as much avocado pulp as possible and mash or pulverize in a food processor.

3. Mix together the sour cream, mayonnaise, lime juice, hot sauce, scallion greens, cilantro leaves, chili powder, coriander and salt. Fold into the mashed avocado pulp.

4. Fold in the shrimp. Fill the reserved avocado skins. Refrigerate until very cold.

5. To serve: Set avocados on mixed baby lettuce greens divided onto 4 plates.

6. Optional: Seed and chop plum tomatoes and toss them with 1 part white balsamic vinegar to 3 parts extra virgin olive oil with a little salt and pepper. Arrange them on the lettuce. Bring a pepper mill to the table.

Shrimp St. John's

Yield: 4 Servings

1 pound medium shrimp

3 tablespoons butter

⅛ teaspoon grated nutmeg

1 shallot, minced

½ pound small white mushroom caps, left whole

2 tablespoons butter

2 tablespoons flour

Optional: 2 tablespoons light dry sherry

1½ cups warm milk

½ cup heavy cream

½ teaspoon salt

⅛ teaspoon white pepper

Individual shallow baking dishes or 1 large baking dish

¼ cup freshly grated Parmesan or Romano cheese

1. Remove shells and veins from raw shrimp. Set aside.

2. Melt 3 tablespoons butter. Add the nutmeg and shallot. Add the mushroom caps. If small mushrooms cannot be found, slice larger ones into halves or quarters. Cook until mushrooms begin to take on color. Remove from the heat and set aside.

3. Melt 2 tablespoons butter in a saucepan over medium heat. Stir in the flour. Slowly stir in the wine. Stir in the warm milk with a wooden spoon, smoothing the sauce with a wire whisk as it cooks. When the mixture thickens, stir in the heavy cream. Add the salt and pepper. Stir in the mushrooms with their sauce. Add the shrimp and cook only until the shrimp turn pink on both sides.

4. Fill 4 ramekins. Sprinkle grated cheese over the tops. Place under the broiler. When the tops become brown, serve immediately.

Duck

Duck is considered white meat. Because they are birds of flight, however, the breast meat is darker than chicken and turkey breast.

RECIPES:

Wild Duck in Marsala Sauce

Sauces for Wild or Domestic Duck

Roasted Duck with Natural Gravy

Wild Rice with Pecans

A Duck in Thyme

Brandied Duck Pie in Short Crust

Sautéed Duck Breasts with
Mushrooms and Glazed Baked Onions

Duck Breasts with Anise

Duck Breasts with
Bananas and Tangerines

Duck Breasts with
Blackberries and Cassis

Duck Breasts with Kumquat Sauce

Duck Pâté

Paola's Tuscan Pâté

Duck is considered "white" meat. Because they are birds of flight, however, the breast meat is darker than chicken and turkey breast. Wild duck is dryer and the meat darker than domestic duck. The meat is not as tender because they get more exercise and produce less body fat. All fat must be removed from wild ducks as from other game because it will give the meat an "off" flavor. Anyone who has tasted wild duck will never again be satisfied with its domestic cousin. Young wild ducklings are a gourmet prize for the experienced hunter. Game birds require different cooking procedures than those found in the freezer compartments of grocery stores. After dressing game birds, they should soak in water for two hours in the refrigerator to remove excess blood. It is best to marinate them overnight in a wine or vinegar base to mellow the flavor.

The following is an easy marinade followed by simply broiling the meat.

Wild Duck in Marsala Sauce

3 young ducklings to serve 6

Leafy tops from a whole stalk of celery, chopped

1 clove garlic, chopped

4 bay leaves

Handful of fresh tarragon leaves, or 1 teaspoon dried

Handful of fresh thyme leaves, or ½ teaspoon dried

Handful of fresh flatleaf parsley

1 teaspoon black pepper

¼ teaspoon mace

¼ teaspoon nutmeg

4 whole cloves

2 cups Marsala sweet wine

½ pound butter, melted

3 cups fine unseasoned bread crumbs

6 thick slices Italian or French bread

4 tablespoons butter, melted

Marsala Sauce (recipe below)

1. Wipe the birds with a damp cloth and split them into halves along the backbone. Pound the halves with the flat side of a cleaver.

2. Combine the first 11 ingredients in a bowl, beginning with the celery and ending with the wine. Add the duck halves, spooning the marinade over to cover. Marinate, covered, overnight in the refrigerator.

3. Drain and dry the ducks. Strain the marinade, reserving the Marsala and discarding the spices.

4. Dip the duck halves in the melted butter and cover with the bread crumbs. Set under a broiler and cook until done, turning over and basting often with the melted butter.

5. Broil the bread on one side. Turn over and brush with melted butter. Broil until bubbly and brown. Set a duck half on each slice and cover with Marsala Sauce.

Marsala Sauce:

2 tablespoons butter

2 tablespoons plus 1 teaspoon all-purpose flour

1¼ cups beef broth

1 cup strained marinade from the ducks

Salt and pepper to taste

1. Melt the butter. Slowly stir in the flour over medium-low heat. Slowly stir in the beef broth and cook until slightly thickened. Slowly stir in the marinade, cooking until thick. Add salt and pepper to taste.

Secrets for Domestic Duck

When domestic duckling is prepared correctly, the fat that gives it a bad reputation will be mostly eliminated. The following technique alleviates virtually all the fat. The lengthy preparation is quite simple, and well worth the effort. The good news is that it can be prepared in advance, making it one of the easiest company dinners to serve. Allow about 1 to 1½ pounds raw weight per person. Raw boneless meat yields about 3 servings per pound after cooking, or 3-4 ounces meat per person when cooked.

1. Preheat oven to 500°F.

2. Slice the duck in half lengthwise down the breast. Turn the ducks over and cut down along both sides of the backbone. Remove the bone and set aside. Cut off the wing tips to combine with the backbone, neck, giblets and liver and set them into a pot with water to cover. They will become the base for natural duck gravy.

3. Cut off all excess fat without exposing the flesh. Wash the duck halves well and place them skin side up in a pan approximately 3-inches deep. Give them room so they do not overlap. With a small, sharp knife, slit the skin and fat underneath in a crisscross pattern, being careful not to cut into the flesh.

4. Sprinkle well with salt. Cook 30 minutes, uncovered. Remove from oven and discard the amazing amount of fat that has poured out of the duck. Lower the oven temperature to 350°F.

5. When ducks are cool enough to handle, take a small, sharp knife and cut away the rib bones and tough cartilage. Combine with the reserved bones for the gravy.

6. Combine 1 teaspoon flour with 2 cups white wine or apple juice and stir until blended. Optional: Add ½-ounce brandy. Pour the mixture over the duck and roast, uncovered, for 1½ hours, basting occasionally. If mixture becomes too thick, stir in more wine.

Sauces for Wild or Domestic Duck

Natural Gravy

1. Combine the backbone, wing tips, breast bones, neck and gizzards and cover with water. Add 1 sliced onion, 2 ribs celery, a handful of fresh thyme leaves, 1 bay leaf and a whole garlic head. Bring mixture to a boil. Reduce heat to medium-high. Cover the pot and boil gently 1 hour. Taste for salt and pepper. Cool to room temperature. Strain the soup into another pot. When the duck is cooked, spoon the gravy drippings from the pan into the soup. To make gravy, combine 1 tablespoon butter with 1 tablespoon flour for each cup liquid. Stir the butter and flour together in a saucepan over very low heat. When it begins to color, stir the duck stock slowly into the saucepan, cooking over medium heat until the gravy thickens to your liking.

Bing Cherry Sauce

Yield: 4 Cups

1 cup red Dubonnet or Port wine

16 ounce can pitted Bing cherries with their juice

½ teaspoon ground cloves

½ teaspoon ground cinnamon

½ cup black currant jelly

1 tablespoon arrowroot

1. Combine the Dubonnet with the juice from the canned cherries in a saucepan, reserving ¼ cup of cherry juice. Add the cloves, cinnamon and currant jelly. Bring to a boil, stirring until smooth. Reduce heat to low. Stir the arrowroot into the reserved cherry juice and add to the sauce, stirring until thickened. Stir in the cherries to serve.

Framboise Sauce

Yield: Approximately 1 Cup

10 ounce package frozen raspberries

½ cup Kirschwasser brandy

¼ cup Chambord liqueur

1 teaspoon arrowroot combined with 2 tablespoons warm water

1 pint fresh raspberries

1. Defrost the frozen berries. Force them with their juice through a sieve or fine strainer to remove seeds. Pour the strained liquid into a saucepan with the Kirschwasser and Chambord and bring to a boil, stirring. Lower heat to medium. Combine the arrowroot and water and stir into the sauce over low heat until slightly thickened. Do not allow mixture to boil.

2. Fold in half the fresh berries directly before serving. Pour sauce over the duck and sprinkle fresh raspberries around the plate.

Orange Sauce

Yield: Approximately 3 Cups

2 navel oranges

2 teaspoons arrowroot combined with
   2 tablespoons warm water

1 cup Valencia orange juice

1 teaspoon lemon juice

1 cup orange marmalade

1 tablespoon brandy or cognac

3 tablespoons Grand Marnier or orange liqueur
   of choice

½ cup almonds, blanched and slivered

1. Peel the outer orange skin of the navel oranges. Slice the peel into thin slivers. Combine the slivers with water to cover in a small saucepan. Bring to a boil. Lower heat and cook 15 minutes. Drain and set aside.

2. Cut the pith off the oranges and remove the segments from their membranes with a small sharp knife. Refrigerate.

3. Stir the arrowroot into the water and combine with the orange and lemon juice in a saucepan. Bring to the boiling point, stirring, but do not boil. Lower heat to simmer and stir in the slivered orange peel.

4. Stir in the marmalade, brandy and Grand Marnier and cook, stirring, until mixture is smooth and thick.

5. Stir in orange segments directly before serving. (You do not want the oranges to cook.) Spoon the sauce over the roasted duck, sprinkling almonds over and around the outside edge of the plates.

Cranberry-Currant Sauce

Yield: Approximately 3½ Cups

12 ounces fresh cranberries, mixed with 1 cup granulated sugar

2 cups Zante Currants

Juice from 1 small lemon (1 tablespoon)

⅓ cup Tawny Port Wine

⅓ cup Crème de Cassis

1 full teaspoon cornstarch

1. Combine the cranberries, sugar, currants, lemon juice, Port, Crème de Cassis and cornstarch in a saucepan. Stir to combine. Bring to a boil, stirring. Reduce heat to low and cook 5 minutes. Baste the cooked duck with the sauce and set the rest aside to reheat before serving.

To Finish:

1. Preheat oven to 350°F. Baste the ducks again and roast until very hot and crisp. Serve extra sauce and natural gravy on the side.

The first time the Danti family came from Florence, Italy, I arranged a dinner party in their honor, choosing my specialty, Duckling à l'Orange, as the main course. When the plates of crisp duckling arrived at the table, their youngest child stared wide-eyed at the julienne orange peels adorning the Grand Marnier glaze. "Mamma." She said in Italian. "Perphe Zia Valeria serve il dolce su un piatto con l`anatia`" ("Why is Aunt Valerie serving dessert on the plate with the duck?") Paola very politely explained that the sauce was a French delicacy, but it was obvious she shared her daughter`s gastronomic preference for sweets reserved for the dessert course. The next time I cooked duck for Italian friends, it was served with its own natural gravy.

Roasted Duck with Natural Gravy

Yield: 3 young ducklings, approximately 4 pounds each

Make the Duck Broth:

Backs, wing tips, necks and gizzards from the ducklings (Save livers for pâté)

1 large onion, cut into quarters

2 celery ribs, cut up

1 sprig fresh rosemary, or 1 teaspoon dried

1 tablespoon thyme leaves, or 1 teaspoon dried

Handful tarragon leaves, or 1 teaspoon dried

1 large clove garlic, split

1 teaspoon salt

½ teaspoon black pepper

4 cups water

1 tablespoon brandy

1. Cut the duck in half along the backbone and through the breast. Cut along the other side of the backbone and remove it. Cut off wing tips and combine with the backs, necks and gizzards to a pot with the onion, celery, rosemary, thyme, tarragon, garlic, salt, pepper and water. Bring to a boil. Cover. Reduce heat to medium and boil gently 1 hour. Stir in brandy. Strain. Cool to room temperature and refrigerate.

Note: It is difficult to determine the number of servings from poultry. If an appetizer or large salad has been served first, and the poultry is accompanied by numerous vegetables, a portion of one-quarter duck will be sufficient. A general rule of thumb is one-half duck per person, which will allow an ample amount left-over for another meal.

(Continued)

ROASTED DUCK WITH NATURAL GRAVY *(Continued)*

Roast the Ducks:

Salt

½ cup dry white wine

1 ounce Grand Marnier liqueur

1 tablespoon brandy

1 teaspoon flour

2 tablespoons dark molasses

1. Preheat oven to 500°F.

2. Remove all excess fat from the duck halves. With a sharp knife, slash the skin of the ducks in a crisscross pattern, being careful not to cut into the flesh. Set skin-side up in a baking pan. Sprinkle salt over the skin and place in the oven 30 minutes. Remove ducks from the pan. Discard the liquid fat from the pan.

3. With a boning knife, carefully remove the rib cage from underneath, leaving the leg and wing bones in tact.

4. Preheat oven to 350°F.

5. Combine wine, liqueur, brandy and flour in a bowl. Pour over the ducks. Roast, uncovered, in a preheated 350°F. oven 1 hour. Brush the skins lightly with molasses. (This gives the finished product a marvelous brown glow.) Reduce temperature to 325°F. and roast another 15 minutes.

To Finish:

1. Remove any congealed fat from the top of the duck broth. Melt 2 tablespoons butter. Stir in 2 tablespoons flour. Slowly add the broth over medium heat, stirring constantly. Bring to a boil and continue cooking until it thickens into gravy. Taste for salt and pepper.

Accompany with Wild Rice with Pecans. (recipe on next page)

Wild Rice with Pecans

Yield: 6-8 Servings

6 ounce package wild rice

½ cup dried porcini (Italian mushrooms found in gourmet shops)

4 tablespoons butter

1 medium onion, chopped into small pieces (not minced)

2 ribs celery, chopped into small pieces (not minced)

½ cup yellow bell pepper, chopped into small pieces (not minced)

1 teaspoon salt

1 teaspoon pepper

3 cups water

⅓ cup roasted pecan pieces

1. Soak mushrooms 10 minutes in warm water to cover. Discard water and rinse mushrooms well. Cut into small pieces.

2. Melt butter in the top of a double boiler over direct heat. Sauté onion, celery and pepper over low heat until they are limp but not colored.

3. Add water and bring to a boil. Stir in rice, salt, pepper and chopped porcini. Bring all to a boil, stirring. Cover. Reduce heat to low and cook 50-60 minutes, stirring often. Set pot into simmering water in the bottom of the double boiler. Leave in its water bath until ready to serve.

4. Place pecans on foil or a baking sheet in a 250°F. oven 15 minutes. Stir into the rice directly before serving.

A Duck in Thyme

Yield: 4 Servings

2 young ducks, approximately 2-3 pounds each   Salt and pepper

Marinade:

¼ cup brandy or cognac   Handful of fresh thyme, or 1 teaspoon dried
2 cups Cabernet Sauvignon wine   ½ teaspoon ground allspice
1 large Florida sweet onion, chopped   1 bay leaf

1. Clean, rinse and cut each duck into six pieces. Remove excess fat. Sprinkle with salt and pepper.

2. Combine marinade ingredients in a large pan. Place duck in the pan and spoon the marinade over. Cover and refrigerate overnight or several hours, turning the duck several times for it to marinate evenly.

3. Remove duck from the marinade and set aside. Strain marinade and reserve.

To cook the duck:

4 tablespoons unsalted butter   2 tablespoons all-purpose flour
2 tablespoons olive oil   1 cup beef broth
2 cloves garlic, minced   2 large carrots, finely chopped
½ pound white mushrooms, cut into large
    chunks

1. Combine butter and olive oil in a deep skillet. Heat to the sizzling point and set the duck pieces in, skin side down. Cook over medium-high heat until brown. Turn and cook on the other side. Remove duck from the skillet. Lower heat to medium.

2. Add the garlic and mushrooms and cook until the mushrooms are soft. Stir in the flour. Slowly stir in 1 cup of the marinade. Add the beef broth, stirring until smooth. Add the carrots.

3. Add duck pieces and bring to a boil. Lower heat to medium-low and cover the skillet. Cook 1 hour or longer, until the duck is very tender.

4. Remove duck from the skillet. Bring the gravy to a hard boil and pour around the duck pieces to serve.

Note: This is marvelous accompanied by wide noodles to absorb the delicious gravy.

Brandied Duck Pie in Short Crust

Yield: 8-10 Servings for hors d'oeuvre

Short Pie Crust Recipe (recipe, page 258)

1 duck, 5-6 pounds after cleaning

Salt and pepper

¼ pound unsalted butter, softened

2 cloves garlic, peeled and split

2 bay leaves

Handful of fresh thyme leaves, or 1 teaspoon dried

Handful of fresh oregano leaves, or 1 teaspoon dried

Handful of fresh marjoram leaves, or 1 teaspoon dried

1 large onion, quartered

1¼ cups chicken broth

2 tablespoons butter

2 tablespoons all-purpose flour

¼ cup brandy or cognac

¼ cup chopped parsley

¼ cup chopped chives

2 Red Valencia oranges, peeled and cut into segments

1. Make Short Crust Basic Pie Dough (recipe, page 258).

2. Cut duck into quarters and remove the skin and fat. Sprinkle the meat with salt and pepper.

3. Combine butter, garlic, bay leaves, thyme, oregano, marjoram, onion and chicken broth in a deep skillet or pot. Add duck pieces and bring to a boil. Cover and reduce heat to medium-low. Cook slowly 1½ hours. Remove from heat and cool to room temperature. Strain broth.

4. Cut duck meat into small, uniform pieces and set aside.

5. Melt butter. Stir in flour. Slowly add strained broth and brandy, stirring until smooth and thickened. Stir in duck. Correct seasoning with pepper and salt to taste.

6. Fill cooled pie crust. Bake in a preheated 350°F. until very hot.

7. Sprinkle with parsley and chives. Set orange segments around the top of the pie. Serve immediately.

Sautéed Duck Breasts with Mushrooms and Glazed Onions

Yield: 4 Servings

2 duck breasts, boned and skinned and cut into halves

Salt, black pepper

2 large portobello mushroom caps

2 shallots, minced

1 clove garlic, minced

Flour for dredging

4 tablespoons extra virgin olive oil

4 tablespoons butter

3 ounces brandy or cognac

1 cup heavy cream

2 tablespoons minced flat leaf (Italian) parsley

1. Wash and dry duck breasts. Sprinkle with salt and pepper and set aside.

2. Wipe mushrooms clean with damp paper toweling. Remove the stems. If mushrooms are dirty, rinse quickly but do not soak. Cut into thick slices. Set on paper toweling to dry completely.

3. Peel and mince shallots and garlic.

4. Dredge the breasts in flour, shaking off excess. Heat oil in a large skillet. Cook breasts on both sides until brown on the outside and pink to rare within. Remove from the skillet to paper toweling. Discard oil and wipe out the pan.

5. Melt the butter in the skillet and cook the mushroom slices and cook until just tender. Do not overcook. Remove them to a plate. Set the shallots and garlic in the pan and cook over low heat until soft, approximately 2 minutes. Add the brandy and bring to a boil. Remove from heat and slowly pour in the cream, stirring constantly. Return to the heat and cook, stirring over low heat, until mixture reaches a velvet consistency and is very hot. Return the mushrooms and duck breasts to the skillet and spoon the sauce over. Divide among four plates. Serve with Glazed Onions (recipe on next page) and sprinkle minced parsley over all.

Oak Haven Farm off Wolf Branch Road a few miles from Mount Dora and Far Reach Ranch off SR 561 outside Tavares offer U-Pick for Florida's answer to Georgia's sweet Vidalia onion. The large white Pegasus onion is a milder version of the Vidalia that has captured the fancy of Central Floridians. The Gran X is also mild, but not as soft as the Pegasus. The flavor of these onions pulled directly from the ground instead of the produce department of the supermarket is eminent beyond comparison.

Glazed Onions

Yield: 4 Servings

4 whole sweet Florida onions	Pinch of white pepper
4 tablespoons butter, melted	¼ cup Orange Marmalade
¼ teaspoon salt	2 tablespoons Grand Marnier liqueur

1. Preheat oven to 350°F.

2. Peel onions and cut a small hole in the top. Place in a shallow baking dish.

3. Combine butter, salt, pepper and marmalade in a small pan and cook, stirring, over low heat until mixture is smooth. Pour the mixture over and bake approximately 30 minutes, or until glazed.

Note: Onions may be filled with creamed spinach, mashed potatoes, or squash. Cut a circle into the centers ¼ from the bottom before baking. Chop centers fine. Sauté in a little butter until soft and add to vegetables. Fill the last 15 minutes of cooking.

Duck Breasts with Anise

Yield: 4-6 Servings

4 duck breasts, 1 pound each (2 ducks)

2 tablespoons dry sherry or Marsala wine

2 tablespoons granulated sugar

2 tablespoons Tamari sauce

1 large clove garlic, grated

1 teaspoon anise extract or 1 ounce Sambuca or Anisette liqueur

3 tablespoons light corn syrup

1 scallion, green part only, finely-chopped

2 fresh tarragon leaves

3 tablespoons sesame oil

½ pound fresh or canned straw or shiitake mushrooms

2 tablespoons cornstarch

1¼ cups duck or chicken stock

8 cups total: thin strips of green zucchini, yellow peppers and fennel

Fresh or canned pineapple cubes

Chopped fresh tarragon leaves

1. Combine sherry, sugar, Tamari, garlic, anise, corn syrup and scallion greens. Marinate the breasts several hours or overnight.

2. Remove from marinade and pat dry. Score the skin of the duck breasts to allow fat to escape. Lightly salt duck breasts. Brush with sesame oil and cook in a preheated 500°F. oven 10 minutes. Pour off fat. Brush heavily with marinade. Reduce heat to 325°F. Return duck to roast until done to your liking. Duck breast should be served pink. Do not overcook or meat will be tough.

3. Sauté the mushrooms over medium heat in the remaining sesame oil until done to your liking. Do not overcook. Remove to a warm platter.

4. Stir the cornstarch into the sesame oil. Add the duck (chicken) stock and stir over medium heat until thickened.

5. Cut the vegetables into thin strips (julienne) and steam until tender but firm. Place a mound in the center of 4 plates. Slice the duck breasts into strips on the bias and set on top of the steamed vegetable strips. Spoon the sauce over. Decorate with pineapple. Sprinkle chopped tarragon over to serve.

Duck Breasts with Bananas and Tangerines

Yield: 4 Servings

4 boned and skinned duck breasts

6 tablespoons butter

Salt, pepper

½ cup orange blossom honey

½ cup Persian lime juice

Juice from 1 Ponkan or Sunburst tangerine

½ teaspoon grated nutmeg

2 finger bananas

1 Ponkan or Sunburst tangerine to decorate

1. Wash and dry the duck breasts.

2. Melt the butter in a skillet and dip the breasts in to coat. Remove the breasts to a plate and sprinkle with salt and pepper.

3. Stir honey, lime and tangerine juice into the remaining melted butter and cook over medium heat, stirring into well blended. Add nutmeg. Add duck breasts and cook over medium heat, covered, for 5 minutes. Turn breasts over, cover again and cook another 5 minutes, or until slightly pink within. Do not overcook.

4. Peel and slice bananas in halves lengthwise and add to the pan. Cook, uncovered, until bananas are hot, but not soft. Serve immediately.

Blackberries grow wild throughout Central Florida. Like the Muscadine grape, one only needs to plant and let nature do the rest. They will eventually take over any fence they can climb.

Duck with Blackberries and Cassis

Yield: 4 Servings

4 boneless duck breasts, 1 pound each

Salt, pepper

2 tablespoons clarified butter

½ cup dry white wine

2 ounces Crème de Cassis liqueur

½ cup reduced duck broth or concentrated chicken broth

8 boiled and peeled whole fresh chestnuts (Purchase canned chestnuts out of season)

1 tablespoon arrowroot

¼ cup cool water

1 pint blackberries

1. Preheat oven to 325°F.

2. Remove the skin and fat from the duck breasts. Lightly salt and pepper all over. Sauté in a shallow skillet skin-side down in the clarified butter until light brown. Turn and sauté the other side. Remove breasts to a shallow roasting pan.

3. Add wine and Cassis to the skillet and bring to a boil, stirring. Add broth. Pour over the duck breasts.

4. Roast breasts 25 minutes for rare, 30 minutes for medium, 35 minutes for well-done, basting every 8 minutes. Add chestnuts to the pan the last 10 minutes of cooking to absorb the flavor of the gravy.

5. Slice breasts on a diagonal into 4 or 5 strips. Transfer to individual plates.

6. Pour the gravy from the roasting pan into a saucepan.

7. Combine arrowroot with cool water and stir into the gravy. Bring to the boiling point, stirring, and spoon over the duck breasts. Decorate with blackberries and chestnuts to serve.

Duck Breasts with Kumquat Sauce

Yield: 4 Servings

4 boned duck breasts with skin

Salt to sprinkle

1 teaspoon minced gingerroot

1 teaspoon minced garlic

1 tablespoon minced shallot

1 tablespoon unsalted butter

½ teaspoon all-purpose flour

1 teaspoon brandy

1 teaspoon Grand Marnier liqueur

½ cup dry white wine

1 tablespoon minced fresh thyme leaves

½ cup Kumquat Preserves (recipe, page 44)

1 tablespoon Grand Marnier liqueur

¼ cup reduced duck (or chicken) stock

Preserved kumquats for garnish

Optional: Chopped scallion greens for garnish

1. Preheat oven to 500°F.

2. Cut small slits through the skin of the breasts into the fat. Sprinkle with salt. Place in a shallow pan and roast 10 minutes, or until the skin begins to turn color and the fat has escaped. Remove from oven and pour off fat.

3. Combine ginger, garlic and shallot in a saucepan with the butter. Cook over low heat until soft. Add flour, brandy and Grand Marnier, stirring until smooth. Add wine and thyme leaves and bring to a boil, stirring. Cool to room temperature. Pour over duck breasts to marinate several hours in the refrigerator.

4. Preheat oven to 375°F.

5. Place breasts in a shallow baking pan with the marinade. Heat the kumquat preserves with the Grand Marnier and brush the skin heavily. Roast 15 minutes, or until done to your liking. Turn oven to broil and set duck breasts on upper rack. Broil until glaze is almost black.

6. Remove the breasts to a cutting board. Combine the gravy from the pan with the reduced duck stock and bring to a boil in a saucepan. Slice the breasts into thin strips on an angle and portion onto four plates. Spoon the sauce over to serve. Decorate with whole preserved kumquats and chopped scallion greens.

Brandied Duck Pâté

Yield: 2 Cups

½ pound bulk pork sausage (Jimmy Dean®
   original recipe lower fat)

Livers from 2-6 pound ducks, approximately
   8 ounces

6 tablespoons butter

2 tablespoons minced shallot

1 teaspoon grated garlic clove

½ teaspoon ground thyme

½ teaspoon salt, or more to taste

¼ teaspoon black pepper, or more to taste

¼ teaspoon mace

⅛ teaspoon nutmeg

1 bay leaf

3 tablespoons brandy or cognac

⅓ cup heavy cream

1. Cook sausage. Drain and discard fat. Cut sausage into pieces.

2. Remove any fat and connective tissue from the livers. Do not use the gizzards or hearts in pâté.

3. Melt butter in a skillet over low heat. Add the shallot, garlic, thyme, salt, pepper, mace, nutmeg and bay leaf. Cook over low heat 10 minutes.

4. Stir in livers. Cover and cook approximately 5 minutes, or until the livers are done. Do not overcook or livers will take on a bitter flavor.

5. Add sausage. Add brandy and bring to a quick boil. Remove from the heat immediately to cool.

6. Remove and reserve bay leaf. Place the liver mixture into a food processor with the steel blade. Pulverize to a thick, coarse paste. Add cream, 1 tablespoon at a time, turning the machine on-off several times to incorporate. Taste for salt and pepper.

7. Spoon pâté into a 2-cup crock or soufflé dish. Place the bay leaf on top. Cover and refrigerate overnight or several days for best flavor.

8. Serve with Danish black bread triangles or crackers.

Paola's Tuscan Pâté

This recipe originates from my good friend, Paola Danti, from Florence, Italy.
Chicken livers may be substituted.

Yield: 16 Toasts

1 clove garlic, minced

1 medium onion, minced

1 tablespoon minced capers

4 anchovy fillets

½ cup extra virgin Italian olive oil

¾ pound lean ground sirloin

¾ pound duck or chicken livers, trimmed of sinew

½ teaspoon dried sage, or 1 teaspoon minced fresh leaves

½ teaspoon salt

¼ teaspoon black pepper

2 tablespoons Chianti wine

1 teaspoon tomato paste mixed with ¼ cup water

½ cup strong beef broth

16 thin slices Italian bread (If large, cut into halves), toasted on 1 side only

1. Mince the garlic, onion, capers and anchovies in a food processor.

2. Heat olive oil in a skillet. Add the mixture from the food processor. Add the ground sirloin and cook, stirring constantly until meat is cooked. Add livers and cook until just done, but still soft. (Liver cooked too long becomes bitter.)

3. Add sage, salt and pepper.

4. Remove from heat and put into a food processor with a steel blade. Turn on-off a few times to create a smooth paste. Return to pan and stir in wine and tomato paste.

5. Slice bread as thin as possible. Toast one side under the broiler and brush the other with the beef broth. Spread thick with the pâté. Serve at room temperature or place into a 300°F oven for a few minutes to warm.

Note: In Italy, this is called Crostini Di Fegatini, meaning "Little Crusts". They are served on individual plates as an appetizer, garnished with fresh basil leaves.

Wood Duck

Recipes for Wood Duck, Quail and Cornish Game Hen are interchangeable. The Wood Duck is the most prolific bird to hunt in Central Florida. The headwaters of the St. John's River in east Central Florida have a vast expanse of marshes within a few minutes drive of the Kennedy Space Center an hour from Orlando's Disney World.

RECIPES:

*Baked Wood Duck
with Tangelos and Bananas*

*Butterfly Gingered Wood Duck,
Quail or Cornish Game Hen*

*Curried Wood Duck, Cornish
Game Hen or Quail Crêpes*

*Wood Duck or
Game Hen with Tarragon*

*Meyer Lemon Wood Duck,
or Game Hen*

Quail Pie

Wood Duck, Quail or Cornish Game Hen

Recipes for Wood Duck, Quail and Cornish Game Hen are interchangeable. The wood duck is the most prolific bird hunted in Central Florida. The headwaters of the eastern part of the St. John's River have a vast expanse of marshes that create a habitat for wildlife and waterfowl within a few minutes drive of the Kennedy Space Center an hour from Orlando's Disney World. Although Quail can also be found, most people choose to hunt in one of the many available ranches or hunting preserves, where hunters equipped with guns or crossbows are accompanied by trained bird dogs. Whereas the weight of the wood duck averages 1.4 pounds, the tiny quail tips the scale at approximately 6 ounces. And, yes! Snipe is a real bird that weighs about 4 ounces, similar to the woodcock. Contrary to the great hoax perpetrated by older siblings and camp counselors of our youth, snipe are not found with a flashlight in the depths of the woods at midnight. Nor do they have to be gathered in a gunny sack. Many a dark night was spent by innocents terrified of creepy sounds made by the older group who muffled giggles while they hid out in glee. But, make no mistake. The snipe is a weird bird with large eyes located far back on its head that can see forward, backward, to the side, and up and down without moving its head while its bill is stuck in the ground eating. There are no recipes dedicated to snipe in this chapter, but, should you bring one home, follow one for quail. The Cornish Game Hen, which is plump and juicy and can be found in the frozen food section of most supermarkets, is not actually a game bird at all, but a small breed of chicken weighing between 1 and 1½ pounds.

The touch of sweet honey coupled with Key lime, juicy Orlando Tangelo and savory finger bananas enhances fish as well as chicken. This sauce is also an enhancement to our St. John's River fresh Bass.

Baked Wood Duck with Tangelos and Bananas

Yield: 4 Servings

4 wood ducks, skinned and boned, legs and wings in tact

6 tablespoons butter

Salt, pepper

½ cup honey

½ cup Key lime juice

½ teaspoon grated nutmeg

2 Orlando Tangelos, peeled, quartered, seeds removed

2 yellow ripe but firm finger Bananas, peeled and cut into halves

1. Melt the butter in a saucepan. Dip the duck to coat lightly with the butter. Remove to a shallow baking dish and sprinkle all over with salt and pepper.

2. Stir honey and lime juice into the melted butter in the pan and cook over medium heat until well blended. Pour over the duck.

3. Place under the broiler to lightly brown. Spoon the sauce over. Set oven temperature to 375°F. Cook 25 minutes, or until done. Add tangelos and bananas and cook another 10 minutes.

Note: Cornish hens may be substituted for the wood duck. Leave the skin on while cooking. This sauce is also lovely with Bass. Clean and skin the fish, but leave it whole with the head intact. Grill the fish over low gas heat or white coals, basting often to retain moisture.

Cornish hens are easier to obtain than wood ducks, but the tender, juicy little wood duck is a very special treat. If you substitute Cornish hen for wood duck, purchase one that weighs one pound only.

Butterfly Gingered Duck or Cornish Game Hen

Yield: 4 Wood Ducks or Cornish Game Hens

4 wood ducks, about 16 ounces each, or
   Cornish game hens of the same weight

Salt and pepper

2 tablespoons olive oil

2 tablespoons black sesame seed oil

2 cloves minced garlic

2 minced shallots

2 tablespoons minced fresh ginger

1 teaspoon dried marjoram

¼ cup white wine

¼ cup chicken broth

8 white, firm large mushrooms

1. Preheat oven to 400°F.

2. Slice the ducks open along the backbone, but not through the breasts. Skin-side down, slice along the other side of the backbone and remove it. With a small, sharp knife, carefully remove the tiny ribs, tail and any extra fat. Wash and dry on paper toweling.

3. Sprinkle with salt and pepper. Place the ducks in a shallow baking dish.

4. Combine the olive and sesame seed oils in a saucepan. Add the garlic, shallots, ginger and marjoram and cook over very low heat 10 minutes. Spoon half the mixture over the ducks, turning them several times to gather the flavors. Arrange skin side up and roast 15 minutes. Reduce oven temperature to 300°F. and cook the wood duck another 20-30 minutes, or until tender. (Cornish hens will cook in less time, or approximately 15 minutes.) Remove the ducks to a heated platter.

5. Add the wine and broth to the remaining oil mixture and bring to a boil. Boil 1 minute. Lower heat to simmer. Add the whole mushrooms and cook 1 minute longer. Pour in the juices from the pan, stirring to incorporate. Spoon a bit over the duck and pour the remaining gravy into a gravy boat to serve on the side.

6. Set duck on top of Corn Bread Stuffing made with Jalapeño or Southern Corn Bread. (recipes, page 91 and 92)

Curried Wood Duck, Cornish Game Hen or Quail Crêpes

Yield: Approximately 6 cups cooked meat to fill 24 Crêpes

Blender Sweet Crêpes, (recipe, page 67)

4 wood ducks, split

¼ cup olive oil or 4 tablespoons unsalted butter

2 shallots, finely diced

2½ cups chicken broth

½ cup Chardonnay wine

½ pound sliced white mushrooms

2 tablespoons butter

3 tablespoons all-purpose flour

1 tablespoon Madras curry powder

1 teaspoon ground turmeric

1. Make Blender Sweet Crêpes, omitting the sugar and vanilla (recipe, page 67). For a lighter crêpe, substitute concentrated chicken broth for the milk and water.

2. Split and clean the wood ducks and sprinkle with salt and pepper.

3. Heat the olive oil and simmer the shallots until they become soft but not colored.

4. Add the ducks. Add 1½ cups of the chicken broth and all the wine. Cover and cook over medium heat about 20 minutes, or until the ducks are cooked through. Cool and strain the sauce. Remove skin and bones and slice the duck meat into strips. Set aside.

5. Sauté the mushrooms in the butter. Stir in the flour. Add the remaining broth, curry powder and turmeric and stir until smooth. Add the strained sauce and bring to a boil, stirring, until thick and smooth.

6. Place a good amount of duck in the center of the uncooked side of each crêpe. Spoon some of the sauce over and fold one side of the crêpe to cover the mixture. Close the other side over the first. Place flap side down on an oiled, sided cookie sheet. Brush each crêpe with a little butter.

7. Bake in a preheated 350°F. oven until hot.

8. Place two crêpes on each plate or a heated platter and spoon sauce over.

Note: Steps 1-6 may be done in advance.

Wood Duck or Game Hen with Tarragon

Large appetites may require two ducks or hens to satisfy. In this case, double the recipe.

Yield: 2 Servings

2-16 ounce wood ducks or game hens

Grated rind and juice of 1 orange, preferably
  Parson Brown or Ambersweet

½ teaspoon Kosher salt

½ teaspoon pepper

Paprika

2 handfuls of tarragon leaves

4 tablespoons melted butter

¼ cup dry white wine

1 tablespoon Pernod anise liquor

1. Cut birds open down one side of their backbone. Cut along the other side and remove the backbone. Using a small, sharp knife, remove the tiny ribs under the breast.

2. Grate the orange rind and squeeze the orange over the birds. Sprinkle with salt and pepper and paprika.

3. Spread the birds butterfly fashion skin side up on top of the tarragon leaves in a shallow pan and brush with the melted butter.

4. Place under a broiler and broil until the skin turns brown.

5. Change the oven setting to 350°F. Combine the wine with the Pernod and pour into the pan. Roast the birds 35 minutes, or until done.

Meyer Lemon Wood Duck or Game Hen

Yield: 4-8 Servings, depending upon the appetite of guests

8-16 ounce wood ducks or Cornish game hens

Salt and pepper

Juice from 1 large Meyer lemon
  (Approximately ¾ cup)

2 cloves garlic, minced

4 tablespoons melted butter or extra virgin olive
  oil

2 tablespoons Grand Marnier

½ cup Valencia orange juice

Grated rind of Valencia orange

½ cup Pinot Blanc wine

1. Preheat oven to 350°F.

2. Slit the ducks (hens) along the backbone. Cut away the backbones and spread the open. Wash under cold water, removing any blood, small tails and extra fat. Sprinkle well with salt and pepper. Squeeze lemon juice over both sides. Mince the garlic and rub well all over. Brush with melted butter or oil.

3. Place birds skin side down over an open gas or wood fire until well browned. Remove.

4. Set the birds in a shallow pan, skin side up. Brush heavily with melted butter or oil. Brush with the Grand Marnier. Add orange juice, grated orange rind and Pinot Blanc wine to the pan. Roast 35-40 minutes, or until very tender but not dry.

5. Strain the gravy from the baking dish into a saucepan. Bring to a boil and pour over the birds to serve.

Note: Pinot Blanc is dryer than Chardonnay with less intensity and flavor. If you cannot locate this wine, use Chardonnay.

Quail Pie

Yield: 6 Servings

Baking Powder Dough (recipe, page 268)
Approximately 6 quail, 1¼ pounds total weight
3 tablespoons Port wine
1 teaspoon salt
½ teaspoon pepper
¼ teaspoon nutmeg
1 teaspoon powdered basil
6 slices thick cut bacon
1 tablespoon butter
2 tablespoons all-purpose flour

½ cup sweet German Riesling wine
1 cup coffee cream
2 tablespoons heavy cream
1 cup smoked ham, coarsely chopped
1 tablespoon scallion greens, minced
1 pound tiny white button mushrooms
6 ounces small cooked Belgian carrots
10 ounce package baby green peas
1 pound tiny pearl onions

1   Dip the quail into the Port. Remove and shake off excess.

2. Combine salt, pepper, nutmeg and basil and rub into the quail.

3. Wrap a slice of bacon around each and secure with a toothpick.

4. Preheat oven to 450°F.

5. Set the quail in a shallow pan. Bake 20 minutes. Remove from oven.

6. Melt butter. Stir in flour, wine and creams and cook over low heat until sauce thickens. Remove from heat.

7. Stir in ham, scallions, mushrooms, carrots and peas.

8. Pour boiling water over onions. Leave 10 minutes. Peel and add them to the sauce.

9. Cut quail into fairly large pieces. Chop bacon. Add to the sauce.

10. Roll out pie crust and cut into 2 circles to fill the bottom and cover the top. Spoon in quail mixture. Cover the pie tightly with the top circle of crust. Cut slits to allow steam to escape.

11. Bake 15-18 minutes, or until nicely browned. Allow to stand at room temperature 10 minutes before serving.

Note: Wood Duck and Cornish Hen will necessitate longer cooking time.

TURKEY

The Chain-O-Lakes Gobblers chapter of the National Wild Turkey Federation (NWTF) is an organization fiercely dedicated to the preservation of wild game and fowl. When it was founded in 1973, there were an estimated 1.3 million wild turkeys and 1.5 million turkey hunters. Today there are approximately 5.4 million wild turkeys and approximately 2.6 million turkey hunters.

Turkey

Hunting in Central Florida:

Contrary to the misperception of those who disapprove of hunting, the person who takes to the wild during legal season is rarely a gun brandishing, fired up, beer chug-a-lugger, running through the woods in camouflage hootin' and hollerin'. Most hunters are responsible owners of guns dedicated to teaching safe handling of all weapons, from guns to bows and arrows.

Hunting may be called a sport, but it's a serious sport, not to ever be taken lightly. Stringent rules in Osceola, Florida, allow hunters only muzzle loading guns, shotguns, and crossbows and bows and arrows to fell venison, wild turkey and boar. If you wish to bring dogs to track and chase, you'll have to travel to Louisiana. Hunting here is not killing for fun. Responsible hunters never kill more than they can eat. Leftovers are carefully cleaned and packaged for the freezer.

The Chain-O-Lakes Gobblers chapter of the National Wild Turkey Federation (NWTF) is an organization fiercely dedicated to the preservation of wild game and fowl. President, Dale S. Wessling, gathers this gaggle of gallinaceous gobblers to collect their herd of hunters and convinces them to empty their freezers of their precious stash saved from hunting season. Once a year they cook up a feast for the conservation of the wild turkey and the preservation of the turkey hunting tradition in the town square of Leesburg, All proceeds from the banquet go directly to the JAKES program (Juniors Acquiring Knowledge, Ethics and Sportsmanship for young people to learn the principles of wildlife management), WITO (Women in the Outdoors who wish to be introduced to outdoor activities and trained as outdoor educators), and Wheeling Sportsmen, a program for the disabled, which has merged with NWTF to become the largest disabled outreach program in the country.

At one time, wild turkey in its uncivilized state ranged over much of the country, but over-hunting caused the species to dwindle, particularly in the northeast. When the National Wild Turkey Federation was founded in 1973, there were an estimated 1.3 million wild turkeys and 1.5 million turkey hunters! NWTF volunteers and partners joined forces, raising more than 135 million dollars which have been spent on over 15,000 projects benefiting wild turkeys throughout North America. One of the successes of this 325,000 member grassroots, nonprofit organization with members in fifty states, Canada and eleven foreign countries has been the protection and restocking of wild turkeys, resulting in the present estimated figure of 5.4 million wild turkeys and approximately 2.6 million turkey hunters. NWTF also supports scientific wildlife management on public, private and corporate lands as well as wild turkey hunting as a traditional North American sport. Funds are used for the purchase of equipment to parks, planting and refurbishing of wildlife management areas, research projects and purchase of land for public hunting.

The Florida wild turkey, also referred to as the Osceola, is found only on the peninsula of Florida. Smaller and darker in color with less white veining in the wing quills than the eastern wild turkey, its feathers are an iridescent green and red. The subspecies was first described in 1890 by W.E.D. Scott, who named it for the famous Seminole Chief, Osceola, who led his tribe against the Americans in a twenty-year war that began in 1835.

The wild turkey must be handled differently than those we purchase in the market although recipes may be interchangeable. The flavor of the two is slightly different, with the flesh of the wild turkey having more color and a more piquant and interesting taste. The wild bird does not have the body fat of his domestic cousin and, therefore, should not be seared or cooked in too hot an oven.

Deep Fried Turkey

The art of deep-frying a whole turkey is a Cajun-southern tradition foreign to most city folks. The method produces incredibly juicy meat and crispy skin, and it takes less than one hour to cook a whole bird. Before you attempt to deep fry your bird, the following guidelines should be carefully followed:

1. The best size of a whole turkey to fry should not exceed 12 pounds, although larger birds are fried every day.

2. Purchase a gas burner that outputs about 180,000 BTU's to service small and large turkeys, and a 7-10 gallon pot with a basket or rack. Turkey fryers are sold in most home supply stores. They can be found under $100 and include the burner, pot, lifting rack and thermometer.

3. Purchase at least 5 gallons of oil for the cooking.

4. Purchase a flavor injector from a specialty cook shop.

5. Combine liquid sauces to inject into the turkey. Or, purchase Creole seasoning or dry seasoning of your choice to rub over and under the skin. Or, simply sprinkle with kosher salt and heaps of garlic powder. Chain of Lakes Seasoning (recipe, page 245) works well with fried turkey. To inject it, add water or white wine and stir to create a liquid seasoning.

6. Purchase a candy thermometer to measure oil temperature. Purchase a meat thermometer to determine the temperature of the turkey.

7. Purchase oven mitts to keep from getting burned.

8. Use oils with high smoke points. Peanut and grapeseed oils have the highest smoke points and also insure the best flavor and aroma, but the cost escalates the price of the meal. Combine them with canola or safflower oil.

9. Temperature of the cooking oil should be 350°F. If it drops below 340°F., it will be absorbed into the turkey. Temperature of the cooking oil should not exceed 365°F., or it can begin to smoke and catch fire. Most people bring the oil temperature to 375°F. and lower it immediately to 350°F. when the turkey is inserted.

10. A fire extinguisher is a handy tool to have near-by.

11. The outside of the turkey must be completely dry of water for the hot oil not to pop up and splatter the unsuspecting chef.

12. Do not stuff turkeys for deep frying.

13. Remove the tail and extra flaps of skin and fat before frying. When frying an Osceola turkey, you probably will want to remove and discard the long legs also. The body of the wild turkey is lean and the legs thin and muscular, unlike his domestic cousin who lies around all day basking in the sun gorging himself on corn.

(Continued)

DEEP FRIED TURKEY *(Continued)*

14. Whole turkeys require approximately 3 minutes per pound to cook. They are done when the internal temperature of the breast reaches 170°F. and the internal temperature of the thigh reaches 180°F. Turkey parts, such as the breast, wings and thighs require approximately 4-5 minutes per pound to reach their temperature points.

15. The turkey will have ultimate flavor and be easier to carve if allowed to rest 30 minutes after removing from the oil. Wrap it in aluminum foil for the juices to circulate through the meat, making it tender.

16. Allow the oil to cool completely before disposing. The cool oil can be strained through a fine mesh cloth and stored in a cool place several months to use again.

17. And, most important, never fry turkey in-doors, even in a garage or under an overhang attached to the house, or on a wooden deck that could catch fire. Place the outdoor gas burner on a level dirt or grassy area. The grease will stain concrete.

Fried Turkey Breast Blackman

Breast from 8-10 pound Osceola turkey

Seasoned salt or Cajun seasoning of choice

2 whole heads garlic

Peanut oil, or another liquid vegetable shortening of choice

Step One:

1. If you have a turkey fryer, it will have a built-in rack. If you do not, create a cradle out of a large, heavy coat hanger and insert it all the way into the cavity to hold the middle of the turkey. Tie the top with a heavy cord with a large 'hangman's loop' at the end long enough to hang over the edge of the fryer to pull the turkey out.

2. Set the turkey breast into a large soup pot and pour in the oil to cover completely. This will gage the amount of oil needed to fry without splashing over the top of the fryer. Remove the breast from the oil and pat dry.

3. Carefully separate the skin from the flesh of the breast without tearing or cutting into the meat. Pull it up, inserting your fingers to separate. With a small sharp paring or oyster knife, puncture a one-inch hole in both breasts. Peel the cloves from 1 head of the garlic and split the cloves in half. Insert the halves into both sides of the breast. Spoon some seasoning into the holes, pushing it into the flesh as deep as possible. Rub seasoning over the outside of the flesh. Pull the skin over, smoothing it into place. Then, pin it down tightly with toothpicks.

Step Two:

1. Heat the oil to 280°F. Peel the remaining head of garlic, leaving the root intact and toss it into the oil. Let it saturate the oil with flavor 30 minutes. Scoop it out with a slotted spoon and bring the oil to 350°F.

2. Preheat oven to 300°F. Set the turkey on a rack into the oven only until it becomes hot but has not begun to cook. (This is an amazing technique of Chet Blackman's because it is so logical. When a cold turkey is placed into oil, it absorbs the oil as it cools down. While inhibiting the cooking process, it also causes the oil to bubble up over the edges.) Lower the hot turkey breast into the hot oil and fry 4-5 minutes per pound, or until a meat thermometer reaches 170°F. and the breast is tender. If the oil bubbles, raise and lower the turkey several times until it reaches the heat of the oil.

3. Remove the breast from the oil and allow it to drain a few minutes. It's best to wait 30 minutes for easy carving.

Note: This same technique is used to fry a whole turkey. The whole turkey should fry about 3-4 minutes per pound to reach a temperature of 180°F when a thermometer is inserted into the deepest part of the thigh. Cooking time should be approximately 35-45 minutes for a 10-12 pound turkey.

Turkey with Dumplings

Yield: 6 Servings

4 pound turkey breast, wild or domestic

Salt and black pepper

¼ pound butter, melted

6 leeks, white part only

4½ cups water

2 large Florida Granx or Pegasus mild sweet onions, peeled and cut into quarters

6 ribs celery, cut up

½-inch piece ginger, minced

¼ teaspoon grated nutmeg

Small handful fresh dill, chopped fine

1 pound baby carrots

1. Remove the skin from the breast and cut the meat into squares approximately 2 inches in diameter. Sprinkle with salt and pepper. Melt the butter and toss with the turkey squares.

2. Preheat oven to 375°F. Place the white part of the leeks on aluminum foil and roast until very brown, or approximately 15 minutes.

3. Combine the leek with the remaining ingredients in a soup pot. Bring to a boil. Skim off any dark froth that bubbles on top. Cover. Reduce heat to medium. Boil gently 1 hour. Serve with Old Fashioned Dumplings. (recipe, below)

Old Fashioned Dumplings

This recipe comes from my Great Grandmother's notes, written somewhere around 1890.

Yield: 12-15 Dumplings

2 cups all-purpose flour

4 heaping teaspoons double acting baking powder

¼ teaspoon baking soda

½ teaspoon salt

Small pinch white pepper

1¾ cups whole milk (Chicken broth may be substituted)

1. Sift dry ingredients together into a bowl. Stir in milk.

2. Drop the mixture by large tablespoons on top of the cooking turkey and vegetables. Dumplings should not fall into the gravy, but steam on top. It may be necessary to pour off some of the liquid into another pot to keep warm while the dumplings cook. Cover the pot and cook over medium heat 35 minutes. Lower heat to simmer and continue cooking another 20 minutes, or until light and fluffy.

Wild turkey takes longer to roast than its domestic cousin because it is not as tender. Unless it is fried, I suggest browning it quickly with high temperature to seal in the juices before cooking it in a slow oven for a tender finish. The Osceola turkey is smaller than its Alabama wild cousin. Ten to twelve pounds is usually the maximum weight. The same seasonings and method of cooking will enhance any turkey, wild or domestic.

Roasted Turkey

Yield: Approximately 8 Servings

12 pound wild or domestic turkey

Salt and black pepper to sprinkle

Ground coriander to sprinkle

2 cloves garlic, peeled

2 ribs celery, chopped

1 large onion, chopped

1 small apple, chopped

1 Red navel or Parson Brown orange, cut into quarters

¼ cup olive oil

4 tablespoons melted butter

Sweet Hungarian paprika

1. Wash the turkey inside and out.
2. Sprinkle the turkey cavity with salt, pepper and coriander. Insert the garlic. Stuff the cavity with the celery, onion, apple and orange.
3. Sprinkle salt and pepper over the outside of the turkey and underneath the legs and wings. Sprinkle with the coriander.
4. Combine the olive oil with the melted butter and brush the outside of the turkey. Sprinkle with paprika. Rub it into the skin with your fingers or brush it in to create a reddish cast. Cover tightly and refrigerate overnight.
5. Preheat oven to 425°F.
6. Set a poultry holder or rack into a roasting pan. Rub the rack with oil. Place the turkey on its side on the rack and roast, uncovered, 30 minutes. Turn it over to its other side and roast another 30 minutes.
7. Reduce temperature to 300°F. Pour 1 cup hot water into the bottom of the roaster. Turn the turkey on its back (breast facing up). Roast approximately 2 hours longer. The turkey is done when the leg moves easily in its joint and the juice runs clear when a knife is inserted into the leg joint. The most accurate way to know it is cooked through is to insert a meat thermometer into the thickest part of the thigh muscle. When it registers 180°F., the turkey is done.
8. Remove the turkey from the oven and allow it to rest 20 minutes, covered lightly with aluminum foil. Remove the garlic, celery, onion, apple and orange from the cavity. Carve in the kitchen or at the table.

Note: 10-16 pound turkey should roast 15 minutes per pound. Larger birds should roast 12 minutes per pound, although it must be stated that it is unusual for the Osceola turkey to exceed 12 pounds in weight. Allow longer for a turkey cooked at the icy stage of defrosting. Fresh turkey cooks faster than that which has been frozen. Check periodically.

Alligator Tail

Most folks just cut up the alligator tail and deep fry it until tender. But, then, most folks in Central Florida just cut up everything and fry it until tender!

Alligator Tail

The first time I tasted alligator was at a canal-front dive somewhere in Lake County. A huge pile of piping hot crispy fried strips arrived with traces of wet fat dripping onto the platter. They were accompanied by a spicy tomato salsa for dipping. Biting into them produced the same sensation as that of a rather tough clam strip, but the chewy substance proved to have a more scintillating flavor than clams. When I inquired where one could purchase alligator tail, the proprietor-chef said, "Don't know. I git em from back o here. Just aim 'tween thar eyes and whack off thar tail. Tail can't be more than three feet long, though, or it'll be tough."

Most folks just cut up the alligator tail and deep fry it until tender. But, then, most folks in Central Florida just cut up everything and fry it until tender! Question any good hunter how he prepares wild turkey and venison, and he'll tell you the best recipe is no recipe. "When game is absolutely fresh, it doesn't need any embellishment. Cut out the muscle and connecting tissue, chop it into chunks, roll it in salt and pepper, dip it in flour and fry them golden. Serve a store-bought spicy sauce or salsa on the side, and dig-in."

Chain of Lakes Alligator Tenders

Yield: Approximately 6 Servings

1 pound alligator tail meat, fat and sinew removed

1 cup Seasoned Garlic Oil (recipe, page 246)

1 cup all-purpose flour or cornmeal

2 tablespoons Chain of Lakes Seasoning (recipe, page 245)

Canola or vegetable oil, mixed with peanut oil, or grape seed oil, if available

1. Pound alligator tail with a mallet to tenderize.

2. Cut alligator tail across the grain into thin strips. Roll in the oil.

3. Mix flour and seasoning in a plastic or paper bag. Toss in alligator strips and shake until coated.

4. Heat oil to 360°F. in a deep fryer. Drop strips in one at a time. Fry until strips float at the top.

These have a consistency similar to the conch fritter. They are hot and spicy and fun to nibble on with cold, cold beer.

Alligator Cocktail Fritters

Yield: Approximately 12 Fritters

1 pound alligator tail meat, finely ground

1 Florida sweet onion, chopped fine

1 green bell pepper, chopped fine

1 clove garlic, minced

½ cup all-purpose flour

2 teaspoons baking powder

⅛ teaspoon mace

½ teaspoon dry mustard

1 teaspoon salt

2 extra large eggs, beaten

2 tablespoons melted butter

1 tablespoon Worcestershire sauce

Optional: 1 teaspoon Florida hot sauce

Canola or peanut oil, or a combination

1. Grind the alligator or pulverize in a food processor. Add the chopped onion, pepper and minced garlic and pulverize with the alligator in the machine.

2. Sift the flour with the baking powder, mace, dry mustard and salt.

3. Beat the eggs. Add the flour mixture. Add the melted butter, Worcestershire and hot sauce, and combine with the alligator mixture.

4. Pour canola or peanut oil or a mixture of both into a skillet 1-inch deep. Heat to 380°F (the bubbling stage). Drop the batter 1 tablespoon at a time into the hot oil, turning the fritters over with a slotted spoon as they brown. Remove when browned on all sides.

Serve with Key Lime wedges and Tartare Sauce (recipe, page 262).

Beer Fried Alligator Tail

Yield: Approximately 6 Servings

1 pound alligator tail meat, fat and sinew removed

Regular beer (not light)

Pepper, garlic salt and onion powder

All-purpose flour for dredging

¾ canola oil mixed with ¼ peanut oil to fry

Deep fryer or pot

1. Slice alligator tail across the grain into thin strips about the length of your index finger.

2. Soak the pieces in beer overnight.

3. Drain and dry the pieces. Sprinkle lavishly with pepper, garlic salt and onion powder.

4. Pour flour into a plastic bag and coat the alligator strips.

5. Heat the combined canola and peanut oil to the boiling point and drop the alligator pieces in one at a time. Deep fry until golden brown.

Alligator with Shallots and Thyme

Yield: Approximately 6 Servings

1 pound alligator tail, fat and sinew removed

¼ cup Bearss lemon juice

¼ cup Ruby Red grapefruit juice

2 tablespoons extra virgin olive oil

1 finely-chopped red bell pepper

1 finely-chopped green bell pepper

2 minced shallots

¼ pound butter

½ teaspoon dried thyme

¼ teaspoon turmeric powder

½ teaspoon black pepper

Salt to taste

¼ cup dry white wine

Toast points

1. Slice alligator tail very thin on the diagonal across the grain.

2. Squeeze lemon and grapefruit juice over and toss well. Add the olive oil and toss again.

3. Cover and refrigerate at least 1 hour.

4. In a deep pan, Sauté the peppers and shallots in the butter until soft but not colored. Add the thyme, turmeric and pepper. Add salt to taste. Add white wine. Stir in the alligator slices and cover the pan. Simmer over low heat 20 minutes.

5. Spoon over toast points and serve immediately.

Note: The alligator slices may also be sautéed separately from the sauce as follows:

> *¾ cup fine bread crumbs*
> *¾ cup all-purpose flour*
> *1 cup half-and-half, or ½ cup milk, ½ cup coffee cream*
> *3 beaten eggs*

Combine the ingredients into a batter. Dip the slices into the batter and line them on a sheet of waxed paper in the refrigerator for at least 1 hour. Melt a combination of half butter, half olive oil to just cover the bottom of a shallow skillet. Sauté the cold pieces until lightly browned. Set them into the sauce and continue cooking over low heat until very hot. Serve immediately.

Florida alligators are aggressive only during mating season when it's wise to keep a safe distance from their gigantic heads moving in pairs through the connecting lakes of Lake County's Chain of Lakes. The remainder of the year they are really quite placid, unless you're a small cat or dog that wanders too close to the marshy shoreline where a sleepy alligator can sniff out a prized gourmet meal. They couldn't care less about the human specie, unless threatened or fed by tourists naive enough to believe they can be domesticated. The minuscule brain of this reptile cannot differentiate between "people feed me" and "people are feed", and the alligator who expects a handout and doesn't get one simply mistakes the human for his expectant meal.

Alligator with Cilantro and Garlic

Yield: Approximately 6 Servings

1 pound alligator tail, fat and sinew removed

2 whole heads garlic

3 tablespoons olive oil

¾ cup dry white wine

1 tablespoon minced shallot

1 tablespoon olive oil

Pinch of ground thyme, or ¼ teaspoon chopped fresh thyme

⅛ teaspoon grated lemon peel

⅛ teaspoon grated nutmeg

Salt to taste

1 tablespoon brandy

¼ teaspoon freshly ground black pepper

⅛ teaspoon hot Hungarian paprika, or white pepper to taste

¼ pound butter, clarified to create 6 tablespoons

½ cup heavy cream

¼ cup chopped cilantro leaves

1 cup fine bread crumbs

4 tablespoons salted butter, cut up

1. Pound alligator tail meat with a wooden meat tenderizer mallet. Cut the meat across the grain into small pieces and set aside.

2. Preheat oven to 250°F.

3. Slice off the top of each head of garlic, exposing cloves, and spread slightly apart. Place in a small baking dish. Spoon the oil over and cover dish with aluminum foil. Bake until cloves have softened, about 45 minutes.

4. Peel cloves and place in a food processor or blender with ¼ cup of the wine.

5. Cook shallot in the olive oil over low heat until soft. Add remaining ingredients, reserving the cream and cilantro. Cook over low heat another 15 minutes.

6. Stir in the cream and cilantro. Remove from heat and let stand 10 minutes. Divide into 6 shallow casserole dishes. Sprinkle with bread crumbs. Dot with butter and bake 5 minutes at 350°F.

Venison

The more tender cuts from the loin are grilled and fried in the open. The less revered cuts are more interesting to work with, lending themselves to a variety of spices and sauces.

RECIPES:

Venison Steaks with Currant Sauce

Grilled Boneless Loin

**Crockpot Sandwiches
with Red Cabbage**

**Chet Blackman's
Bodacious Barbecued Venison**

Hickory Fried Venison

Venison Stroganoff

Venison Kebabs

Venison Burgers

Roasted Leg of Venison

Venison Ragoût

Venison and Duck Pâté

Fig Sauce

Figs Dubonnet

Florida venison are a tender, mild flavored meat, low in fat and cholesterol. They are raised in controlled areas of free range, where they are grass-fed and unadulterated with hormones or steroids.

The preparation of most cuts of wild venison requires more resourcefulness than the hunt that brought it to the kitchen, although old timers still choose to simply cut the meat into medallions to deep fry. More particular chefs hang venison for at least two weeks to lessen the strong flavor. The tenderloin, rib chops and steaks may be broiled, sautéed or grilled over gas, wood or charcoal. Because the fat of deer meat is not marbled as in cattle, trimmed cuts are very low in fat. A 3.5 ounce broiled beef T-bone steak contains approximately 15.4 grams of fat as opposed to 6.4 grams of fat found in venison steak. In order to keep them from becoming dry, these steaks and the chops cut from the ribs should be eaten rare or medium rare and seasoned at the table with salt, freshly ground pepper and melted butter, and, perhaps, a light red wine sauce served on the side.

Accompaniments to venison and wild turkey are basically the same. Wild rice or risotto, green beans with almonds or pine nuts, baked squash or pumpkin mashed with cumin, coriander, ginger and butter and returned to its shell, and, of course, cranberries of any description and sautéed apples or applesauce to soften the palate. Venison is best served with champagne, but a hearty, fruity wine is most pleasant with all game.

The loin of the venison is as tender as the finest prime cuts of beef. The first taste of fresh loin chops, boneless tenderloin and filet mignon will become a memorable gourmet experience.

Venison Steaks with Currant Sauce

Yield: 4 Servings

Make the Currant Sauce:

3 tablespoons red currant jelly

1 tablespoon yellow mustard

2 tablespoons chili sauce

1. Combine ingredients in a saucepan. Bring to a boil, stirring. Lower heat to simmer to keep warm.

Make the steaks:

4 venison tenderloin steaks

Salt and pepper

4 slices bacon

1. Sprinkle salt and pepper over the steaks.
2. Wrap a slice of bacon around each, securing the open flap with a toothpick.
3. Heat a griddle or non-stick shallow skillet. Cook the steaks quickly on both sides.
4. Set steaks on plates and cover with the sauce.

Grilled Boneless Loin

Yield: 4 Servings

2 large portobello mushrooms
6 tablespoons unsalted butter
1 clove fresh garlic, crushed
Salt

Coarse black pepper
4 filets of venison from the loin, cut 1- inch thick
4 slices French bread, toasted on one side only

1. Clean mushrooms but do not soak in water. Remove stems. Slice. Melt 4 tablespoons of the butter in a skillet. Peel and crush (or chop) garlic and cook over the lowest heat for 1 minute. Carefully add mushrooms and cook quickly over medium-high heat 2 minutes only, turning with a spatula so they will not break into pieces.

2. Sprinkle filets lightly with salt and pepper. Melt 2 tablespoons butter and brush the steaks on one side. Place on a hot grill and brown. Turn, brush again, and brown on the other side. Sprinkle with salt and freshly ground pepper.

3. Place a slice of French bread on each plate, toast side down. Set a filet on top of each and spoon the mushrooms and sauce from the pan over. Serve with Piquante Boggess Sauce on the side (recipe, page 262).

Accompany with Portobello Garlic Potatoes (recipe, page 109)

Note: Check desired temperature with a meat thermometer, or press the tops with a fork. If very spongy, meat is rare. The firmer the meat is to the touch, the more done it is within. If too rare for your taste, remove the filets to the mushroom pan and cook for a minute over medium heat. Do not overcook.

Bob Tranum is an active member of the Chain-o-Lakes Gobblers chapter of the NWTF. Each hunting season he brings fresh venison to my kitchen. Although he shares only the shoulder and rump, I'm not ungrateful because I know that the more tender cuts from the loin are grilled and fried in the open among the camaraderie of these preservationists. I personally feel that the less revered cuts are more interesting to work with, lending themselves to a variety of spices and sauces.

Crockpot Sandwiches with Red Cabbage

Yield: 8-10 Servings

2 pound piece venison shoulder or rump

Black pepper

1 medium onion, chopped fine

2 cloves garlic, grated or minced

3 cups dark beer (not light)

2 tablespoons balsamic or red wine vinegar

½ teaspoon ground allspice

2 whole cloves

1 large dried bay leaf, or 2 fresh

3 juniper berries, crushed

1 branch rosemary

½ cup tomato ketchup

2 tablespoons granulated sugar

1 teaspoon Kosher salt

Electric crockpot

2 teaspoons all-purpose flour

Kaiser or sub sandwiches rolls (Hoagie)

1. Sprinkle the meat with black pepper, rubbing it in with your fingers.

2. Combine the remaining ingredients. Marinate the meat 48 hours in the refrigerator.

3. Remove meat from marinade. Pat dry with paper toweling. Sprinkle kosher salt on both sides. Brown the venison quickly over high heat in a skillet. Remove the meat to the crockpot and pour the marinade over. Turn the control to high. Cover. Cook 5-6 hours, or until tender. Cool. Refrigerate overnight.

4. Discard fat from the top of the gravy. Remove meat and slice very thin across the grain on the diagonal. The meat will fall apart. That's good.

5. Pour gravy into a pot with 2 teaspoons flour. Stir. Heat, stirring to the boiling point. Add venison. Reduce heat to simmer. Taste for salt and pepper.

6. Pile high on Kaiser or hoagie rolls.

7. Serve with Red Cabbage on the side.

Red Cabbage with Apples:
Yield: 8-10 Servings

1 red cabbage

1 Central Florida sweet onion

2 Granny Smith apples

½ cup red wine

½ teaspoon chopped dill

1 tablespoon dark brown sugar

1 cup or more beef broth

1 tablespoon red balsamic vinegar

Salt and black pepper to taste

1 tablespoon butter

1. Chop or shred the cabbage and onion. Peel, core, and chop the apples.

2. Combine with the wine, dill, and brown sugar in a heavy pot and cook, covered, until tender approximately 20 minutes, stirring in the broth as needed to keep cabbage moist. Stir in the balsamic vinegar.

3. Season with salt and pepper to taste. Stir in the butter directly before serving.

The most tender cuts of venison come from the ribs and loin. They can be broiled or grilled. When venison is fresh, it should be moist and springy, but not soft. If you purchase the meat frozen, check to see it is tightly wrapped and there is no frozen liquid surrounding it to indicate it has been thawed and refrozen.

Trim off excess fat and cut out sinew before cooking. The fat of any wild animal gives off a gamey taste. Venison becomes tough when overcooked or cooked over high heat. Wrap venison cuts in bacon or pork fat to keep it from drying out during the cooking. Roast at 300°F. (150-180₉C) approximately 15-20 minutes per pound.

Chet Blackman is the former Mayor of Leesburg and annual chairman of the Gobbler's Charity Feast.

Chet Blackman's Bodacious Barbecued Venison

Yield: 15-18 Servings

8 pounds venison leg, trimmed of fat and connective tissue

Everglades® Seasoning* or Chain of Lakes Seasoning (recipe, page 245) or commercial spicy barbecue sauce

½ cup melted butter

2 large pieces heavy aluminum foil

6 slices thick sliced bacon

Smoker (Chet has a 1,000 gallon wood smoker in case company drops in unexpectedly)

Gravy: 1 cup beef broth, ½ cup Marsala or Port wine, ½ cup red currant jelly, 1 tablespoon all-purpose flour.

1. Cut venison into large chunks or thick pieces diagonally across the grain.

2. Sprinkle heavily with Everglades® or Chain of Lakes Seasoning and toss with melted butter.

3. Place chunks on a double layer of foil. Top with bacon. Bring edges of foil up all around and seal tightly by turning over each other.

4. Heat the wood in the smoker to 200°F. Cook 4½ hours.

5. Open the foil and pour gravy into a pot. Spread out the meat. Cook, uncovered, 1 hour longer, or until the top of the meat forms a crust.

6. Allow the cooked venison to rest 20 minutes. Slice into ³/₁₆-inch thickness. Combine pan juices with Gravy recipe and stir over medium heat until thickened to pour over meat.

Note: If you season with Chain of Lakes Seasoning (recipe, page 245), mix 2 teaspoons Ponderosa lemon juice and 1 teaspoon Worcestershire sauce with ¼ cup of the dry seasoning to create a paste.

Note: Everglades Seasoning is made in LaBelle, Florida. It can be ordered from Everglades Foods, Inc., P.O. Box 595, LaBelle, Florida 33975, or call 1-800-689-2221.

Hickory Fried Venison

Yield: 8 Servings

¼ Saddle of Venison, approximate weight 4 pounds trimmed.

Hurricane Bay Hickory Marinade®, manufactured by Florida Gourmet Foods in Deland, Florida

All-purpose flour

Canola or vegetable oil, mixed with peanut oil, or grapeseed oil, if available

1. Cut venison into chunks. Saturate with the hickory marinade and refrigerate 48 hours.
2. Remove venison from the marinade and pat dry with paper toweling.
3. Pour flour into a plastic or paper bag. Toss in venison and shake until coated.
4. Heat oil to 360°F. in a deep fryer. Drop venison pieces in one at a time. Fry until venison floats at the top.

Venison Stroganoff

Yield: 6 Servings

2 pounds Venison tenderloin

3 tablespoons unsalted butter

2 large shallots, sliced very thin

1 pound white mushrooms, sliced thin

2 tablespoons tomato ketchup

1 teaspoon dry mustard

2 tablespoons all-purpose flour

2¼ cups broth made from venison bones, or concentrated beef broth

Optional: ½ ounce black truffle peelings

⅓ cup Madeira wine

1 cup sour cream

1. Slice the venison into fairly thick strips. Sprinkle lightly with salt and black pepper. Set aside.
2. Melt 1 tablespoon of the butter in a large, heavy skillet. Peel and slice the shallots and mushrooms. Cook over low heat until soft but not colored. Remove to a serving platter.
3. Add remaining butter to the skillet. Sear the venison quickly over high heat on both sides. Do not overcook. Beef should be rare at this point. Remove slices to the platter with the mushroom mixture.
4. Mix the ketchup with the mustard and stir into the skillet with the juices from the beef. Stir in the flour. Add the beef broth, stirring over medium heat until thickened.
5. Mix the truffle peelings with the wine and stir into the gravy. Turn heat to simmer. Return the meat and mushroom mixture to the skillet. Stir in the sour cream and serve immediately.

Note: Serve with cooked wide egg noodles on the side that have been tossed with salt and butter or oil.

Venison Kebabs

Yield: 8 Skewers

2 pounds venison tenderloin

4 tablespoons extra virgin olive oil

2 cloves crushed garlic

1 teaspoon cumin powder

1 teaspoon coriander powder

1 teaspoon ground ginger powder

1 tablespoon chili powder

2 teaspoons salt, or to taste

½ teaspoon black pepper

½ cup venison or beef broth

2 large green bell peppers, cut into 1-inch squares

2 large red bell peppers, cut into 1-inch squares

24 boiler onions

16 medium mushrooms

8 plum tomatoes, seeded and halved

1. Cut the venison into 1-inch squares Combine oil, garlic, seasonings and broth and marinate several hours.

2. Alternate the meat and vegetables on the skewers. Broil or grill, basting frequently.

Note: Before placing the onions on the skewers, cut off the root ends and drop into boiling water for a few seconds. The outer skins will slip off easily when you peel them under cold, running water.

Venison Burgers

Yield: 4 Burgers

1½ pounds ground venison

¾ pound pork sausage with sage

½ cup cold water

1 teaspoon salt

1 teaspoon pepper

1. Combine ingredients and form into burgers. Refrigerate until very cold. Grill or pan fry. Serve with the same accompaniments as beef hamburgers.

Note: The addition of water keeps the burgers from drying out during the cooking.

Roasted Leg of Venison

Yield: 8-10 Servings

Cooked Marinade:

1 large onion, chopped fine

3 celery ribs, chopped fine

3 large garlic cloves, grated or chopped fine

Handful fresh parsley leaves, chopped fine

2 large bay leaves

6 juniper berries, crushed

1 teaspoon crumbled sage leaves, or ½ teaspoon
   dried

1 teaspoon whole allspice berries

1 tablespoon minced fresh thyme leaves

Several fresh tarragon leaves, chopped fine

2 cups red Burgundy wine

½ cup olive oil

Whole leg of venison, well-trimmed

1. Reserving the olive oil, combine the rest of the ingredients in a pot and bring to a boil. Reduce heat to medium and cook gently 15 minutes. Cool to room temperature. Strain. Add the olive oil.

2. Wipe the venison meat well with a red vinegar-soaked cloth and marinate the leg or loin or haunch of the venison in the refrigerator at least 36 hours. Remove and pat dry with paper toweling to cook, reserving the marinade for basting.

To Roast:

Flour seasoned with salt and pepper

8 strips thick cut bacon or larding pork cut into
   long strips

1. Preheat oven to 450°F.

2. Season the flour with salt and pepper. Dredge the meat and shake off excess. Wrap the meat with the bacon and place in a roasting pan. Roast at 450°F. 20 minutes. Reduce temperature to 325°F. Baste heavily with the marinade. Roast 20 minutes per pound, basting every 15 minutes. The leg should be thoroughly cooked without any traces of pink.

3. Serve with currant sauce on the side.

Sauce:

1 cup red Burgundy wine

2 tablespoons red wine vinegar

3 tablespoons granulated sugar

2 tablespoons lemon juice

12 ounces red currant jelly

1. Bring ½ cup of the wine to a boil with the rest of the ingredients. Boil 5 minutes, stirring. Remove from the heat and stir in the remaining ½ cup wine. Cook gently another 5 minutes. This sauce may be made several days in advance. Warm to serve with Roasted Leg or Loin of Venison or lamb.

Venison Ragoût

Yield: 6-8 Servings

3-4 pounds meat from the shoulder or leg of venison

¼ cup chopped porcini dried mushrooms

1-2 cloves garlic, minced

1 green bell pepper, chopped

1 large onion, chopped

1 tablespoon minced fresh parsley

1 teaspoon minced fresh thyme

1 teaspoon minced fresh oregano leaves

Several young rosemary branches

Several fresh basil leaves

1 bay leaf

1 cup Cabernet Sauvignon red wine

1¼ cups rich beef broth (10 ounce can)

3 tablespoons tomato paste

14.5 ounce canned diced tomatoes of choice

Salt and pepper

Flour to dredge

1 cup vegetable oil (or, to cover the bottom of a large deep skillet)

8 or more red bliss potatoes

Baby carrots, or large carrots, sliced thick

1. Rinse the porcini mushrooms with warm water. Soak in hot water to soften. Pour off the water. Rinse again. Chop fine.

2. Combine mushrooms, garlic, green pepper, onion, parsley, thyme, oregano, rosemary, basil, bay leaf, wine, beef broth, tomato paste and diced tomatoes in a large container and cover the venison. Marinate in the refrigerator 48 hours.

3. Preheat oven to 350°F.

4. Remove the venison from the marinade and cut into large pieces, approximately 2-inches in diameter. Season with salt and pepper. Put flour in a bag and add a few at a time to coat.

4. Cover the bottom of a large skillet with vegetable oil over high heat. Brown the meat on both sides and remove to a roasting pan.

6. Pour the marinade over. Cover the roaster tightly and set into the oven. Cook 3 hours, or until very tender. Cool completely. Refrigerate overnight for the flavors to incorporate.

7. Return to the roaster and in a 300°F oven. Cook 35-40 minutes, or until very hot.

8. Cover carrots with water and boil until tender. Cut a small strip around each potato so the skins will not "pop". Cover with water and cook until tender.

9. Spoon venison and gravy into a large deep serving dish with the carrots and potatoes. Serve with fresh bread or rolls to mop up the gravy.

Note: Ragoût freezes beautifully.

Venison and Duck Pâté

Yield: 10-12 Servings

Approximately 6 ounces livers from 2 ducks (Do not use gizzards or hearts)

8 ounces tenderloin of venison

4 ounces white mushrooms, sliced

2 large shallots, peeled and sliced

2 large cloves garlic (not elephant), peeled and sliced

1 teaspoon salt

1 teaspoon black pepper

⅛ teaspoon ground allspice

½ teaspoon ground thyme

4 ounces thick cut bacon

1 jumbo graded egg, beaten

1 ounce black truffle peelings or 1 tablespoon truffle oil, if available

2 tablespoons cognac or brandy

Best Flaky Pie Crust (recipe, page 264)

8-inch fluted deep tart or spring-form pan

1 jumbo graded egg yolk, beaten with 2 tablespoons milk

1. Preheat oven to 350°F. Roll the pastry dough thin and cover the bottom and sides of the pan or spring-form. Set a piece of parchment paper on the bottom and fill pan with dried beans. Bake 10 minutes. Remove from oven to cool.

2. Combine livers, sliced venison, shallots, garlic, mushrooms, salt, pepper, allspice and thyme and toss together.

3. Cook bacon until done but not crisp. Add liver mixture and simmer, covered, over lowest heat, until just done, turning several times. Do not overcook or livers will become bitter and Venison tough. Cool to room temperature.

4. Pulverize with the juices from the pan in a food processor.

5. Beat the egg. Mix the truffle peelings (oil) with the cognac and fold into the pâté.

6. Fill with the pâté. Roll out remaining pastry dough to cover the top. Cut out thick shapes of hearts with a cookie cutter from remaining dough and set them around the top. Refrigerate 1 hour.

7. Preheat oven to 400°F.

8. Brush the top crust with the egg yolk-milk mixture. Bake 20-25 minutes, or until golden brown. Remove from oven to cool slightly.

9. Refrigerate overnight. The flavors are best when made a day or two in advance. Serve as an hors d'oeuvre with thinly sliced black bread or as a first course with Fig Sauce or Figs Dubonnet (recipes follow).

Figs in Central Florida?!? Yes! We can grow figs in Central Florida, although they are certainly not prolific. It's sort of a backyard thing, where we relish the small crop when they ripen. The Black Mission Fig from California may be substituted.

Fig Sauce

2 cups Chianti wine

¾ cup light brown sugar

2 pounds very ripe Florida Green Ischia figs

1. Combine wine and sugar in a deep pot. Bring to a boil. Remove stems from whole figs and add. Boil 5 minutes, turning figs over several times with a spatula.

2. Reduce heat to medium and place a cover over the pot on a tilt to allow the steam to escape. Boil gently another 5 minutes. Cool to room temperature.

3. Pulverize in a food processor for sauce. Serve warm or cold.

Figs Dubonnet

1 pound Florida Green Ischia figs

1 cup Dubonnet (apéritif) wine

1 teaspoon cinnamon

1 tablespoon granulated sugar

1. Set the figs, wine, cinnamon and sugar in a shallow pan, so the figs will be covered by the Dubonnet mixture.

2. Bring to a boil. Cover and simmer gently 10 minutes. Remove cover to cool before refrigerating.

Miscellaneous

RECIPES:

Chain of Lakes Seasoning

Spicy Herbal Seasoning

Seasoned Garlic Oil

Clarified Butter

Parmesan Garlic Croutons

Crème Fraîche

Genoise Cake

Ganache Frosting

Praline Topping

Orange Butter

Eggs Benedict

Sorrento Onion Soup

The mixture of spices with sugar is similar to Jamaican Jerk. I have named it Chain of Lakes because the spices within create a mucky brown color; the unfortunate result of one hundred years of tampering with our once beautiful Harris Chain of Lakes. The headwater lake, Lake Apopka, is where much of the problem began because of the run-off of pesticides and fertilizer from the Zellwood corn farms. As it flowed into Lake Beauclair, Lake Dora, Lake Eustis, Lake Griffin (the headwater of the Ocklawaha River), Lake Harris and Little Lake Harris, these lakes were directly affected, first by the muck farms and now by the attempt to restore Lake Apopka. It will most likely take a generation of years and millions of dollars to restore what nature gifted to us.

Chain of Lakes Seasoning

Yield: ½ Cup

2 tablespoons ground allspice

3 tablespoons dark brown sugar, packed

2 tablespoons garlic salt

1 teaspoon (more or less, as desired) cayenne
   pepper

1 teaspoon ground thyme

1 tablespoon onion powder

1 teaspoon cinnamon

¼ teaspoon nutmeg

½ teaspoon chili powder

1. Combine ingredients into a plastic bag. Shake well to combine. Pour into an airtight container to store at room temperature indefinitely.

To marinate game or fowl:

1. Rub a thin layer over the entire surface. If cuts of meat are thick, slit the flesh in several places and insert the rub.

To grill or cook in pan:

1. Brush the meat with melted unsalted butter or seasoned oil and grill slowly over lowest gas setting or white coals. If you cook in a pan on a stove or over an open grill, do so in an iron skillet. A heavy non-stick pan will also work. Cook over very high heat. After grilling or pan frying, brush again with olive oil or melted butter. Remove from the heat and cover for just a minute for ultimate succulence.

Note: Jamaicans use allspice (pimiento) branches mixed with charcoal for the unique flavor synonymous with their food. Any aromatic wood added to the barbecue grill will enhance the flavor.

Spicy Herbal Seasoning

½ teaspoon ground thyme

½ teaspoon ground oregano

¼ teaspoon black pepper

½ teaspoon hot Hungarian paprika or a pinch of cayenne pepper

½ teaspoon salt

¼ teaspoon garlic powder

½ teaspoon onion powder

1. Measure ingredients into a small plastic bag and shake to incorporate. Pour into a small airtight container.

Seasoned Garlic Oil

Yield: 1 Liter

1 liter olive oil

1 branch rosemary

3-4 chopped basil leaves

1 sprig fresh oregano, or 1 teaspoon dried

1 sprig fresh thyme, or ½ teaspoon powdered

4 large cloves garlic, peeled and quartered to fit into the neck of the bottle

¼ teaspoon cayenne pepper

1 full teaspoon ground black pepper

1. Insert the spices and seasonings into a liter bottle of oil to marinate. Store in a cool place or refrigerate.

Note: Bring the bottle to the table to use as a substitute for butter. Brush on French or Italian bread and heat or toast for Portobello Bruschetta (recipe, page 103). Toss with pasta and top with Parmesan or chopped Gorgonzola cheese, with or without the addition of fresh chopped plum, tomatoes. Use as a base for escargot. Brush on fish or chicken to broil or grill. Add vinegar to use as a salad dressing. Add salt as needed for each recipe, but not as part of the marinade.

Clarified Butter

Unsalted butter is best for clarified butter. You lose approximately one-third of the volume when you separate the milk solids, so gauge amounts before clarifying. Below are three methods.

Stove Top Method:
1. Melt butter in a small saucepan. Bring just to the bubbly point, but do not boil. Remove from the stove and skim off the top foam. Allow to stand until lukewarm, and, wither strain through cheesecloth or pour off as much yellow liquid as possible, leaving the white milk at the bottom. You can also refrigerate the clarified butter as is and remove the yellow top when solidified, warming it before use.

Oven Method:
1. Put the butter into a small dish and melt at 325°F. until it begins to bubble. Remove from the oven to cool and follow the directions for the Stove Top Method.

Microwave Method:
1. This is easiest of all. Cut up the butter and set into a glass cup. Lightly cover and microwave on high for 30 seconds. Pour off the yellow clarified butter and discard the milk solids.

Parmesan Garlic Croutons

1 pound loaf French or Italian bread
½ cup Seasoned Garlic Oil (recipe, page 246)
1 tablespoon salt

1 tablespoon black pepper
1 cup grated Parmesan cheese

1. Preheat oven to 250°F.

2. Slice bread rather thick. Cut slices into cubes.

3. Remove the bread cubes to a plastic bag and pour in the seasoned oil, salt and pepper. Shake well, turning the bag upside down. Add the Parmesan cheese over and repeat.

4. When the bread is saturated with the oil mixture, separate the cubes and place on a baking sheet. Do not pile. You may have to do this in batches or on two baking sheets. Leave in the oven 1 hour or longer until cubes are dry and crisp. Cool and store in an airtight container. These may be frozen.

Genoise Cake

2 (9-inch) Layers

4 tablespoons unsalted butter, clarified to make 3 tablespoons

1 teaspoon vanilla

1 cup sifted all-purpose flour

¾ cup granulated sugar

4 jumbo graded eggs

2 9-inch round cake pans

1. Preheat oven to 350°F. Line bottoms of pans with parchment paper.

2. Combine butter and vanilla and keep warm in a bowl over simmering water.

3. Combine sugar and eggs in a bowl. Set the bowl over a pot of simmering water, and beat the mixture with a hand electric beater set on high speed until almost white in color. It will have tripled in bulk and have a very thick consistency.

4. Sift ⅓ of the flour over the egg mixture. Fold in by hand. Add the remaining flour a little at a time. Spoon 1 cup of the batter into another bowl and combine with the warm butter and vanilla, folding together with a rubber spatula. When combined, fold butter mixture completely into the batter.

5. Spoon batter into the pans. Bake 25 minutes, or until cake bounces back when touched in the center.

Ganache Frosting

Yield: 3½ Cups

1½ cups heavy cream
4 tablespoons unsalted butter
4 tablespoons granulated sugar

⅓ cup strong liquid coffee
14 ounces semisweet chocolate chips or finely-chopped chocolate

1. Combine the cream, butter and sugar in a saucepan. Cook together, stirring constantly, until mixture reaches the boiling point. Stir in the coffee.

2. Put the chocolate in a bowl and pour the boiling mixture over it. Do not stir until the chocolate has melted (about 5 minutes). Stir with a whisk until just smooth. Do not over-stir. Set aside, covered with plastic wrap or wax paper, until cool. Refrigerate approximately 2 hours, or until ganache begins to thicken.

3. Place the bottom layer of a 9 or 10-inch cake upside down on a cake plate. Spread ½ of the ganache over. Refrigerate until set, approximately ½ hour. Return the other half of the ganache to the refrigerator.

4. Set the remaining layer over and pour ganache over the top. Spread it around the sides. Refrigerate the cake until the ganache has set.

Note: If the ganache thickens to the point it cannot be poured, allow it to come to room temperature before attempting to cover the layers.

Praline Topping

Yield: 4 Cups

3 cups sugar

½ cup water

4 cups whole blanched almonds

Baking sheet

1. Preheat oven to 275°F.

2. Boil sugar and water over medium heat, stirring and washing down sugar residue clinging to the sides of the pan with a pastry brush that has been dipped ice water.

3. Cook the syrup until it turns a light brown. Add almonds and stir until all nuts are coated and syrup begins to bubble.

4. Transfer to a cookie sheet. Bake 45 minutes. Cool to room temperature.

5. Put the almonds into a plastic bag. Chop or smash almonds with a hammer until pulverized. Store tightly covered.

Orange Butter

Filling or frosting for cakes

Yield: 3 Cups

⅓ cup Valencia orange juice

½ pound unsalted butter, softened

2 tablespoons Grand Marnier liqueur

Grated rind of 1 Valencia orange

4 cups sifted 10X powdered sugar

1. Combine ingredients in a bowl and beat with an electric mixer until smooth. Spread between layers and over cake.

Eggs Benedict

Yield: 4 Servings

1 small sweet Florida onion, chopped

1 clove garlic, crushed

1 small red bell pepper, chopped

1 small yellow bell pepper, chopped

2 tomatoes, peeled, seeded and chopped

¼ pound small whole American white mushroom caps

2 tablespoons butter

Salt and pepper

Pinch of cayenne pepper

8 thick slices French bread or English muffins, toasted

16 slices smoked ham, sliced thin

1 tablespoon butter

1 cup water

1 teaspoon salt

8 eggs, cold from the refrigerator

Hollandaise Sauce (recipe, page 258)

1. Sauté the onion, garlic, peppers, tomatoes and whole mushroom caps in 2 tablespoons butter. Add salt and pepper to taste, and a pinch of cayenne pepper. Remove from the heat and set aside.

2. Toast the bread and set 2 slices on each plate. Top each with 2 slices ham. Set in a warm place.

3. Melt 1 tablespoon butter in a skillet. Add 1 cup water and 1 teaspoon salt. Bring to the boiling point. Take the eggs directly from the refrigerator and crack them into the water. (The whites remain intact when they enter the water cold.) Lower heat to medium and watch carefully for the point at which you like them cooked. Remove the eggs with a slotted spoon to drain. Set an egg on top of the ham. Spoon Hollandaise Sauce over each (recipe, page 258).

4. While the eggs cook, return the sautéed onion mixture to the stove to become very hot. Divide among the four plates.

Sorrento Onion Soup, Quick and Easy

2 Servings

1 large sweet Sorrento or Vidalia onion

2 tablespoons butter or butter substitute

1 tablespoon cream sherry

1 tablespoon brandy or cognac

1 tablespoon Wondra® Sauce and Gravy flour

10-ounce can Campbell's® beef broth

½ - ¾ can water to taste

2 slices French bread, cut to cover the soup crock

2 slices mozzarella cheese

¼ cup grated Parmesan or Romano cheese

1. Slice the onion into thin circles. Cut the circles in half.

2. Sauté the onion in butter until soft. Add the sherry and cognac and continue to cook over low heat until onions take on color.

3. Stir in the flour.

4. Stir in the beef broth and water and bring to a boil, stirring constantly. Lower heat to simmer and cover until ready to serve.

5. Toast the bread on one side. Fill 2 individual oven-proof soup crocks with the soup.

6. Set a slice of bread on top, toasted side down. Set a slice of mozzarella cheese on top of each. Cover mozzarella with grated Parmesan. Set under the broiler to bubble and brown. Serve.

Sauces

RECIPES:

Buerre Blanc Sauce

Cilantro Sauce for Seafood

Citrus Butter for Fish

Citrus Sauce for Crêpes

Vanilla Sauce

Cucumber-Dill Sauce

Dijon Mustard Sauce

Hollandaise Sauce (Blender Method)

Lemon Sauce for Shrimp

Mayonnaise

Spicy Mayonnaise

Meyer Lemon Sauce

Mustard Sauce

Mustard Sauce Too

Oriental Sauce

Pesto Sauce

Quick Red Horserasish

Piquante Boggess Sauce

Red Cocktail Sauce

Tartare Sauce

Buerre Blanc Sauce

Yield: Approximately 2 Cups

¼ cup minced white scallion bulbs

2 tablespoons white balsamic vinegar

½ cup dry white wine

1 teaspoon salt

⅛ teaspoon white pepper

1 pound cold unsalted butter, chopped into small pieces

Optional: 1 or more cloves garlic, minced

1. Bring scallion bulbs and vinegar to a boil in a saucepan. Boil 5 minutes. Strain into the top of a double boiler or bowl set over simmering water.

2. Add the butter, a little at a time, beating with a hand electric mixer or wire whisk. When all the butter has been added and the sauce thickens, pour over broiled or grilled fish to serve.

Cilantro Sauce for Seafood

Yield: 2 Cups

1¾ cups mayonnaise

1 tablespoon Dijon mustard

2 tablespoons white horseradish

1 tablespoon chopped cilantro leaves

Salt and pepper to taste

1 tablespoon Key or Persian lime juice

Cilantro leaves for garnish

Optional: Chopped anchovies and capers

1. Combine ingredients, stirring well. Mix with cold seafood for salad, or serve hot in ramekins. This is also an excellent accompaniment to broiled fish.

Citrus Butter for Fish

Yield: ½ Cup

1 tablespoon Key lime juice

2 tablespoons juice from the Hamlin or Blood orange

1 tablespoon juice from the Sunburst Tangerine

1 tablespoon juice from the Ruby Red grapefruit

1 teaspoon minced fresh ginger

¼ pound cold butter

1. Combine juices with the ginger over medium heat and cook, stirring, 5 minutes. Stir in dried fruit. Cut in butter, stirring until blended. Do not boil.

2. Spoon over baked or blackened fish.

Citrus Sauce for Crêpes

Yield: 1¼ Cups

¼ cup granulated sugar

½ cup freshly squeezed juice from Florida Blood orange

2 tablespoons Meyer lemon juice

1-ounce Kirsch liqueur

2-ounces Cointreau liqueur

1-ounce Grand Marnier liqueur

1. Combine sugar, orange and lemon juice, Kirsch, Cointreau and Grand Marnier in a saucepan and bring to a boil. Remove immediately from the heat. Cool and pour into a glass container. Refrigerate, covered. This may be made several days and up to a week in advance.

At Table:

4 tablespoons Clarified Butter, unsalted (recipe page 247)

Rind of 1 large red Blood or Red Valencia orange, slivered very thin without any white pith

Rind of 1 Meiwa (oval) kumquat, slivered very thin

12 dessert crêpes

2 ounces brandy, such as Martel, Courvoisier or Remy Martin

1 ounce Grand Marnier

Réchaud or shallow pan set over an open flame

2 forks - 1 ladle

1. Heat the sauce before bringing it to the table.

2. Melt the butter in the pan and stir in the slivered rinds. Add the sauce. Add the crêpes, one at a time, folding them into halves or squares or rolling them with the help of two forks. As each one is folded, push it to the side to make room for the others. Bring the sauce to a boil and pour some of the brandy into a ladle. Ignite it with a match, and add it to the sauce. Pour in the rest of the liqueur and allow it to flame while you ladle the sauce over the crêpes.

Note: This is a beautiful show. Learn the technique and enjoy the applause. Henri Charpentier (1880-1961) credited himself as the inventor. He recounts his apprenticeship as a "commis des rangs" (assistant waiter) at the Café de Paris in Monte Carlo when he was fifteen years old in his book The Henri Charpentier Cookbook. Edward, Prince of Wales, son of Queen Victoria, was apparently dining with friends when Henri was instructed to heat the sauce for the crêpes and serve them. He became so flustered that he spilled some into the fire, which ignited the entire pan. A child dining at the table was so delighted that the Prince requested the flaming dessert be named Crêpes Suzette in her honor. The sauce above is my version of the original - different but similar in concept.

Vanilla Sauce

Yield: 2½ Cups

4 extra large egg yolks

1 cup whole milk, hot but not boiling

1 cup heavy cream, hot but not boiling

½ cup granulated sugar

1 tablespoon vanilla

Optional: 2 tablespoons Kahlúa or Grand Marnier liqueur

1. Separate eggs, reserving the whites in an air-tight container in the refrigerator.

2. Heat the milk and cream together in a saucepan or microwave 1 minute, stir, microwave 30 seconds longer.

3. Stir ¼ of the warm mixture into the yolks and pour through a strainer into a saucepan.

4. Cook over medium heat, stirring constantly with a wooden spoon 7-8 minutes, or until mixture begins to thicken. Do not allow mixture to boil. Dip a stainless steel spoon into the mixture. When a thin layer adheres to the spoon, the sauce is done. Remove from the heat and stir in vanilla (and liqueur). Lower heat to simmer and cook approximately 30 seconds or until blended.

5. Strain into a container. Cover and refrigerate at least 24 hours. The sauce will thicken in the refrigerator and remain fresh up to 1 week. Serve in a sauceboat to accompany the soufflé or with fresh berries.

Note: This is more difficult than the recipe appears. A few seconds can make the difference between a beautiful sauce and a curdled disaster. The sauce does not thicken. It changes consistency. When you feel it change, dip the spoon in immediately. When you remove the spoon, a very thin amount will adhere to it.

Cucumber-Dill Sauce

Yield: 8 Cups

4 cups homemade Mayonnaise (recipe, page 259)

2 cups thick sour cream

2 tablespoons white horseradish

3 cups chopped scallion greens

½ cup peeled, seeded and chopped cucumbers

½ cup chopped fresh dill weed

½ cup tiny capers, or chopped large capers

¼ teaspoon white pepper, or more to taste

½ teaspoon sea salt, or more to taste

1. Combine ingredients and serve in a sauceboat to accompany sautéed Talapia, Bass, or Blue Crab recipes.

Dijon Mustard Sauce

Yield: 1⅓ cups

½ cup Dijon mustard

½ teaspoon dry mustard

½ cup mayonnaise

⅓ cup sour cream

½ teaspoon chopped dill weed

1 teaspoon chopped fresh tarragon leaves

1 teaspoon Persian lime juice

1. Combine ingredients and refrigerate.

Note: May be doubled several times.

Hollandaise Sauce (Blender Method)

Yield: Approximately 1½ Cups

4 extra large egg yolks

2 tablespoons Bearss lemon juice

½ teaspoon salt

Pinch cayenne pepper or dry mustard

¼ pound (1 stick) unsalted butter, melted

Optional: 1 teaspoon minced fresh parsley

1. Place yolks in blender. Turn on-off to blend. Add lemon juice, salt and cayenne or mustard (or both). Turn on high speed 10 seconds. Turn motor off. Add a drop of butter and turn on high speed for a few seconds. Turn off. Add 2 drops and do the same. Turn on high speed and begin pouring the butter in a thin slow stream. As it thickens, continue adding butter until mixture is thick.

2. Remove to the top of a double boiler set over boiling water. Stir constantly while mixture reaches the boiling point to secure safety of egg yolks. Do not allow it to boil or it will curdle. Sauce may be held, covered, over hot water no longer than one hour. Spoon over asparagus or Eggs Benedict (recipe, page 251).

Note: if mixture must stand for any length of time, pour the sauce into a glass bowl set into hot water. If mixture becomes too thick or lumps, add a tablespoon or two of cold water and stir over simmering water.

Lemon Sauce for Shrimp

Yield: 2 Cups

¼ cup minced white scallion bulbs

1 tablespoon Worcestershire sauce

½ teaspoon salt

1 cup lemon juice of choice

1 cup dry light sherry

½ cup unsalted butter, softened

¾ cup yellow mustard

1. Mince the scallion bulbs fine. Combine with the Worcestershire, salt, lemon juice and sherry in a saucepan.

2. Mix the butter with the mustard together until smooth and add to the saucepan. Boil 5 minutes, stirring constantly. Serve over grilled or broiled shrimp.

Note: This sauce will keep in the refrigerator several weeks.

Mayonnaise

Yield: Approximately 2 Cups

4 extra large egg yolks, room temperature

½ teaspoon salt

⅛ teaspoon white pepper

⅛ teaspoon dry mustard

3 tablespoons fresh lemon juice

1¾ cups vegetable oil

1. Beat egg yolks in a glass bowl with a hand electric beater on medium speed for about 30 seconds.

2. Add salt, pepper, mustard and lemon.

3. Add oil, drop by drop, on medium speed. As mixture begins to thicken, begin to pour the oil in a slow, steady stream until it is very thick.

Spicy Mayonnaise

2 tablespoons white horseradish

2 tablespoons chopped fresh dill weed

1. Stir into completed Mayonnaise by hand.

We are fortunate to have Meyer lemon trees in our grove in Central Florida. Each mammoth delicate fruit yields an excess of a half cup juice. The trees are so prolific that the lemons weigh the limbs to the ground. Each year we invite children in the area to pick them to sell for the benefit of their churches and schools.

Meyer Lemon Sauce to Accompany Fish and Shellfish

Yield: Approximately 1¼ Cups

3 tablespoons Meyer lemon juice (Other lemons will do, but not as well)

1 cup mayonnaise

1 tablespoon minced cilantro leaves (Dill may be substituted, if it is your preference)

½ teaspoon seeded and minced chapolte peppers or jalapeño peppers

1 tablespoon minced scallion greens

1. Stir together in the top of a double boiler over simmering water until warm. Serve with crab cakes, soft shell crab or grilled fish.

Mustard Sauce

Yield: 2 Cups

½ cup yellow mustard

1 tablespoon white horseradish

2 teaspoons Dijon mustard

1 cup mayonnaise

2 tablespoons Meyer lemon juice

1 tablespoon finely chopped curly leaf parsley

Tiny capers to top

1. Combine above ingredients, stirring smooth.

Mustard Sauce Too

Yield: 2 Cups

1 cup mayonnaise

1 cup strong mustard (Dijon is best)

1 tablespoon white horseradish

1 teaspoon lemon juice

Optional: Pinch of cayenne pepper

1. Mix together and refrigerate 1 hour or longer.

Oriental Sauce

Yield: Approximately 3½ Cups

This is a marvelous accompaniment to dip shrimp or serve with grilled or broiled fish.

⅓ cup Chinese hot mustard

⅓ cup rice wine vinegar

⅓ cup Tamari natural soy sauce

½ cup Orange Blossom honey

1 tablespoon fresh ginger, peeled and finely chopped

1 teaspoon fresh garlic, peeled and finely chopped

⅓ cup sesame oil

1½ cups Italian olive oil

½ cup chopped scallion greens and thinly slivered white bulbs

Key limes or Meyer lemons to garnish

1. Reserving the scallions, combine all ingredients in a blender. Turn on high and blend. Refrigerate.

2. Sauce will keep several weeks.

Pesto Sauce

Yield: Approximately 2 Cups

2 cups firmly packed minced fresh basil leaves

8 large cloves garlic

3 ounces walnuts

½ teaspoon salt

½ teaspoon black pepper

⅓ cup extra virgin olive oil

Extra virgin olive oil to top

1. Wash and dry basil leaves. Peel and slice garlic cloves. Place together into a food processor and mince. Add walnuts and mince again. Add salt, pepper and oil and turn machine on-off to blend.

2. Spoon into airtight containers. Pour olive oil over the top so pesto will not turn brown.

Quick Red Horseradish

Yield: Approximately 1 Cup

½ cup bottled white horseradish   2 ounces cooked fresh beets (1 medium beet)

1. Purée in blender. This is so much better than the bottled red found in the supermarkets.

Piquante Boggess Sauce

Yield: 3½ Cups

10 ounce jar yellow mango chutney   ¼ cup Worcestershire sauce
1 cup chili sauce   ¼ cup A-1® sauce
1 cup ketchup   Florida hot sauce to taste

1. Mix together. Serve on the side with grilled tenderloin of venison or game fish.

Red Cocktail Sauce

Yield: 2 Cups

2 cups chili sauce   Optional: 1 tablespoon sweet pickle relish
4 tablespoons white horseradish

1. Combine ingredients together and refrigerate.

Tartare Sauce

Yield: 3½ Cups

2 cups mayonnaise   4 tablespoons minced parsley
4 tablespoons minced scallion greens or chives   4 tablespoons minced olives with pimentos
4 tablespoons minced dill pickles   1 tablespoon Bearss lemon juice

1. Chop ingredients very fine with a chef's knife, not in a food processor. The sauce will remain fresh several days in the refrigerator.

Pie Crusts

RECIPES:

Best Flaky Pie Crust

Sablé Pastry

Pecan Crust

Short Pie Crust

Sweet Pie Shell for Tarts

Baking Powder Dough

Best Flaky Pie Crust

Yield: 3 (9-inch) single crusts for a crowd or to freeze

5 cups all-purpose flour

1 teaspoon salt

1 tablespoon granulated sugar

1 teaspoon baking powder

8 ounces solid vegetable shortening, or 4-ounces vegetable shortening mixed with 4-ounces lard

¾ pound salted butter, softened

½ cup ice water

1. Sift together flour, salt, sugar and baking powder.

2. Combine shortening and butter. Work in flour ⅓ rd. at a time.

3. Slowly work in the ice water until dough is soft and pliable. Refrigerate in a covered bowl or wax paper several hours.

4. Bring to room temperature. Separate into thirds. Roll to fit 3 (9-inch) pie plates, leaving ¼-inch excess around the sides. Pinch the dough around the edges to create a fluted design. Refrigerate until very cold before baking, or cover and freeze for later.

5. Preheat oven to 350°F.

6. For precooked or fresh fruit pies, set the crust into the oven directly from the refrigerator or freezer and bake approximately 15 minutes, or until lightly browned around the edges. Cool completely before filling.

7. To fill with ingredients to be baked in the crust: Spoon ingredients into cold shell and bake immediately, timing individual pies according to recipe.

Sablé Pastry shell for fruit tart

Yield: 1 (8-inch) Tart

6 ounces unsalted butter

6 ounces 10X powdered sugar, sifted

2 jumbo eggs, lightly beaten

3 tablespoons heavy cream

12 ounces sifted all-purpose flour

1 whole egg mixed with 1 yolk for the glaze

1. Preheat oven to 350°F.

2. Beat butter and sugar until light and fluffy.

3. Add eggs, one at a time, beating well after each addition.

4. Beat in cream.

5. Add flour all at once, beating until mixture is smooth. Wrap in wax paper or plastic wrap. Refrigerate several hours.

6. Roll out pastry into ½-inch thickness. Line an 8-inch tart ring and place a circle of parchment paper on top. Sprinkle center with hard, dried beans.

7. Bake 20 minutes. Remove beans and paper. Bake until pastry is golden.

8. Mix 1 whole egg with 1 yolk. Brush the crust all over. Return to oven for 2 minutes to glaze.

Pecan Crust

Yield: 9-inch tart

½ cup unsalted butter, softened

6 tablespoons light brown sugar, packed

1 cup all-purpose flour

¾ cup finely chopped pecans

9-inch fluted tart pan with removable bottom

1. Combine butter, brown sugar and flour.

2. Chop pecans fine in a food processor and add to butter mixture. Mix well until thoroughly incorporated.

3. Press dough on the bottom and up the sides of the tart pan. Refrigerate at least 1 hour, or until dough is cold and firm. Dough may be frozen, covered.

4. Preheat oven to 375°F.

5. Line the crust with foil and fill with dried beans. Bake 10 minutes. Remove beans and foil and bake until the crust turns a golden brown.

Short Pie Crust

Yield: To fill the bottom of an 8 or 9-inch pie plate

2 cups all-purpose flour

1 teaspoon salt

½ teaspoon baking powder

½ cup (¼ pound) solid vegetable shortening or lard

4 tablespoons unsalted butter

Ice water to bind

1. Sift flour, salt and baking powder together.

2. Cut the shortening and butter into small pieces and blend with the flour mixture. Do not overwork, or the dough will become tough.

3. Work in just enough ice water to hold the dough together. Refrigerate 30 minutes or longer.

4. Roll crust out on a lightly floured flat surface to approximately ¼-inch thickness or thinner. Line an 8 or 9-inch pie plate, leaving one to 1½ inches hanging over the edges. Fold the excess crust up and then back to make an upright rim and flute with your fingers. Prick dough closely and deeply with the tines of a fork on the sides and bottom. Refrigerate or freeze 30 minutes or longer.

5. Preheat oven to 375°F. Fill or bake approximately 10-12 minutes, or until lightly browned at the bottom.

Note: If crust is to be filled with fruit, brush the bottom with an unbeaten egg white or sprinkle with toasted plain, fine bread crumbs.

Sweet Pie Shell for Tarts

Yield: Shell for 9-inch tart or numerous individual tarts

¼ pound unsalted butter, cut up

½ cup all-purpose sifted flour

1 teaspoon granulated sugar

¼ teaspoon salt

½ teaspoon baking powder

2 extra large egg yolks

2-3 tablespoons cold water to bind

1 egg white to brush pastry before baking

1. Work first 6 ingredients together, adding enough water to hold dough together so it will not break apart when rolled on a lightly floured surface.

2. Roll out dough and fit into the bottom and sides of an 8 or 9-inch fluted tart pan with a removable bottom. Or, fill individual tartlet pans. Refrigerate or freeze until very cold.

3. Preheat oven to 375°F.

4. Remove tart shell from refrigerator. Brush with the egg white. Bake 8-10 minutes, or until lightly browned. Cool to room temperature.

5. Fill tart shell(s) with fresh berries. Sprinkle powdered sugar on top to serve. Or, fill the bottom of the shell Crème Patisserie (recipe, page 19). Top with a variety of fresh berries, arranging them in circles according to color. Blueberries around the outside circle, bananas or white peaches creating the middle circle and raspberries in the center will simulate the American flag for patriotic holidays. Drizzle chocolate sauce around individual tarts in a zigzag pattern for a special presentation.

Note: Bananas and peaches must be brushed with citrus juice or glaze (melted apple jelly) to keep them from changing color.

Note: The secret of a light and flaky pie crust is to refrigerate the shell and place it into the hot oven while it is very cold.

Baking Powder Dough

Yield: Top and bottom crusts for meat or poultry pies

2 cups all-purpose flour

4 teaspoons baking powder

1 teaspoon salt

2½ tablespoons solid shortening (vegetable or lard)

¾ cup 2% milk

1. Preheat oven to 450°F.

2. Sift dry ingredients together. Blend in the shortening with a pastry blender or fork.

3. Make a well in the center and add the milk all at once. Stir only until the flour is moistened.

4. Set on a lightly floured surface and work into a ball. Flatten. Turn one side over the other. Flatten again. Roll ½-inch thick into two circles. Cover the bottom and sides of an 8-inch pie plate with one circle. Reserve the other for the top.

5. Fill with meat or poultry. Cover the top with the crust. Cut small slits for steam to escape.

6. Bake 15-18 minutes, or until crust is brown.

Epilogue

A cookbook dedicated to the Bounty of Central Florida would not be complete without fried catfish and hush puppies.

A cookbook dedicated to the bounty of Central Florida would not be complete without fried catfish and hush puppies. Since every southerner already knows the definition and derivation of the hush puppy, this explanation is for readers who live above the Mason-Dixon Line. When southern folk fried their catfish by the light of a camp fire, the excess cornmeal breading that fell off the fish into the boiling fat was thrown to the dogs as a treat. Legend has it that Confederate soldiers hiding near Union camps fed the crisp bits to their dogs to hush their howling so they wouldn't be detected. "Hush, Puppy!"

Since there are as many recipes for hush puppies as there are old Florida fishermen, forgiveness is requested for any additions, subtractions and substitutions for those fondly remembered.

Hush Puppies

Yield: 6-8 Servings

2 cups white cornmeal

2 tablespoons all-purpose flour

1 tablespoon + 1 teaspoon baking powder

½ teaspoon baking soda

1 teaspoon salt

2 cups whole buttermilk

1 jumbo graded egg, beaten

6 tablespoons chopped sweet onions

Oil or fat to half fill a deep fryer with a basket insert

1. Heat the oil to the boiling point, 370°F.
2. Sift dry ingredients together.
3. Stir in the buttermilk, the beaten egg and the chopped onions.
4. Immerse the basket into the boiling fat to become hot. Drop the batter by small spoonfuls into the basket. When the hush puppies are done, they will float to the top. Drain on paper toweling.

Hush Puppies

Yield: 6 Servings

2 cups white cornmeal
2 tablespoons all-purpose flour
1 tablespoon baking powder
1 teaspoon salt

⅛ teaspoon cayenne pepper or 1 finely-chopped small jalapeño pepper
1 jumbo graded egg, beaten
2 cups half-and-half
Oil or fat to half fill a deep fryer with a basket insert

1. Heat the oil to the boiling point, 370°F.

2. Sift the dry ingredients together.

3. Add egg and half-and-half, stirring well to combine. (Add the jalapeño.)

4. Immerse the basket into the oil to become hot.

5. Drop the batter by level tablespoons into the basket. Fry 3-5 minutes until they turn golden brown and float to the top. Dry on paper toweling.

Hush Puppies

Yield: 6 Servings

2 cups stone ground cornmeal
2 teaspoons baking powder
1 teaspoon salt
½ teaspoon black pepper

1 tablespoon granulated sugar
1 jumbo graded egg, beaten
2 cups milk
Vegetable oil to half fill a deep fryer with a basket insert

1. Heat the oil to the boiling point, 370°F.

2. Sift the dry ingredients together.

3. Add the beaten egg and milk, stirring to combine.

4. Immerse the basket into the oil to become hot.

5. Drop the batter by level tablespoons into the basket. Fry 3-5 minutes until they turn golden brown and float to the top. Dry on paper toweling.

Classic Fried Catfish

Yield: 4 Servings

2 cups yellow cornmeal

2 teaspoons baking powder

1 teaspoon salt

½ teaspoon cayenne pepper

Optional: ½ teaspoon garlic powder

4 large catfish fillets or a 4 whole small catfish

Vegetable oil to half fill a deep skillet

1. Sift dry ingredients together.

2. Cut the catfish into fillets or remove the heads, tails and skin from the whole fish and wash the insides well.

3. Heat the oil to 350°F.

4. Dip the fish into the batter and shake off excess. Fry until golden brown. Drain on paper towels.

Beer Battered Fried Catfish

Yield: 4 Servings

8 or more catfish fillets, boned and skinned

2 cups all-purpose flour

1 teaspoon salt

Pinch white pepper

Pinch cayenne pepper

3 extra large eggs, separated

12 ounces beer, not light

¼ cup melted butter

1 part peanut oil to 4 parts canola oil for frying

1. Wash and dry the fish fillets. Refrigerate, covered.

2. Sift flour, salt and peppers together into a bowl.

3. Mix the egg yolks into the beer. Stir into the flour mixture. Stir in the melted butter. Cover the bowl and leave 1 hour at room temperature.

4. Beat the egg whites very thick but not stiff. Fold into the batter.

5. Pour enough oil into a deep skillet to cover the fish. Heat the oil to the bubbling point.

6. Cover the fillets with the batter, letting excess drip back into the bowl. Fry until golden brown, approximately 3-4 minutes. Do not overcook.

Index

HORS D'OEUVRES

JAMS AND JELLIES

KUMQUATS

LEMON

LIMES

MISCELLANEOUS

MUSHROOMS